ADVENTURES IN CODE

ADVENTURES IN CODE

The Story of the
Irish Software Industry

John Sterne

The Liffey Press

Published by
The Liffey Press
Ashbrook House
10 Main Street
Raheny, Dublin 5, Ireland
www.theliffeypress.com

A catalogue record of this book is
available from the British Library.

ISBN 1-904148-59-X

Printed in Spain by GraphyCems.

CONTENTS

ABOUT THE AUTHOR

John Sterne became aware that software development was different from other industries while working as a journalist in the early 1980s. He wrote about information technology in various newspapers and magazines for more than a decade, then severed his ties with the print medium and moved online. In March 1992, he launched *IT's Monday*, a weekly news publication that borrowed a sales model from the software industry and applied it to journalism. Customers paid an annual licence fee to receive special interest news stories by e-mail. *IT's Monday* is understood to have been the first commercial publication in Europe that was delivered in this way. John edited weekly issues for nearly eleven years and sold the title in January 2003. John holds degrees in history and sociology and has contributed to EU research projects on new applications of information technology. He lives in Dublin with his partner Eileen and their son Rory. *Adventures in Code* is his first book.

ACKNOWLEDGEMENTS

This book is based on a series of interviews with more than 50 key participants in the Irish software story. Their recollections and insights enabled me to identify the most important projects, products and events from the earliest attempts at product development to the present day. They discussed their contributions to the industry, often disclosing facts that had never previously appeared in the public domain, and steered me towards other information sources. The interviewees gave their time freely, sometimes over two or three sessions, so that this book could be written. I am indebted to all of them.

Thanks also to Vicente Ortiz Lopez, Colm Reilly, Cormac Sheridan and Brian Trench, who read parts of the work in progress and provided helpful comments.

For my parents

Prologue

A SMOKE-FILLED ROOM

Meeting Tom McGovern was always an enlightening experience. But, in an era when there were no restrictions on smoking in the workplace, it could also be an ordeal. He received his visitors in a tobacco fog. McGovern's office on Merrion Square was in the area of central Dublin where generations of legal, financial and medical consultants had advised their clients. It seemed like an appropriate base for a technology intellectual. McGovern's views on the state of the Irish computer market or on government strategies for industrial development or on the global trends in software engineering were always worth hearing. He was a philosopher as well as an entrepreneur. But his observations came floating through a wreath of cigar smoke.

System Dynamics was the first software company in the country and Tom McGovern was its boss. By the 1980s, he was widely regarded as the senior statesman of Irish software. He acted as the public face of the industry, representing it on trade associations and on national and international expert committees. He was active in the IBM users group and chaired the Irish Computer Services Association. He helped to plan the first computing education programmes in the universities. He also invested in new ventures and acted as mentor to a variety of start-ups.

His own company had been formed back in 1968 by a team of former IBM Ireland employees. They split away from the computer corporation in order to offer an alternative source of expertise to the organizations that had installed its machines. Similar businesses sprung up all over the world in the late 1960s. IBM had come under pressure from the

American anti-trust authorities to permit more competition in its customer base. In 1969, the US government filed a charge, claiming that it was acting as a monopolist. IBM responded by publishing separate software and service prices for the first time. This unbundling action allowed a new generation of firms to compete against IBM. The new ventures hoped to win software development and support contracts that would previously have gone to the computing giant. Most were founded by former IBMers who saw this as a faster way to advance their careers than by working their way up the corporate hierarchy.

The launch of System Dynamics was part of this worldwide phenomenon. Its founders included Paddy Doyle, a charismatic figure with industry experience in the US, and Fred Kennedy, who wanted to move into research and development. Both men had strong technical reputations from their time at IBM. By 1970, however, both had left the company. From then on Tom McGovern and Nick Spalding led the business. Spalding had a reputation as a brilliant IBM systems programmer and became the leading technologist in System Dynamics. McGovern took over as managing director. He stayed in this role for the next 22 years and remained the company's majority shareholder until 1994.

In the early years, System Dynamics styled itself as a "technical consulting house" rather than as a software company. But its services included bespoke programming for computer installations. The company tried to establish long-term relationships with the computer departments of large enterprises, bidding for successive consulting assignments, supplying technical staff on temporary placements, undertaking applications development projects and running training courses. System Dynamics initially worked on IBM's mainframe platforms. But in the mid-1970s it began to implement less expensive minicomputers from Data General and Digital Equipment. The company's business model thus adapted to changes in computer hardware, but it always involved hands-on services.

Former colleagues remember Tom McGovern as a visionary for the software industry as a whole, an excellent communicator and a shrewd spotter of technical talent. But he was also rather conservative when it came to running his company.

His openness to new concepts was evident when he penned some comments for the first issue of *Irish Computer* magazine in 1977. He suggested that the new publication should discuss "the prospects for indigenous export-oriented software enterprises in Ireland and the type of support which should be provided by the state". He also floated the possibility that software might be supplied in packaged form instead of written to order. This was futuristic stuff. In 1977 most computers were still running custom-built applications and the first Irish-developed software product was still a couple of years away.

In contrast, McGovern was never keen on developing products inside System Dynamics. Consulting services offered more stability and enabled the company to keep its costs low. But its growth was fitful and interrupted by a couple of major crises. According to one former executive, the company struggled to survive on an overdraft facility and would never have had enough money to move into the package business. Nonetheless, McGovern steered the firm through the 1970s and 1980s, when it employed more than 60 staff. He delegated much of the day-to-day operations management to colleagues like Martin Walsh, who became his chief lieutenant. This allowed him to give more of his own time to other activities.

System Dynamics was always run like an old-style family firm. The managing director maintained a tight proprietorial grip that irritated some of his senior managers. In 1988, a group led by Walsh broke away and set up a rival services company called Delphi Software. This was not unlike the split from IBM that had created System Dynamics 20 years earlier. McGovern reorganized and stabilized his company again, but the breakaway was a traumatic event. He suffered a heart attack shortly afterwards.

Tom McGovern's interests ranged far beyond System Dynamics by this time. He held non-executive roles in ventures that were much more daring and more ambitious than his own firm.

Jim Mountjoy became a regular visitor to the smoke-filled room in the mid-1980s. He was introduced to McGovern by Michael Purser, an early System Dynamics employee who had left the company to become a lecturer at the computer science department in Trinity College Dublin. Purser had also set up his own firm, Chaco Computer Consultants, in 1976. Chaco acquired a reputation as the most technology-centred software company in town, employing a bunch of Trinity's brightest graduates. Michael Purser had alerted Tom McGovern to the growing demand for telecommunications software and proposed that they set up a new services company in this area. Jim Mountjoy was also interested in this project. Most of his career had been in telecommunications, but he had spent the previous five years as an administrator and policy adviser at the National Board for Science and Technology and wanted a new job with a private company. McGovern and Purser had both been involved in a recent inter-university networking project and had exchanged ideas about a new venture.

The end result of these discussions was the launch of a communications software design company, Baltimore Technologies. Formed in 1984 with Jim Mountjoy as managing director, it borrowed its name from a fishing port in west Cork, reflecting Mountjoy's roots in that part of the country. In the early years Chaco and System Dynamics held equal shareholdings in Baltimore Technologies, but Chaco acquired the whole business in 1987 and the two companies merged under the Baltimore name. It won a series of development contracts, mostly in electronic messaging and network management.

According to Mountjoy, Tom McGovern's investment in Baltimore was typical of his approach to new technologies and new lines of business. He liked sideline projects that might lead to opportunities for System Dynamics at a later date. McGovern supported Baltimore Technologies, Mountjoy says, because of his awareness that computing and telecommunications had started to converge.

Jim Mountjoy regularly sought McGovern's opinions and advice. "Most people need someone to go to who will give a perspective on things," he says. "Tom could do that and he was always available. He would be the guy that I hold in the highest regard."

The relationship between Michael Purser and Jim Mountjoy, on the other hand, deteriorated in the late 1980s. Their disagreements prevented

Mountjoy from leading Baltimore in the way that he wished. He quit the company in March 1990 and set up a new venture, Euristix, in the following month. Tom McGovern became a shareholder in Euristix and continued to act as a mentor to Mountjoy. Euristix initially offered contracting services at the high skills end of the communications software business and moved into software product development later on. McGovern's belief in Mountjoy's vision eventually netted a massive return. But this was a posthumous success.

Tom McGovern died in April 1994. He was only 55 years old. Within a few months, a British company, Arrival Holdings, acquired System Dynamics for a very modest price. Arrival scaled down the Dublin organization and assigned most of its staff to international projects. Baltimore Technologies changed hands two years later for a six-figure sum. Here again, the company's valuation was much lower than it could have been in earlier years.

The value of Euristix, in contrast, soared in the 1990s. Fore Systems purchased the company in 1999 for five million shares and stock options with a reported value of $81 million. This figure more than doubled when, within a matter of weeks, Marconi agreed to buy out Fore's shareholders in a cash transaction at a premium price. Each of the five million shares was now worth $35.00. Tom McGovern had held one of the largest stakes in Euristix. The Fore-Marconi deal provided his family with a multi-million dollar windfall. It was as if he had left a jackpot lottery ticket sitting in the drawer of his desk.

System Dynamics reverted to Irish ownership in 1996 and is still trading today. But it is seldom cited as a role model by other Irish firms. Euristix, on the other hand, has been hugely influential. It succeeded by creating highly specialised software applications and attracting a global customer base. Unlike System Dynamics, it took high risks.

The contrast between these two companies deserves attention, because it shows how the software industry has followed a different path in Ireland than in other countries.

Software development started as a service business, where the buyers always expected some degree of tailoring in the code, and where it was important for the companies to be located near their customers. Local firms provided skills and services to local computer installations in cities all over the world. System Dynamics followed this model. As the industry evolved, however, a new breed of software product developers emerged. This strategy was much more expensive and entailed far greater risks than selling services. Most companies, therefore, continued to focus on their local customers. As the product trade grew, however, there was less demand for custom-written applications and these firms spent more of their time installing and supporting packaged software.

The package creators were the risk takers. Most came from a small number of industry clusters. One of the few clusters outside the United States evolved in Ireland. The proliferation of small export-driven businesses produced a cottage industry with global reach.

By the turn of the century, hundreds of Irish software companies had shipped thousands of packaged products. Very few achieved financial returns on the same scale as Euristix. Only a small percentage, indeed, have ever achieved annual revenues of $5 million or more. But this industry has become self-sustaining and the processes and pitfalls of product development are now well understood. The old-style owner-managers were superseded by serial entrepreneurs who learned how to adapt to shifts in the technology and discontinuities in the market. Many also acquired a knack for selling into the US, where buyers were traditionally reluctant to consider non-American technologies.

Back in the 1970s, when software development started to look like an industry in its own right, Ireland was one of the least likely places in the world for it to sink roots. The country had been slower than others to adopt computers. Expenditure on the technology was significantly below the European average. There were no national research and development programmes for software. The government was adjusting the education system so that it would turn out more technicians for American-owned assembly plants. Industrial policy, indeed, revolved around inward investment and the incentive programmes that the Industrial Development Authority (IDA) devised to attract foreign corporations into the country.

The packaged software companies introduced a game with very different rules. In the early 1980s, a group of young companies proved that software products could be developed in Ireland and sold internationally. Their successors in the following decade had more technical competence, achieved much higher sales and acquired an unprecedented degree of international influence. This was almost entirely an indigenous success story. There were a few foreign companies that made notable contributions, usually by choosing to work with the same technologies as their native neighbours. In general, however, overseas firms treated Ireland as a distribution or support centre, not as a location for developing software.

Almost by accident, the software industry produced a native-born, post-IDA model for Ireland as a whole.

The software product companies contributed to the economic expansion that the country experienced in the closing years of the twentieth century. That growth was rooted in an acceleration of global trade and in demographic factors. A bulge in the population increased the number of employed people at an unprecedented speed. The social aspects of the boom were no less important than the economic change. Ireland experienced a general rise in confidence and expectations in the late 1990s. The software industry played a key role here. These attitudes had already been apparent among the package developers of the previous decade. The cultural revolution started with the code cutters and it started long before the Celtic tiger cliché was coined.

Even the most successful ventures, though, never grew up to be large organizations. Most Irish-owned software companies rise and fade in less than a decade, leaving little trace. This is a story of small firms that appear in waves and company builders who jump from one venture to the next. Software is the most volatile of industries and new contenders proliferate after every shake-up. The number of exporting firms thus keeps on increasing and the value of their cumulative sales continue to rise — even in the bad years.

Software professionals seem to regard history as a rude word. Their companies are constantly preoccupied with forthcoming product releases and seldom look back at the past. It is not always acknowledged, therefore, that the successes of the 1990s were preceded by two decades of hard graft. Each generation of start-ups included pioneer companies that broke down barriers and provided role models for others to follow. Insight, RTS and Intelligence Ireland set the trends in the 1980s. Glockenspiel and Iona followed in the early 1990s and Aldiscon and Euristix were hugely influential later in the decade. Each of these eras threw up a different crop of companies with different business models. Each generation has learned from its predecessors' trials and errors.

There has never been much public awareness of this industry and this history. Most software companies, indeed, have been quite content with their low profile. Their executives have little time for public relations, especially within Ireland. If they ever court outside attention, it is among industry analysts abroad. Few software leaders join business federations or involve themselves in national politics. The best developers enjoy high prestige within the technical community, but are seldom interested in how they are perceived by others.

The software development community in Ireland, nonetheless, has a fascinating story to tell. This book aims to tell it.

Chapter 1

FIVE GENERATIONS OF IRISH SOFTWARE

Getting Started in Maynooth

Tom Moore joined the software industry by buying a book about the Basic programming language and teaching himself to write a payroll application. He quit his job with an engineering group in 1982 and formed a software company in Maynooth. "There was a gung ho environment then that is not there now," he recalls. PCs had come into vogue. Accountants were discovering the usefulness of spreadsheets. Amateur developers could afford to buy computers for the first time. When it became possible to create a product on just one desktop machine, people drifted into software development from all points on the careers compass.

Moore's company, Manser, set out to produce a material requirements planning package for personal computers. Large manufacturers had already benefited from this sort of application on expensive minicomputers. He wanted to provide small factories with the same capabilities. Manser made its first sale in 1984 to his former employer.

By then, however, he had become aware that many similar PC-based products were coming onto the market. Some were being imported and adapted to suit local conditions. Others were developed by small Irish companies like Omnicorp in Limerick and Microman in Dublin. There were few differences among these offerings, apart from the brands of computer on which they ran. Customers' expectations were low, especially in areas like information presentation, and most users were satisfied with a minimal set of functions.

The key to success was to find a reseller with real customers and to make the software work on the brands of microcomputer that it was authorised to sell. Manser's product started on an ACT Sirius machine, moved to Digital Equipment's Rainbow and eventually ended up on an IBM PC.

Tom Moore says that he did not feel that he was part of an embryonic industry. He did not even pay much attention to what the other material requirements planning software firms were doing. The important thing was that affordable computer hardware had enabled enthusiasts to make a living from software in a way that had not previously been possible.

Software development, he says, was not yet regarded as a profession in the early 1980s. But software work was changing fast. It certainly looked very different than it had done ten or twenty years earlier.

Generation One — Just Another Service

Once upon a time, the tiny club of computer installations in Ireland were known as the "twelve apostles". PC stood for "peace commissioner". Mainframes were more expensive than office buildings and a mechanical calculator could cost more than the user's salary. Computing in the 1960s revolved around big boxes and the corporations that built them. Insofar as there was any public awareness of the technology, it was perceived as a threat to existing employment, not as the foundation for new businesses or careers.

In those early years, most software was supplied by the system makers. The rest was usually written by employees of the user organisations and the majority of these were in the public sector.

A state-owned sugar factory in Thurles became the country's first computer installation in 1958. The machine, an ICT 1201, read in data from punch cards and used the same medium for data output. The manufacturer, International Computers and Tabulators, subsequently evolved into ICL, which continued to design and sell its own computers until the late 1990s.

IBM's first computer shipment followed in 1960, when the ESB electricity company acquired a Model 650 plus six accounting machines.

By the end of 1961, IBM claimed ten "data processing" customers. Soon afterwards, it supplied the first computer in an Irish university when the School of Engineering at Trinity College Dublin installed an IBM 1620. This box used paper tape rather than punch cards as its input-output medium.

In the mid-1960s, the country's first minicomputer, a Digital Equipment PDP 8, went into service at the air traffic control centre in Shannon Airport, and Honeywell joined ICL and IBM in the mainframe trade. In 1966, the Revenue Commissioners began a long association with Honeywell, which eventually became Bull, as the main supplier of computers for tax processing.

The high point for Irish computing in the 1960s came towards the end of the decade. When the national airline, Aer Lingus, introduced an IBM-based passenger reservations system, it employed the coolest technologies of the age. This was the first online computing project in Ireland, connecting a mainframe with remote terminals. The mathematical processes behind its query response routines were hailed as "world class".

By this time, separate communities of data processing specialists had clustered around each of the three main vendors. IBMers constituted one fraternity. ICL types congregated in a separate club. Honeywell people belonged to another. The first generation of programmers emerged in this environment and pursued careers within their own vendor communities. Some worked for the computer maker and then joined one of its customers. Others learned their craft in one user organisation — the large employers ran internal training programmes — and were then poached by another.

No one talked about "geeks" or "nerds" in the 1960s. But computing practitioners were commonly known as "whiz kids". This was not a complimentary term. The data processing brigade did not fit comfortably into established workplace politics. At a time when trade unions were apprehensive about technological change, the whiz kids represented a disruptive force. Mainframe computers threatened to devalue the skills of clerical workers and to disrupt familiar practices and pecking orders. The whiz kids were the human minders of this technology.

Usually, in fact, they were young men who had started their careers in some other line of work and been selected for re-training when their employers decided to install a computer. The vendors supplied aptitude tests that picked out those individuals who could make sense of a flow-chart. The whiz kids worked long hours and socialised together. They improved their skills on training courses provided by the computer companies. They used their contacts in these firms to advance their careers. Job mobility was high in the vendor-specific communities and they could gain promotion and responsibility at a relatively young age.

If, however, these proto-geeks wanted exposure to the most advanced systems or to learn the latest software development methodologies, Ireland was not a good place to be. In computing terms, the country was underdeveloped and the projects were on a smaller scale than elsewhere. Ambitious programmers looked abroad, and especially to Britain and Canada, for bigger challenges and better rewards.

When the first generation of software companies appeared, they added another strand to the vendor-centric job market. System Dynamics, Applied Management Systems (AMS), GC McKeown, Chaco Computer Consultants, Software Development Services and Honeywell partner IMPC were essentially service providers with skills for hire. They offered technical consulting, software development and training and found customers in the public service, finance institutions and the larger manufacturing firms.

In-house software teams retained their primary role in the data processing environment of the 1970s. Organisations like Bank of Ireland, Irish Life and the government's Central Data Processing Services continued to select and train their own programmers. It was often difficult for the independent consultants and contractors to get a share of the big data processing budgets. Sometimes they provided extra hands when the internal computing departments were really busy. In general, however, they fared better among organisations that did not already employ computing staff. The service companies encouraged these to install their first computers and developed software for the systems.

Brendan Doherty describes this as missionary work. A former IBM Ireland system engineer, he had added to his software experience in Canada, Costa Rica and Venezuela before he joined System Dynamics in 1975. The general business community, he recalls, had a rather limited understanding of what computers could and could not do. System Dynamics offered them an explanation, analyzed their business processes and advised them how to proceed. Software development was just part of a bundle of services that the independents provided.

The 1970s was also the decade of the computing bureau. These services appeared when mainframe users realised that they could make money out of selling spare data processing time on their machines. ICS Computing, for example, grew out of Ulster Bank. Cara Data Processing was an offshoot of the computing department at Aer Lingus. Smurfit Computing emerged from a large printing and packaging company. These service organisations were closely aligned with specific computer vendors and run by people who had worked for the system manufacturers. They were not interested in writing software. They provided payroll processing to companies that could not afford to run their own computer departments and they grew by targeting smaller firms. A cluster of data preparation companies formatted the punch cards that contained user data. Some of these employed dozens of machine operators. The bureau operations and the data prep firms soon became the public face of Irish computing.

By 1977, the computing services industry consisted of about 30 companies with a total workforce of just 300 people. Add in the data preparation firms and the total was closer to 500. This was generation one of the Irish software industry. But the majority of its employees never wrote or modified any code.

Generation Two — Pack It and See

Packaged software came in with the minicomputer. And the minicomputer had a bigger impact on software development in Ireland than in most countries.

Economic development during the 1970s was all about attracting foreign companies. The Industrial Development Authority (IDA) selected sites on the edges of provincial towns and arranged for these to be zoned for manufacturing. It then enticed international — but predominantly American — companies to set up branch plants in these locations, easing their path with employment grants and tax incentives.

Most of the new arrivals had very limited responsibilities. They usually undertook product assembly and configuration tasks or back office support services for customers in Europe. From the perspective of the inward investors, the main attraction of Ireland was that they could adjust their internal accounting procedures and benefit from low tax liabilities. The managers of the branch plants knew how easy it would be to transfer the assembly work to cheaper locations. They looked for strategies to deepen their employers' commitment to Ireland. Software competence was one such strategy.

Back in the US, most manufacturing organisations ran mainframes. But few could justify installing an IBM System/370 or one of its equivalents in a small satellite facility. The minicomputer offered these firms an alternative platform at a much lower price point. And there were plenty of models to choose from. In the minicomputer trade, new names like Digital Equipment, Data General, Nixdorf and Prime competed against IBM and ICL. Because their systems cost less, these vendors did not provide as broad a range of customer services as the mainframe makers. This presented the independent service companies with new business opportunities.

If the Irish factories had installed the same computers as their counterparts in the US, the parent companies could have shipped over the software they already used for financial management or production planning. The smaller systems, however, required different software and a different set of computing skills. The assembly plant managers were keen to experiment with minicomputer applications on behalf of their employers. They did not, however, want to employ teams of programmers to write customised software. They looked for tried and tested applications that could be supervised by a financial controller and run by an operator or two.

IBM scored most of the early successes. It introduced the System/32 in 1975. Many of the IDA-backed projects installed this machine and its successors. IBM also introduced Maapics, an off-the-shelf software product, that provided manufacturers with most of the functions that they needed. Coming from the US, though, it was not designed to support the multi-currency, multi-country operations of international companies. Here again, the local computing firms could fill the gap.

Software that worked on one site could be reproduced for other customers with the same sort of computer. Some service companies imported application packages and hawked them around the assembly plants. Others started to build products of their own.

This process was hardly unique to Ireland. But the unusually strong orientation of the market towards minicomputers made it happen faster. Companies like AMS and Cops and RTS concentrated on software for IBM's System/3x family. Mentec and GC McKeown and Online Computing worked on Digital Equipment platforms. Memory Computer introduced software for Prime computers and MA Systems for ICL machines. Most of the IDA-backed plants were in the provinces and regional software suppliers began to appear outside the Dublin area.

Some of the software sellers had previously been involved in bureau services, but most generation one service companies found it hard to make the transition to products. Cara, for example, bought the rights to a hotel administration package that ran on Philips minicomputers. It won three or four high value sales a year and the package became a standard for Trust House Forte and for Sheraton in Europe. Cara, however, never treated its software division as a strategic part of its operations. It was much easier to satisfy its parent group, Aer Lingus, by running payroll processing services or by reselling data communications equipment. The company failed to grow the software business and allowed it to wither away gradually.

The younger breed of product developers was much more willing to take risks. They chalked up their first sales abroad in the early 1980s. The majority of this business came from the UK, but two of the new contenders — AMS and RTS — were quick to open offices in North America.

The minicomputer applications companies had already established a model for building software products when the microcomputer arrived in the early 1980s. The low-cost PC accelerated the pace of computerisation and the formation of new software companies. Firms such as Manser were founded by users who were familiar with a specific line of business and knew where it could benefit from PC applications.

Like minicomputer software, the early microcomputer products were pegged to particular computer brands. Differences among hardware makes persisted for much of the 1980s. As the decade advanced, though, most system manufacturers sought compatibility with the combination of Intel processor and Microsoft operating system that became known as the "IBM PC".

Cheap hardware and gradual standardisation lowered the entry barriers to software development still further. More users and enthusiasts jumped into the product business. The PC confirmed and consolidated the primacy of the shrinkwrapped application in a box. The computer industry adapted to a new agenda. Suppliers debated whether the general citizenry would be prepared to pick up keyboarding skills and use their systems. Others started asking whether company directors or doctors or lawyers or government ministers would ever be willing to operate a computer for themselves.

In 1984 — the year that Microsoft Word hit the computer stores — Brian Dugan came to Dublin. A former vice president of Standard and Poor's Corporation in New York, Dugan was the managing director of Ireland's newest state agency, the National Software Centre. His first action was to measure the level of development in the country. He calculated that there were about 250 software companies in Ireland. By the end of 1985, that number had climbed to more than 300.

Not all of these organisations had written their own software products. Some sourced applications outside the country, installed them on a particular computer and gave the bundle a brand name. Dugan expressed surprise at the prevalence of the software package in Ireland. Some small outfits, he discovered, had even designed general purpose products that competed directly against big PC software names like Lotus and Microsoft. Most, however, focused on line-of-business applications for specific industries and professions.

Originality was seldom a priority for these developers. A trade directory published by *Irish Computer* magazine in 1984 listed 24 suppliers with packages for insurance brokers, 18 with software for solicitors and ten that were targeting credit unions. There were no fewer than 12 competing firms with applications for stores that rented out television sets.

Generation two of Irish software was built on derivative products. All too often these were designed for the same accounting, payroll and materials management tasks that hundreds of other packages could perform. The developers' revenues were also unimpressive. Most firms survived on a shoestring. The fledgling industry was perpetually short of money.

By the middle of the 1980s, however, the key characteristics that would differentiate the software industry in Ireland from other countries were already in place. It was made up of hundreds of small companies. It preferred software products over software services. And it was eager to export its wares.

Young software firms did not always fit into mainstream business culture and frequently clashed with the established financial interests. Banks and accountancy companies did not understand their business methods. Lending institutions would not accept that a piece of computer code could be an asset. The only value that they saw was in the tape or disk that held the software. And the financial institutions never shared the developers' optimism about their international sales prospects.

Good programmers can always find workarounds to their problems. Most of the early stage software companies took on service contracts to meet their running costs and to stay solvent while they developed products. In the mid-1980s some started to receive IDA grants — although their value were just a fraction of what was offered to inward investors. Computer hardware companies also encouraged Ireland's embryonic software industry. For example, when Triple A Systems launched its Bankmaster multi-currency banking product in 1981, ICL noticed that the functions of this software would suit banking practices in developing countries. It therefore assisted Triple A Systems, which later changed its name to Kindle, to sell Bankmaster in former British colonies across Africa and Asia. ICL supplied the computer hardware.

Digital Equipment, meanwhile, helped GC McKeown to make inroads into local government authorities in England. And, over in the IBM camp, AMS found international buyers for its Insight financial planning package. The company changed its name to Insight Software in 1983. Within three years this product had achieved cumulative sales of $10 million. RTS also wrote its products to run on IBM minicomputers. From its inception, indeed, the company asserted that this accounting and manufacturing software was aimed at international users. By 1981, it had announced sales to Iceland, Britain and Germany. Four years later, it was running a worldwide network of 20 sales offices.

At the time, no one grasped the real significance of the pioneers' partnerships with hardware vendors. But this was the first manifestation of the software industry's flair for international networking. Big corporations never perceived small companies from a small country as any sort of threat. So they agreed to provide technical assistance and marketing support and sales leads. Networking — the human, not the data communications, variety — gradually became another core characteristic of software development in Ireland and prepared the way for the industry to grow dramatically in later years.

When Brian Dugan surveyed the scene in 1984, he found 2,500 people employed in computing services companies. Most had learned their trade as programmers in user installations, not through the software degree and diploma courses that were set up in the late 1970s.

By the time the first students graduated from these schemes, packaged software had transformed the job market. Users did not employ as many data processing staff as before and the younger graduates had a hard time finding employment. Some emigrated. Some moved over to other lines of work. Some joined special courses that the industrial training agency, AnCO, introduced for unemployed graduates. AnCO gave them an experience of development projects with prescribed user requirements and fixed deadlines. Generation two software firms, however, had surprisingly few jobs to offer to software graduates.

The start-ups kept on coming. CBT Systems produced the Intuition training package and sold it into financial dealing rooms from New York to Hong Kong. It then offloaded the product to another Dublin company, Financial Courseware, and developed new training packages for accountancy, banking and telecommunications. Dillon Technology set up a design and development office in Cork and targeted its multi-currency accounting products at the finance departments of international corporations. Dublin-based Vision tried to combine software development with management consulting and competed against international consulting firms. Glockenspiel developed tools for software technicians instead of packages for end users, championing the Unix operating system and a new programming language, C++.

The most ambitious company of the early 1980s wave, perhaps, was Intelligence Ireland, which developed its own desktop suite of word processing, spreadsheet, database and communications software, aiming to compete globally against major powers like Lotus Development, VisiCorp and Microsoft. Sony accepted Intelligence as a key development partner and it landed international assignments from British Telecom and ICL. Intelligence was as brash as any of the PC hardware vendors and, in its heyday, the company seemed willing to stick its finger into any software pie that might taste good.

A small subset of generation two companies, including Captec and Generics, Baltimore Technologies and Irish Medical Systems, saw the European Commission's Esprit research programme as a way of getting attention abroad. But the European schemes, which kept changing the rules on how commercial a project was allowed to be, never appealed to the majority of development firms. They were not attracted by new concepts in software engineering. They just wanted to write an application, put their name on the package, push it into the market and see if it would sell.

A state support infrastructure for software developers took shape during the 1980s. The IDA assessed business proposals and, if it liked them, awarded grants for employment or research. The National Software Centre offered technical advice and marketing services. Córas Tráchtála provided information on export markets and assisted companies to identify distribution partners, while the National Enterprise Agency began to address the funding gap.

Just as the pieces of this support jigsaw fell into place, however, the software industry started to fall apart.

In 1985, the rate of software company start-ups slowed down significantly. Between 1986 and 1989, one after another, the brightest hopes in minicomputer and PC packages ran into trouble and succumbed to takeovers or shutdowns. These failures punctured the ambitions of other companies that survived the fallout. Redundant programmers were thrown onto a labour market which already had an embarrassing number of unemployed computing graduates. The final phase of generation two was the grimmest time in the history of the industry.

RTS and Intelligence Ireland — companies that had inspired dozens of start-ups in the first half of the decade — were among the first names to disappear. Both were acquired in 1986, but their new owners were very different entities. Management Science America (MSA) — the largest application software company in the world, with annual revenues of more than $150 million — bought RTS in a cash-plus-shares transaction. Three months later, Dedeir Group, a Dublin-based investment company, took over Intelligence Ireland. In both cases, the new owners stated that their acquired businesses would continue to operate as before. MSA, however, became preoccupied with its own struggle for survival. The entire corporation was sold to Dun & Bradstreet in 1990. Dedeir, meanwhile, extracted the data communications knowledge in Intelligence, applied this in a financial software project and allowed the rest of its business to drift away.

CBT Systems, Insight Software and its associate company Vector Software were all acquired by the UK-based Hoskyns Group, which was ranked among the top ten computer service providers in Europe. These companies were reasonably sound, but their principals wanted to move onto other projects.

Kindle held out longer than most. It was backed by a consortium of venture capital firms and the bigger names in banking software offered little competition in its niche market. By 1990, the accumulated sales of its Bankmaster product had risen above $50 million. Ireland's political and financial establishment had come to regard Kindle as the respectable face of Irish software. The company's weakness, though, was that its products were closely identified with third world banking. It made strenuous efforts to sell into other markets, particularly in eastern Europe, with limited success. In 1991, the company was absorbed into ACT Group, a British banking software vendor with a firmer foothold in the western world.

Other package companies failed to find buyers and simply shut down. High-profile casualties like Cops and Software Laboratories were interspersed with the closures of Dashco, Microman, Omnicorp and other less well-known firms.

Most put the blame on money troubles. And on the banks. The financial resources of the 1980s generation were inadequate to sustain a full product cycle or to support an international customer base. Senior executives spent most of their time grappling with cashflow problems instead of advancing their product strategies. Contemporary observers noted, indeed, that the collapsed companies had lacked general management abilities.

Barry Murphy was managing director of Insight Software in the late 1980s. Looking back, he attributes the spate of failures to a combination of poor financial management and unsympathetic financial institutions. The banks, he believes, saw software firms as fly-by-night outfits. Often, he adds, the companies made bad business decisions. "Software is a very simple business," Murphy argues. "It's all about cashflow. If you are not doing your monthly projections you get into trouble very quickly."

The National Software Centre was another casualty of the fallout. The agency belonged to the IDA and the IDA's primary interest was inward investment, not nurturing small software firms. It announced the closure of the NSC in May 1988.

The IDA's interest in foreign software firms, however, increased in these years. Some of these were box-fillers. In 1985, Lotus Development opened up a facility near Dublin airport. Initially its employees did little more than duplicate floppy disks, stuff them, along with user manuals and other documentation, into cardboard packages, and ship them to customers around Europe. Microsoft, Oracle, Ashton-Tate and other corporations followed Lotus into Ireland. IDA officials asserted that these firms would expand the responsibilities of these facilities and might some day design their products in Ireland. This was just wishful thinking. What did materialise, though, was a cluster of companies that sold logistics and localisation services to the big American software vendors. Printing and packaging suppliers took other pieces of this pie. The support companies had little to offer jobless graduates from computer science courses. But this was the sort of software industry that the political and economic establishment could believe in.

A second category of IDA successes involved computer makers and other electronics hardware companies — the big corporations that already had assembly operations in Ireland. The agency encouraged these to hire software teams in the branch plants. Alcatel, Digital Equipment, Ericsson, Motorola, Nixdorf, Prime and Wang joined the new development cluster. Some of these groups, indeed, remained in operation after the companies ceased hardware production in Ireland.

Could it be, perhaps, that a natural order was re-asserting itself? Officialdom in Ireland had usually seen technology as a foreign import. The IDA had brought production activities into the country with the help of tax breaks. The software industry had bucked the usual trend when Irish-based companies had posed as product creators and owners. After the shakedown, however, it appeared that the multinationals were moving back into control. The IDA had discovered a formula for grant-aided software "factories". And government ministers could look forward to audiences with celebrities like Bill Gates or Larry Ellison instead of enduring photo opportunities with tiny businesses that could not persuade the banks to give them an overdraft facility.

The IDA's renewed efforts to attract inward investment had one unintended side-effect. They alerted employers in other parts of the world to the surplus software talent in Ireland. When the agency ran a campaign in Australia, for example, the country's software firms showed little interest in opening offices in Ireland. A number of Australian companies, however, invited experienced software engineers to emigrate.

A document that appeared in 1989 profiled the software industry after a decade of packaged application development. This report was written by a working group that the government had appointed to propose a better support strategy for software development in Ireland. It noted that overseas companies accounted for more than half of the employment in software and computing services — 2,600 in a total workforce of 4,800 — and concluded that industrial policy was already catering well for this side of the industry. It recommended the introduction of new support structures for Irish-owned firms with international potential and that the state should address their financing difficulties and management weaknesses.

The working group, it is now apparent, was looking for more Kindles. Out in the field, however, the code producers had already moved on to a different agenda. A technically elite subset of the software industry surfaced in the second half of the 1980s. These companies did not sell lookalike accounting suites or line-of-business applications for end users. They produced systems software or development tools or communications functions for existing applications. While the box-fillers boasted about the new jobs they were creating, these companies attracted the best developers — the software graduates who wanted technically challenging work rather than a safe job in a big corporation.

Generation three was born in with this cluster. Some of the companies were foreign-owned. These included Merrion Gates Software, data communications specialist Retix, an IBM software laboratory and an information technology centre that ICL had set up in Leopardstown in 1986. The majority, including Baltimore Technologies, Captec and Generics, were homegrown. Glockenspiel, led by the charismatic John Carolan and located in a dilapidated part of Dublin's inner city, was the most elite of this elite. In 1986, it became the first company in the world to ship and support a commercial C++ compiler for applications developers. It went on to pioneer new methods of constructing object-oriented software applications. The Glockenspiel name became well-known among software engineers in North America, where its object technology expertise was highly valued. Back in Dublin, Carolan's company attracted a cultish following of software engineers who wanted to mingle with the masters.

Glockenspiel's dreams turned sour for the usual reason — cashflow difficulties. Computer Associates acquired the company in 1992. To be more accurate, Computer Associates enforced a deal that placed John Carolan at its disposal and bound him into a fixed-term work contract in America. By that time, however, his company had raised the horizons for Irish software developers. And the next wave of firms had begun to appear.

Generation Three — Focus and Differentiate

The National Software Directorate (NSD) started operations in March 1991 with Barry Murphy in the director's seat. The new agency was based inside the IDA's head office and was partly financed by the European Commission's structural fund. Murphy's agenda included a quality management initiative, measures to encourage more campus companies and strategies to assist software firms to bid for major contracts and sell into large corporations. Job creation was no longer an urgent issue. The surplus graduates of generation two had found employment by 1991. The pendulum of skills demand had swung back from the oversupply of the late 1980s. Once again there was talk of a people shortage.

The task of advising companies on best development practices and methodologies, meanwhile, passed to another new organisation — the Centre for Software Engineering at Dublin City University. This was funded through a national programme that aimed to transfer knowledge from the colleges to commercial organisations. The idea was that Ireland should have centres where experts in various fields would monitor international trends, evaluate new technologies and recommend strategies to their client companies. This sort of trend-watching became much easier for all when the internet expanded. But the new centres were seen as strategically important at the start of the 1990s.

What the software industry really needed was better management. It had to sort out the undercapitalisation problems, its limited export competence and the low levels of originality in many products. The software developers had to learn new tactics and the shakeout of the late 1980s was still fresh in everyone's minds.

Barry Murphy served as software director for five years. The third generation of Irish development companies blossomed during this time. Figures compiled by the National Software Directorate show that the industry evolved rapidly in the first half of the 1990s. In 1991 there were around 250 Irish-owned software businesses with 3,225 employees and combined exports of about $90 million. By the end of 1995, the number of companies on the NSD's files had risen to 400 and the export total had jumped to $360 million. According to the directorate, four out of five software development firms were active exporters. The NSD also highlighted the unprecedented size of the largest software companies. By 1995, seven firms had more than 100 employees.

All of the industry data emanating from state agencies during this period, however, should have carried a statistical health warning. The ownership of companies constantly changed through mergers and acquisitions. And it was usually the bigger firms that moved from the "native" category to the "foreign" camp. Each large trade sale left a dent in the indigenous group. The Irish-owned part of the industry kept expanding. But the upward graph was jagged, not a smooth curve.

The government agencies therefore adopted the convention of classifying any business that had originated in the country as indigenous, even when it was no longer under Irish control. They also bracketed the software localisation and logistics providers with software developers. This support industry had achieved a critical mass by the early 1990s and some of the translation and packaging companies had achieved substantial revenues. Their inclusion made the headline figures look more impressive. Even the most cautious statisticians, however, could see that the Irish software industry was on the rise.

The distinguishing characteristic of generation three firms was that they targeted much narrower product niches than their predecessors. The start-ups of the 1980s had been generalists. The new bunch understood the importance of specialisation. They did not want to nibble at one corner of a broad market. They planned to dominate a specific patch — preferably one where no one else occupied a leadership position yet.

There were many examples of highly focused product development in these years. Quay Financial Software — the main operating subsidiary of investment group Dedeir after it gobbled up Intelligence Ireland — applied advanced concepts of information delivery and decision support to financial trading rooms. Datalex offered data access and integration software based on the industry-specific standards and protocols that airlines used. Datacare devised a product that assisted company secretaries to prepare statutory reports. In generation two, both Datalex and Datacare had sold and supported products from other developers. They survived the shakeout and reinvented themselves in the 1990s as software providers to tightly defined communities.

Clustering was another new trick. Whenever several companies in the same region are working in a related area, they tend to advance more quickly than isolated firms. Often they compete. Sometimes they co-operate. More important, though, staff move from one employer to another, resulting in a cross-fertilisation of skills and adding to the overall expertise of the region. Clusters also attract employees to move from other locations.

Many of the new names in the early 1990s belonged to one of three clusters — computer-based training, telecommunications software and middleware — as the developers' toolkits and software that integrated existing pieces of code were known. Software in these categories seldom required features or functions for individual countries and could therefore be sold anywhere in the world.

As a general rule, if a software company was successful in the United States, it could sell everywhere else afterwards. By the middle of the decade, Irish software companies had become vastly better at selling into the US without transplanting their core operations out of Ireland. Glockenspiel had shown that Irish companies selling tools for technologists would meet less resistance abroad than those with line-of-business applications for dentists or dairies or dry cleaners. Generation three produced more companies that wrote software for sale to other software developers. The industry's transatlantic relationships also became more structured, largely through the efforts of the National Software Directorate. Attempts were made to create formal linkages with American associations like the Massachusetts Software Council and the Silicon Valley Software Association. More successful, though, was the participation of Irish companies in the technical groups that set and promoted industry standards.

Generation three was thus characterised by product specialisation, more frequent forays into America and more social networking through industry groups. The star performers, moreover, had not been identified in the report that the government-appointed working group produced in 1989. Most of them had not even existed then.

Each of the three key clusters was led by recognised champions. CBT Systems was the pathfinder in training technology. Aldiscon Information and Euristix showed the way in telecommunications. And Iona Technologies inherited Glockenspiel's mantle as the coolest place where software engineers could work. It also inherited many former Glockenspiel employees.

CBT Systems was already the biggest Irish-owned software exporter at the end of 1991, even though its international sales were worth only a few million dollars. Over the next four years, CBT's annual revenues grew to more than $40 million and most of this business came from the US. In its earlier incarnations, the company had developed courseware for financial management, banking and telecommunications. This time around it focused on training computer users. Niche marketing and industry networking paid off and paved the way for CBT to go public in 1995.

Aldiscon and Euristix both established their reputations in the early 1990s as development contractors to the international telecommunications industry. This work helped them to spot opportunities for product development. Euristix found a niche in element management technology for telecommunications networks. By 1994, Aldiscon had secured two-thirds of the world market for short message service centres — the management systems behind text messaging on mobile phones. The company also won a valuable slice of the market for home location registers, which enable the network operators to provide roaming services to their customers. Aldiscon did not invent short messaging. What it did well was to embrace an industry standard at a critical time — much as Glockenspiel had done with the C++ programming language.

Iona followed the same strategy. And its choice of standard pitched it into direct competition with some of the biggest names in the industry. Iona was a campus company, formed in 1991 by members of the distributed systems group at Trinity College Dublin. They had participated in European research projects on distributed object technology and tracked the attempts to establish standards in this software category. The Object Management Group designated the Common Object Request Broker Architecture (Corba) as a core specification for messaging among software objects. All of the major computer makers set out to release Corba implementations for their own customers. Iona decided that there was also room in the market for a neutral, multi-platform Corba toolkit and rushed to create one. It unveiled this product, Orbix, in 1993, billing it as the first full implementation of Corba on the market — a shrinkwrapped, affordable realisation of the new industry standard. The Object Management Group applauded Orbix. Senior figures in the standards group endorsed the product and praised the completeness of its functionality.

Iona had merely commercialised a piece of technology designed by a committee. It did not even have a seat on that committee. But its understanding of Corba was hailed by the leading authorities in the field. Orbix hit the market with a roar of approval from the voices that mattered. Nothing like this had ever happened to an Irish software product before. The development industry had come of age.

Generation Four — Spend Someone Else's Money

The flotation of CBT Systems on Nasdaq in May 1995 was another landmark event for the industry. The financial rewards that CBT's owners reaped from this action changed the perception that Irish software development firms were the poor relations to the multinational packagers. The flotation also demonstrated that software engineers could interact with financial engineers in Ireland like they did in the United States. This event ushered in the fourth generation of Irish software — the most mercenary phase in the history of the industry.

Barry Murphy spent much of his time as national software director grappling with money matters. He encouraged emerging companies to take the venture capital route to growth. He also tried to promote the Irish software industry as a place where local and international financiers should invest. Murphy joined the investment world in 1996, when he went to work for the Cullinane Group. His successor at the NSD was Jennifer Condon, who had headed the ICL information technology centre in Leopardstown. In the previous decade she had been marketing manager at the National Software Centre.

Looking back, Barry Murphy admits that the changes in attitude in the mid-1990s took him by surprise. The leaders of the newer software start-ups were wildly ambitious and, from the outset, fixed their sights on the international stock markets. "Their confidence bordered on arrogance," Murphy recalls. "They felt that they could develop better software than anywhere else." This generation of entrepreneurs took it as given that they were going to make an international impact.

Likewise, the programmers were not so humble any more. Software workers started asking for higher pay and better benefits. This influenced the career assumptions of Irish students. They left college knowing what share options meant. Everyone wanted to work for the next Iona. They expected to hop from job to job at regular intervals, leaving firms that were starting to look mature and getting into start-ups as early as they could. That meant steering clear of the American-owned branch plants. Working for the multinationals was a fallback for the underachievers.

The national psyche altered in the mid-1990s. The change was never specific to the software development industry, but it was particularly evident there. Its positive side was that it improved the opportunities for creativity and ambition. Its negative side was a mindset that not only tolerated greed, but celebrated it. In previous years, emigration had been the easiest way to accumulate personal wealth. Emigration had now become passé. Staying in Ireland and getting a stake in a technology-based business looked like a quicker route to riches.

Generation two software entrepreneurs viewed external investors as interlopers who wanted to take a share of what was rightfully theirs. Generation three companies were still cautious about dealing with external investors, but more were willing to try. Generation four had no such inhibitions. Funding had never been easier to obtain. Venture capital firms raised and invested unprecedented sums in the late 1990s. The best candidates could also seek backing abroad. CBT's entry to Nasdaq, indeed, spurred some US venture capital funds to start monitoring software development in Ireland. For developers who had struggled through the lean years, there was something seductive about building up a software empire by spending someone else's money.

Commentaries on the software industry in the second half of the 1990s often exaggerated the changes in the funding climate, especially when the authors had a vested interest in the investment cycle. The new age of Irish software was ushered in with a flood of seminars and conferences, newspaper articles and research reports. These hyped up the industry to attract attention from investors, speculating on which Irish companies might go public or get acquired at a premium price. Never mind the day-to-day grind of cutting code or making sales or supporting customers. All the talk was about stock options and share grabs.

The actual volume of investments failed to live up to the rhetoric. By the start of 1997, the total venture capital commitment to the software industry was less than $24 million and a single transaction involving Aldiscon accounted for one-third of this sum. Nonetheless, a new financial infrastructure for software development had evolved.

The second half of the decade was punctuated by acquisition deals that fuelled the hyperbole and placed increasingly high valuations on Irish software firms. Japanese IT conglomerate CSK bought Quay Financial Software in 1995. Logica snapped up Aldiscon for $82 million in 1997. This deal excluded an Aldiscon subsidiary in Northern Ireland, which specialised in standards-based software for wireless data services. The unit was re-branded as Apion and sold to Phone.com in 1999 for $239 million worth of stock. In the same year, Euristix was acquired by

Fore Systems for $80 million. Then Clarus paid $60 million for Software Architects International.

The mainstream media in Ireland had never shown much interest in the software industry, except as a source of recruitment advertising. But they could not ignore transactions on this scale. More personality profiles of technology millionaires appeared in newspapers and business magazines. The chief executives of publicly quoted companies — or companies with aspirations to enter the stock market — could hardly complain. Their chosen strategy obliged them to participate in a public relations process. Only a handful, however, actually made it onto the stock exchanges after CBT Systems. This route was taken by Iona, Trintech, Datalex and, following a change of ownership and a radical overhaul, Baltimore Technologies. Other companies like Aldiscon and Cognotec and Vision may have had higher sales or better technologists. As far as the general public was concerned, however, the small band of software companies that courted publicity constituted an "Irish tech sector".

In reality, Irish software was still an industry of small and very small firms in a constant state of flux. The National Software Directorate continued to measure its growth. When it ran another of its surveys in 1998, the agency identified more than 550 Irish-owned software companies. It calculated that these had 9,300 employees and that their exports totalled about €545 million, which represented 81 per cent of their revenues. The United States had now become the biggest market for their products. By 1998, some 40 Irish software firms had set up subsidiaries in the US and the largest, including Iona, Mentec and Trintech, had networks of regional offices across North America.

This industry profile was unusual, particularly in comparison with the rest of Europe. Most countries employed their software talent to keep local information systems running. A few could also boast concentrations of software skill in large corporations. Ireland, with a population of less than four million and hundreds of small software exporters, did not look like other European economies.

Impressive as their trading figures were, moreover, the Irish software companies' combined revenues were still dwarfed by the exports of the

US-owned software package firms. Microsoft alone generated a much bigger proportion of the gross national product than all the local firms together. During these years, government ministers and industry lobbyists adopted a mantra that Ireland was the world's "biggest software exporter". The country's software exports, they declared, were even higher than those of the United States. In a literal sense, this claim was true — courtesy of Microsoft, IBM and Oracle. But it was also easy for objective observers to dismiss the posturing as a by-product of the tax breaks that the IDA had given to Microsoft and its ilk.

The "biggest exporter" cliché also hid the real achievement of the Irish software developers. The industry had now become self-sustaining. Individual companies remained relatively small, but the export figures kept climbing because there were more of them. The state had pumped resources into a support infrastructure for software warehouses and localisation services, but real value was now being created elsewhere. The political establishment's continuing identification of the software industry with inward investment was unfair, if not insulting, to the home-grown companies.

Teams kept breaking away from the established firms to create new products and to start new businesses. By the turn of the century, there were spin-offs from Iona scattered all over Dublin. Less predictable, perhaps, was a steady drift of executives from the Irish sales offices of international software firms into start-up ventures. For example, Norkom Technologies founder Paul Kerley and Cathal McGloin, who set up Performix Technologies, were both former Cap Gemini consultants, while Paul McBride and Paraic O'Toole left software services contractor Cambridge Technology Partners for careers with product companies Interactive Enterprise and Automsoft. Running a small development outfit is a vastly different job to performing middle management functions in a global organisation. In generation four, however, more people were willing to try jumping this gap.

The turn of the century years also saw employment in software development spread into more regions of Ireland. The industry had always been concentrated in Dublin and in the university cities of Cork, Galway and Limerick. Generation four start-ups also surfaced in places like Dundalk, Waterford, Tralee and Letterkenny. These firms were not created through government incentive schemes. Their establishment was a more organic process. Pressures in the labour market had made it attractive to locate in small towns where there was less risk that good staff would be poached.

Once again a software skills shortage had erupted. Once again the authorities called on the colleges to increase their intakes of undergraduates. Employers not only went trawling the countryside in search of software developers. They also took advantage of rising immigration. Dublin had become a more fashionable place to live. Non-English-speakers, in particular, welcomed opportunities to work in the city. This gave them a chance to improve their language skills as well as to further their software careers.

The National Software Directorate survey of 1998 provided a snapshot of the industry's predominant clusters during these years. It segmented the companies into ten sectors and examined the distribution of employment, sales and exports in each. The computer-based training firms, still led by CBT Systems, accounted for almost one-third of the international revenues, but employed just 11 per cent of the software workforce. Banking and finance applications developers shipped eight per cent of the software exports, but provided 17 per cent of the jobs. Tele-communications software represented eight per cent of international sales and eight per cent of the employment. Companies that wrote bespoke applications employed twice as many people — a surprising statistic given the emphasis on product development. Overall, however, the biggest subset of the industry was an "other niche product" category, which accounted for 17 per cent of employment and 17 per cent of the exports.

According to the NSD statistics, companies with internet-related software were responsible for just one per cent of the export sales in 1998. Virtually every software firm in the land, it is true, was adding web functions to its products and releasing new versions with an "e" prefix to their names. But very few were putting all of their eggs into the internet basket. Some companies, mostly new names, launched software products for web content handling. They found it difficult to close sales. Their mistake was the same one made by the accounting package companies of generation two. Developers from all over the world crowded into web publishing and personalisation and found that the market was rather limited. As usual, the companies that captured niches fared much better.

No software vendor could ignore the rush to build websites in the late 1990s, when all sorts of companies tacked dotcom labels onto their names or declared that their businesses were e-businesses. Software buyers expected products to be internet-enabled and the developers obliged. In general, however, the software firms were minor players in this game. The main protagonists were service companies in the finance, travel, leisure and consumer goods industries, who had also latched onto the easier availability of external finance. Computer hardware suppliers and network service providers also participated in the rush. The main actors, however, were graphic designers and marketing consultants.

For a short while towards the end of the century, the internet boom also reinvigorated the services side of the software business. A rash of new e-business consulting and systems integration firms appeared, offering to add a web dimension to their clients' information systems. Companies like Ebeon, Oniva and Digital Channel Partners aspired to be international advisers and software implementers. They ran extravagant promotions, opened offices abroad, ran up massive expenses and quickly collapsed. The sequence was reminiscent of the software failures in the late 1980s, but it happened within a much shorter timeframe.

There were two significant ways in which the rush to the internet transformed the environment for software product companies.

First, it changed the way that software buyers selected products and the way that the goods were distributed. More vendors put descriptions and demonstrations of their products onto a website or offered free downloads of trial versions. Software sales and marketing gradually moved online, especially for low-cost items.

Second, the evolution of the internet posed fundamental questions about the role of the software product. Pundits predicted that the industry was going to revert to a services model. The traditional package would disappear. Instead, application service providers would rent out software across the internet for a monthly fee and users would no longer need to install applications on their computers. In 1999, Sun's chief executive officer Scott McNealy — always the most quotable of IT bosses — declared that investment in shrinkwrapped software had come to an end. Henceforth, he declared, products would no longer have any value in their own right. Software would become just another service on the web.

These expectations triggered a wave of data centre construction. A new breed of service providers installed racks of servers and storage equipment. They offered to host websites and to manage customers' software applications. They connected the systems to the internet and added back-up services to safeguard against data loss or power cuts. The data centres were fitted out with banks of electricity generators and protected around the clock by squads of security guards.

Like other cities all over the world, Dublin was soon ringed with these establishments. The new services model was also given a specifically Irish twist. In between their profiles of putative technology millionaires, the newspapers now gushed about another wave of inward investment from America. Ireland's data centres, it was argued, could become the European beach-heads for online service ventures from the US. In 1999, the government forecast a hundred-fold increase in the volume of e-business by 2002 and commissioned Global Crossing to ramp up the communications bandwidth from Ireland to the outside world. Once again, the policymakers went chasing after a multinational mirage.

The data centre bubble burst after the turn of the century. Half-built facilities were abandoned. Working centres were sold off for a fraction of their original cost. Some of the buildings became cut-price accommodation for software firms that could make use of their installed bandwidth. In other cases, software development companies provided customers with online applications management by installing a few extra computers in their existing premises.

In retrospect, all the fuss about data centres and web applications obscured the key change in the Irish software industry during the years when external finance was at its most accessible. Generation four saw the birth of a new and distinctive cluster.

Mobile applications overtook middleware, computer-based learning and fixed network telecommunications to become the top priority for new developers. Many of the start-ups, indeed, were founded by veterans of the other clusters. Unlike the companies that went into web content management, moreover, the mobile brigade were able to differentiate their products on the international stage. Alatto Technologies, Am-Beo, Anam, Cape Technologies, ChangingWorlds, Network365, Ossidian Technologies and Xiam were among the developers that started operations at the tail-end of the twentieth century and made an impact in the early years of the twenty-first. This timing enabled them to get going while the venture capitalists were still shelling out finance and to keep growing after 2000 when the money supply tightened up.

Generation Five — Return to the Vertical Markets

Planet Earth was nervous in the final months of 2001. The September attacks on New York and Washington had sent shockwaves through international trade. They had also unleashed a patriotic mood in the US that made selling there more difficult for non-American companies. Enterprises all over the world were spending less money on information technology. Users had ramped up their software purchases before the turn of the century to ensure that their systems would not suffer problems with the date change at the start of the new millennium. They also wanted to be seen to respond to the e-business challenge. After 2000, when these requirements were met, they slashed their software budgets. Industry analysts could not detect any signs of recovery in late 2001.

Against this backdrop, the value of Irish software sales to the US climbed to an all-time high. They increased to €550 million in 2001, up from €460 million in the previous year. The industry's total exports rose by 28 per cent to €1,400 million. In 2002, the growth rate slowed to less than ten per cent. But the export figures kept rising. So did the number of software start-ups that enquired about Enterprise Ireland's support services for client companies.

It was clear, though, that the industry environment had changed and that generation four — with all its arrogance and greed — had had its day. For one thing, no one was talking about a software skills shortage any more. By 2002, indeed, there was mounting concern that software graduates were once again unable to find work as developers. The cycle was familiar. In generation five, though, the scale of the problem increased because of the higher student numbers in the education system and the colleges reported a steep fall in applications for places on their computing courses.

Younger firms, whose first products came to market as the spending freeze kicked in, found the going especially rough after 2001. And the spread into the regions slowed down when the labour market tightened up. Lower office rents and internet access charges in the big cities reduced the appeal of writing software in provincial towns.

The software companies that suffered most, however, were those that floated on the stock markets in the preceding years and those that had accepted large sums of venture capital. When the value of their shares dropped, the investors in these companies wanted to punish someone. It did not matter that valuations were falling everywhere or that the financiers often shared responsibility for bad business decisions. The rules of the game made it clear that chief executives must shoulder the blame in bad times. Several high-profile leaders lost their jobs.

This happened all over the world. But a nationality factor also came into play in Ireland. External investors often replaced founder-managers with chief executives from outside the country, often from the US. This happened too many times to be coincidental and made other companies even more wary of the venture capitalists than before. Some start-ups, indeed, shunned the investment infrastructure and went back to the old practice of living off service projects while they worked on their first products.

For the majority of software development companies, though, the end of generation four was more like a slow puncture than a blow-out. They trimmed their wage costs, slashed discretionary expenditure, scaled down their expansion plans, stopped using PR consultants and treated their existing customers well. The time had come to demonstrate their survival skills. The lessons of the late 1980s were remembered. There was not a crisis on the scale that ended generation two, but there was a general lowering of expectations.

The degree of retrenchment at individual companies in the new decade depended on the type of software they produced. The market contracted most sharply in the financial services and telecommunications clusters, although there was still a healthy interest in new software products among mobile network operators. Middleware and development kits were also problematic, not least because open source groups now offered free alternatives to some of the commercial toolsets. The suppliers of engineering applications, on the other hand, had not experienced any surge in demand in the 1990s and continued on the same steady course after 2001. The market for life sciences software was also buoyant. Geographic information systems were in demand and a new dynamism appeared in information technologies for government.

In 2003, indeed, a developer of public service applications made a sale that is believed to be the largest ever by an Irish software company. Curam Software won a deal worth $22 million in product licence fees alone from the UK Department for Work and Pensions. This involved the Dublin company's software framework for social welfare services, which had already featured in a series of projects at agencies in North America.

Curam was previously known as IT Design and had developed information retrieval products before specialising in social security systems. The company's ability to mix with the most technical breed of software engineers while focusing on a specific line of business was unusual in generation four. But the strategy was rewarded in generation five. Vertical market software developers fared best in the new century. These companies were slow builders that had gradually mastered their chosen fields while the quick buck brigade was splashing out on e-business branding campaigns.

Financial applications vendor Fineos, which started out under the name of Managed Solutions, was another example of the breed. It resembled Curam in the way that it carved out a target market over several years and eventually pulled in major contracts. Qumas, originally known as Westboro Software, grew up in a similar way. It offered bespoke software in the early 1990s and decided later in the decade to specialise in regulatory compliance for the pharmaceutical industry.

Curam, Fineos and Qumas became role models for other software companies that moved into banking and insurance, compliance management and government applications. All three were led by industry veterans who understood how to position software products and how to gain international credibility in their target areas. They knew when it made sense to change the platforms and development techniques behind their software. They were cautious about accepting external investment, but generally maintained good relationships with their financial backers. Their chief executives were never ousted. In all three cases, indeed, the founders stayed in charge for more than a decade.

The clusters that had performed best in the 1990s lost their shine in the first five years of the twenty-first century. The e-learning vendors suffered from corporate spending cutbacks. Software tool vendors faced an even harsher environment. Code inspection specialist Headway Software was arguably the most promising of the younger software engineering tool suppliers, but it went into receivership in 2004. Modelling expert Wilde Technologies saw collaborative development encroaching on its field and decided that it should join the open source movement. Mobile applications software peaked later than middleware, but lost much of its vitality by the middle of the decade. Fewer new names in this cluster released products after 2002.

At the same time, however, the telecommunications software cluster showed signs of recovery. When the telcos' budgets tightened, software firms that understood network planning and management, service activation or customer billing positioned themselves to offer cost-cutting options. Developers like Interactive Enterprise and Shenick won reference sites in all the major geographies. Their rise, indeed, is further evidence that companies with vertical market applications are showing the way ahead.

In summary, the software industry is undergoing another round of renewal with a new set of start-ups and the usual process of attrition among the last bunch. This is business as usual. The international economy, however, is unpredictable and the prospects for software exporters are mixed.

The profile of the Irish software industry is still distinctive. The country does not have a massive workforce of programmers like India or China or the other low-wage economies that offer offshore programming services. It has not matched the technical sophistication of developers in Russia and other parts of eastern Europe. Israel has a much better investment infrastructure for technology start-ups. And Ireland has never thrown up a giant technology corporation like Ericsson and Nokia in the Nordic region or SAP in Germany.

Pessimists sometimes argue that Ireland has become too expensive a place to develop software and that it is only a matter of time before Asian companies take command of the products business as well as providing software services. Optimists say that the global rise in computer literacy will create new markets for Irish middleware and development tools. Some industry analysts say that the packaged software suite is obsolete. Others are identifying more niche requirements in the organisations that depend on those suites. If software is going to be delivered as a hosted service, some feel that Irish developers will lose out to those that are physically closer to the customers. Others say that distance is no obstacle and that they have already made the software-as-a-service model work.

Getting Started in Limerick

Most of the stories in the following pages concern innovators and role models and influencers. The core of the Irish software industry, however, is made up of individuals like Tom Moore, who keep moving from project to project and from company to company. They have never lost their fascination with the way that code gets written and pieced together to perform new tasks.

Manser, the company that Moore founded in the early 1980s, still exists, although he is no longer involved. Two decades later, he is running Taringold, another software products company. This time around, he is based in Limerick. He moved there in the 1990s and co-founded a change management consulting firm.

Taringold, which is housed in an incubation centre for young firms, started to develop a business intelligence application in 2000. It has created a product, called Insata, that seeks to align the actions of individual managers with the overall objectives of a company. Insata — the name denotes "insight through data" — is designed to integrate with existing databases and applications. It is a top-down toolset that drills into data sources as required. Insata takes a different approach to most business intelligence software, which pushes operational data upwards and filters it from level to level. Taringold ran pilot trials of its product in 2002 and completed the first commercial implementation in the following year.

Like Manser, Taringold got started by selling its software into production facilities. Tom Moore points out, however, that the software is not solely for manufacturers and he hopes to apply it in other settings. The first Insata site is a factory in the mid-west because, he says, that is the work environment that he knows best.

"I think that developers put things into a better context now," he comments. There are more standards and norms to guide their product designs. The web browser has become the standard user interface. Database management systems and development environments from different vendors conform with industry norms. Software producers are no longer as isolated as Tom Moore was when he wrote his first PC package.

Developers still follow fads. Taringold, for example, has introduced its own version of extreme programming — a production methodology which, according to its advocates, brings out the coders' abilities by breaking down work into small packages. Essentially, though, extreme programming is just a fashionable approach to writing software in the same way that the PC was a fashionable development platform in Manser's early years.

Now, as then, people form software product companies to create original code. They want to run a business that builds something, instead of a business that sells or supports someone else's work. The future of the Irish software industry still lies in the hands of hundreds of small firms with big ambitions.

Chapter 2

FRONTIER TALES 1

Dreams of Efficiency

Maurice Spillane had a vision in the late 1970s. While working in a German-owned factory in Carlow, where he was responsible for install-ing manufacturing management applications on an IBM System/34 com-puter, he started to think about software quality. Manufacturing compa-nies, he reflected, had become highly efficient. Factories had learned how to co-ordinate the sourcing of materials, to plan production sched-ules and to minimise waste in their processes. Surely these lessons could also be applied to computer code? Software development, he reckoned, looked like old-style manufacturing before quality assurance was intro-duced. Perhaps, he mused, software production could be made as effi-cient as Braun's assembly line for hair dryers.

A quarter of a century has passed and Spillane is still asking this question. Some of his contemporaries from the early days of Irish soft-ware development have retired to tax shelters. Others have moved into property trading, opened wine shops or set up venture capital funds. Maurice Spillane is still pursuing the same ideal. He has made repeated attempts to build a business around his theory. Some of his schemes have been profitable. Others made heavy losses.

Real Time Software (RTS) gave Maurice Spillane an exit route from Braun. Dublin-based RTS was the first Irish company whose mission from its inception was to develop software for export. It was not the country's first software exporter. But its only significant predecessor was Aer Lingus, the government-owned airline, whose in-house computing organisation included an applications software group that co-operated with other carriers. When these airlines wanted a new system or to add extra features to an existing one, they pooled their resources and shared the costs. Aer Lingus took on a disproportionate share of the development work. When it created a subsidiary, Airline Systems Marketing, to resell the software to other airlines, it became Ireland's first homegrown software exporter. By the 1980s, its annual software sales were measured in millions. This extracurricular activity at the airline, however, was almost unknown outside the software community.

RTS, in contrast, was a high profile operation. The IDA-backed network of assembly plants had previously spun off subcontracting firms. When RTS was launched in 1980, it showed that a technology development business could also emerge from an inward investment project. The company's co-founder, Spencer Jenkins, came from another foreign-owned facility — Travenol, which made healthcare products in Castlebar. Jenkins was the technical leader of the new firm. RTS started operations with a staff of six. Maurice Spillane put up the initial finance. Before joining Braun, he had worked as an accountant at a mining company in Zambia and he was able to draw on savings that he had accumulated in Africa.

Like every other software firm at that time, RTS based its product plan around a specific hardware platform — the IBM System/34 mini-computer. According to Spillane, Braun Ireland had become one of the world's most advanced users of IBM's Maapics manufacturing applications, which ran on its System/34. This machine was a big seller in the late 1970s. Maapics had made packaged software more credible and more acceptable. The software, though, had been designed in the US and lacked features for international users. RTS set out to develop add-on modules that addressed these gaps in the suite.

In the early days of the company Maurice Spillane sold his services as a consultant while his colleagues worked on the code. Other Maapics users around Europe were already aware of what he had done at Braun. The electrical goods maker had installed software applications from Germany in its other plants. The Carlow facility was the first to implement Maapics and had modified the package with assistance from Dublin company AMS. It had added data collection, materials planning and downtime monitoring functions and had installed screens on the factory floor at a time when this was unusual and ambitious. "I worked in Braun in complete isolation," Spillane says. "We realised that we were doing something special when IBM UK hired a plane and brought in a bunch of executives to look at what we were doing." He started to receive invitations to speak at Maapics user events and to tell other IBM customers about the innovations in Carlow.

Maurice Spillane conducted market research for RTS at these IBM conferences. One event in Monte Carlo proved to be a real eye-opener. He learned that no one had yet produced multi-currency functions for the accounting and order entry sections of Maapics. The market was more than ready for such a product. RTS brought one out before the end of 1980. The fledgling firm made the first sale in Iceland with assistance from Danny McLoughlin at IBM Ireland. Westinghouse, which ran several production facilities in Ireland, was the second buyer. Then RTS won a major order from pharmaceutical company Boehringer in Germany. IBM Deutschland invited RTS to bid for this business. But the deal was done when Maurice Spillane was introduced to the Boehringer manager in charge of the project. They already knew each other from the conference in Monte Carlo, where they had discovered and discussed their mutual interest in the future of Maapics while waiting for Princess Caroline to perform the opening ceremony.

RTS doubled its turnover every year up to 1985, when it claimed revenues of more than $7 million. By then the company had opened 20 offices around Europe and the US, employed 160 staff and claimed 300 customer installations. Its multi-currency module had spawned a family of financial applications, Spectra, which was available in seven different languages. The enhancements to Maapics became a product line called Propics.

The company, however, was chronically under-funded, especially in comparison with other firms that were developing complementary software for Maapics. Most of these were in America where investors were at hand to back product ideas with hard cash. RTS had to compete against developers like SSA, which was cushioned by $30 million in venture capital. SSA soon became one of the biggest suppliers of manufacturing management software and continues to thrive today with annual sales of more than $500 million.

RTS, meanwhile, was unable to find a friendly banker in Ireland. The financial institutions were only willing to support businesses with physical assets and software products did not count. Maurice Spillane complained to anyone who would listen that the banks were demanding personal guarantees for loans and seemed to be more interested in the value of the borrowers' houses than in their business plans. RTS eventually turned to Bank of Boston for financial services. It also sold a 15 per cent shareholding in the company to 3i, a British venture capital outfit that had opened a branch in Dublin. Ian Armitage, who ran this office, joined the board of RTS. The deal netted just over $1 million at a time when the company needed money to build sales organisations in Germany and the US. It always preferred to sell directly instead of appointing distributors.

"There is no doubt that we tried to do too much with too little," Maurice Spillane says. Looking back, he blames all of the company's difficulties in its later years on investment issues. Critics at that time pointed to the far-flung network of RTS sales offices and suggested that the company had overstretched itself. Spillane maintains that the subsidiaries were doing fine and that RTS was brought down by its lack of financial resources. It did not help that his relationship with 3i turned sour. "What I didn't realise was that we weren't actually dealing with 3i, but with Ian Armitage," he says.

At the end of 1985, it became clear that RTS was going to record a heavy loss for the year. Ian Armitage called a board meeting and declared that the company was in deep trouble. "We weren't in trouble. We were tight with cashflow," Spillane insists. The meeting was acrimonious. Armitage stated that 3i would not put any more money into the organisation. According to Spillane, the director from 3i wanted to scale down the company and appoint a new chief executive. The row worsened. Bank of Boston heard about it and wanted to send in a receiver.

At this point, Maurice Spillane turned to the world's largest software corporation, Management Science America (MSA), to rescue RTS from its external investor. At first he hoped that the US firm would put some money into his business. It was not MSA's policy, however, to invest in other companies. The corporation was only interested in acquiring RTS. According to Spillane, indeed, it had done some research into the packaged software industry in Europe and rated RTS as one of the top three developers. He held preliminary talks with Michael Hunt, the UK-based executive vice president of MSA International and set up a meeting at the US firm's headquarters in Atlanta. When Spillane boarded a transatlantic flight in early 1986 he was horrified to find Ian Armitage on board. He says that they came to blows en route. In the end, MSA struck a deal with Spillane without including the venture capitalist in the negotiations.

MSA took over RTS in 1986, paying a combination of shares and cash. The operation in Dublin was renamed "MSA Medium Systems Division". It shut down in 1988. Maurice Spillane says that all the former RTS employees had found new jobs by the time the office closed. It transpired that MSA had less experience with acquisitions than he had thought. "They fiddled," he says. "They left us in charge of the company without being able to take any decisions. They were too nice to go in and gut the place." When MSA began to chalk up trading losses, however, it put the blame on the Dublin group, not on the army of 800 people that it employed in Atlanta. MSA's own demise followed in 1990, when it was acquired by Dun & Bradstreet.

Before Maurice Spillane left MSA, he floated a proposal to develop a toolset that would generate applications for the IBM AS/400. His superiors rubbished the idea. In 1987, a small team of RTS veterans broke away from MSA, set up Implementors International and created this product. Willie Byrne, one of the original group of six that started RTS, was the technical director of Implementors. Like RTS, the new firm targeted manufacturing and distribution firms. But it offered software that was better tailored to fit the way that they did business. By the end of 1991, Implementors' export sales were running at $350,000 a month, making it one of the biggest Irish software companies in the early stages of generation three.

Implementors lasted until 1995, when it employed more than 30 people, half of whom had worked at RTS. The company's annual revenues increased to more than $3 million, but it failed to raise the funds for further growth. Once again, Spillane says, investment problems killed his company. Once again, indeed, its failure involved a venture capitalist. Implementors had raised $1.7 million from Venture Link in 1990, but Maurice Spillane and Venture Link's principal fell out. At first they disagreed on whether or not the company should build its software to run on Microsoft Windows. Then their personal relationship deteriorated. The end result was that the company was unable to obtain follow-up finance when it needed to raise funds.

Maurice Spillane started over again. He launched Appligenics in 1996 with Fintan Kelly as the head of technology. The mission, as usual, was to create a better way of building software applications, based on the no-waste, no-rework principles that he had seen years earlier in the Carlow factory. Software tools and methodologies have changed over the decades, but Spillane's vision of efficient development has not.

Appligenics is headquartered in England, but its development team is based in Naas. It sells a software development environment that generates Java code for applications that run on any platform and can be accessed through web browsers. The company's sales pitch argues that its technology can make software development less expensive in Birmingham than in India. Spillane claims that the product is unique, because it is designed for applications to be developed by business analysts rather than conventional programmers. They collect and examine the requirements for an application, feed these requirements into the development environment and generate the code.

When Spillane formed RTS, he had his savings from Zambia in the bank. When he started Implementors, he still possessed some of the money that MSA had paid for RTS. In the mid-1990s, he no longer owned a house. All he had were some consulting fees from Implementors' customers. "It was the first time that I started with absolutely no money," he admits. He argues, however, that his experience is not unique. Most Irish software entrepreneurs, he contends, have little to show for their efforts.

Maurice Spillane is still an optimist — not only for himself but also for the industry as a whole. Software development, he believes, is all about investing enough money in the right people. "There is still no understanding that you need to make significant investments in order to get significant returns," he complains.

The Maapics Manipulators

The insights behind the Insight package originated in Canada. Tony McGuire had gone there in 1975. Prior to that he worked for Irish Life in Dublin, but he wanted to deepen his computing skills abroad. McGuire applied for permits in Australia, South Africa and the US as well as Canada. But the Canadian authorities processed his application more quickly than the others, supplying him with the necessary papers within six weeks.

He returned to Ireland in 1979 with practical experience from a database management project at a savings bank. He had also obtained postgraduate qualifications in database technology from a Canadian university. And he had obtained an enthusiasm for disciplined development processes. He was keen to apply this knowledge back home. On his return, however, he quickly discovered that no one else in Ireland shared his interests.

Local software service companies, McGuire recalls, could make good money with unoriginal applications and slapdash methods. "The standard of software that was being put out was appalling," he says. "The prevailing attitude was to throw some kids into a project, throw something together and charge a significant amount for it."

Matt Crotty told Tony McGuire bluntly that he would not find the type of work he wanted anywhere in Ireland. Crotty was the founder of Applied Management Systems (AMS), a minicomputer software supplier that had written accounting applications for IBM systems. In the mid-1970s, when conventional wisdom still held that real software professionals worked on large mainframes, Matt Crotty had decided to install smaller platforms. By the end of the decade, the IBM System/34 minicomputer had become a big seller. AMS knew that its customers' requirements were often very similar and started to produce packages that could be sold to multiple sites.

Like Maurice Spillane at RTS, Matt Crotty spotted an opportunity for new software that would complement IBM's Maapics package in manufacturing organisations. At one point, indeed, the two men considered collaboration on a financial modelling product. They could not agree how to share the rights and went their separate ways.

Matt Crotty had noticed a gap for business intelligence software that could draw data out of Maapics and re-use it in financial profit-and-loss reports. He floated the idea with Tony McGuire. Would he develop a prototype for AMS? McGuire declined Crotty's first approach and accepted a post in Cork as technical manager at Comtech, a Canadian software company with database development plans. It did not take him long to conclude that the Comtech project would never fly. At this point he agreed to take up Matt Crotty's offer if the work could be done through a separate company. He set up Vector Software in a single room at the AMS office in Dublin.

Tony McGuire incorporated some of the new concepts that he had encountered in Canada into the product. He also drew on his experience at Comtech. IBM's Danny McLoughlin chipped in more ideas and referred McGuire to IBM technologists who provided informal advice. A prototype took shape. AMS showed the product to some of its existing customers and began to take orders. The Insight package was released in 1980.

This software sat on top of other applications and manipulated their data in ways that were not possible before. Vector sold licence agreements and maintenance contracts. It refused to give away the source code as other minicomputer software developers had usually done. McGuire insisted that Insight was a product, not a service. The software, though, was not as easy to install and run as the packages of later years. Insight needed local tweaking to make it work. Nonetheless, word-of-mouth contacts among information systems managers made it a success. A single copy sold for more than $10,000 and some organisations bought the software for dozens of computers and locations. AMS financed the development effort from its own resources and proceeded to build up the business through direct sales.

Former colleagues say that Matt Crotty's strengths were in sales and concepts. He delegated the details of making the software work to other people. In the early years of AMS, his team included Pat Chambers, Brendan O'Donoghue and Joe Gorman, all of whom went on to set up other companies that supplied software for IBM minicomputers.

Barry Murphy was another of Crotty's recruits. Like Tony McGuire, he had worked as a mainframe programmer in Irish Life. In 1976, when he was still in his mid-twenties, the insurance firm had placed him in charge of a project to implement a unit-linked policy administration system. This demanded long hours of code inspection and testing. Murphy found gaps in the original specification and delivered an application that worked. When this project was over, Irish Life expected him to return to its nine-to-five regime. But he missed the adrenaline rush that he had experienced during the software roll-out. Murphy did not want to become "one of the lads in the room" again. Then, out of the blue, Matt Crotty called him and offered him a job. He joined AMS in 1977.

"The Irish software industry became very package-oriented in the late 1970s and early 1980s," Barry Murphy recalls. He says, indeed, that it was almost totally centred on bespoke development in 1977 and almost totally product-based just five years later. This was also the period when developers realised that software exports could make far more money than deals in the local market.

In the early 1980s, however, the only way of selling software was to go directly to those installations that had the right sort of computer. Matt Crotty set up a sales subsidiary in Britain called Insight Database Systems and based himself there. He subsequently moved to the US and opened sales offices in New York, Chicago and Los Angeles. Córas Tráchtála, the state agency that assisted exporters, helped AMS to set up its overseas offices. But its officials admitted that they knew nothing about the software trade.

Barry Murphy is generally credited with pulling the Irish organisation into shape while Matt Crotty set up the international offices. AMS changed its name to Insight Software in 1983. Its flagship product began to feature in the annual ICP Million Dollar Awards — a scheme run in the US by International Computer Programs to identify top-selling software. In 1984 the business intelligence package received an ICP award for cumulative sales of more than $5 million.

Back in Dublin, meanwhile, Vector Software took over all development, maintenance and support of the other applications that AMS had written. Insight never became a single-product business. It continued, indeed, to take on contract development projects, including a dealer management system for General Motors Ireland that was later sold to all of the car-maker's subsidiaries in Europe other than Germany.

The biggest software development challenge to Insight and Vector, though, was posed by IBM. By the mid-1980s its minicomputer architecture was nearing the end of its natural life. The system maker designed a new mid-range computer family, the AS/400, which was formally launched in 1988. Tony McGuire tracked the proposals for this new platform and came up with a software product concept that would take advantage of the more powerful relational database inside the AS/400. He aimed the Advanced Management Information System (Amis) at the largest users of the Insight package — groups of companies with operations in multiple territories. Amis was essentially a super-sophisticated spreadsheet — a data analysis product that filtered information in multiple dimensions. Insight released the first edition in 1997, before the AS/400 had shipped, promoting it as an advanced decision support application.

Amis, a premium product with a premium price tag, was not easy to sell. After six months, McGuire himself took on responsibility for international sales — a role that he describes as "very much evangelical". Orders trickled in, mainly from the US and the UK. Customers who bought Amis licences needed consulting and implementation services as well. The sales effort was hampered, however, by persistent rumours that IBM itself was going to release a competing product. It never did. Amis strengthened the reputations of Insight and Vector Software as mid-range system partners to IBM. It also furthered the international expansion of the Dublin-based group. By 1988 the majority of its revenues came from exports.

Early that year, before IBM had formally unveiled the AS/400, Insight Software and Vector Software underwent a change of owner. The Hoskyns Group, a publicly quoted British company that was expanding through acquisitions, bought the sister organisations. Hoskyns had previously sold software for Digital Equipment and Hewlett-Packard computers and wanted to buy in AS/400 expertise. Matt Crotty, the majority shareholder in the group, cut his ties as soon as the deal was agreed. The other senior managers in the group stayed on and were given a two-year sales target by Hoskyns. They achieved that target in twelve months.

"Hoskyns was a good company to work for, but it had nothing to offer on the technical side," Tony McGuire recalls. It liked the idea of having a product development laboratory, but had no previous experience on the products side of the industry. The company culture centred on contract development services. Its business formula was based on project earnings. Its managers spent their time calculating staff utilisation rates and fee levels. In 1988 about 30 per cent of Insight's group business still came from bespoke software. Hoskyns appeared to be much more interested in this work than in the other 70 per cent. But it left the product strategy in place.

Another services-centred group, Cap Gemini, acquired Hoskyns in 1990. Tony McGuire and Barry Murphy both left the company after this second takeover. Cap Gemini dismantled the product development and support operation that they had built. It sold off the Amis product in 1993. McGuire went on to launch and lead other software ventures, but none of these has achieved international success to compare with Insight. Barry Murphy became the national software director.

Between Hardware and Software

When software product development was taking off in the early 1980s, a small set of Irish companies decided to design and build their own computer hardware. Few of these lasted for long, but Mentec found a niche in embedded computing and settled there for the long haul. As a general rule the Dun Laoghaire firm preferred to source whatever software it required from other organisations. Occasionally, though, it bought the rights to key products from their developers. This policy led to the most audacious software acquisition by an Irish company.

Trinity College Dublin lecturer Mike Peirce launched Mentec in 1978 as a computer implementation business that also understood manu-facturing process control. The start-up had an equity base of about $80,000 and a team of former Trinity students to make its customers' systems work. Like all of its contemporaries, Mentec selected a specific computer vendor on whose platforms it would work. Peirce's first choice was minicomputer maker Data General. In 1979, however, Mentec switched its allegiance to Digital Equipment and a long and complex partnership began.

According to Mike Peirce, Digital was the first minicomputer vendor to develop active relationships with original equipment manufacturers (OEMs) — the intermediaries that combined its products with other technologies and brought the bundles to market. It looked for partners that could deliver applications for its PDP computers and the operating systems that accompanied them. Digital differentiated itself from other vendors, such as Data General, by supplying its OEMs with complete and open documentation on both the hardware and the system software. To an engineering firm like Mentec, this was an invitation to explore the fundamentals of the technology that it sold.

Massachusetts-based Digital Equipment had set up a production fa-cility in Galway in 1971 and added a second in Clonmel in 1978. These operations expanded into one of the largest IDA-backed projects in the country. The company also built up a sales office in the late 1970s. It constantly highlighted its manufacturing investments in Ireland and landed much of the available business from government departments, universities and state-owned companies. Soon Digital's revenues from Irish computer users were almost as high as IBM's.

Digital appointed about a dozen OEMs in Ireland to support its bid for a high market share. Mentec quickly established itself as a core part-ner. The others included GC McKeown, which later evolved into a health service applications developer, and Online Computing, which Mentec acquired in 1988. Mentec and McKeown differentiated themselves from the OEM pack by mastering Digital's VAX "supermini" at an early date, while the other partners were still getting familiar with the PDP.

Mentec, which had churned out bespoke software in early years, licensed applications for the VAX from independent developers. The Impcon and Fincon packages for manufacturing management and financial administration came from a company in London. The Dun Laoghaire firm later bought these products outright. It repeated this process some years later with an American software supplier, Visibility. First Mentec became a reseller of Visibility's products. Then it joined with the company's management in a buyout that made it a major shareholder.

In the early 1980s Mentec engineers worked on both of Digital's hardware architectures. They found that the VAX was fine for commercial applications, but too clumsy for real-time processing on the factory floor. "We came from a very strong manufacturing base, sourcing data from sensors," Mike Peirce explains. "As things progressed, Mentec picked up the threads of products that Digital was not promoting." One of these was the J-11 processor. Peirce's company licensed this chip in 1982 and designed its own products around it. It developed a series of single-board computers that was totally compatible with Digital's PDP-11 family, but offered price and performance advantages. Customers embedded these boards into process control systems, telecommunications equipment and the electricity infrastructure.

"We had a baptism of fire with Digital," Peirce says. "When the reality dawned that they had given away a lot, they retracted." The US company cut off the supply of J-11 components. Mentec fought back. According to Peirce, Digital was not accustomed to partners opposing its decisions. American companies, moreover, generally tried to resolve such disputes in the courts. Mentec preferred to use its powers of persuasion, dispatching its executives to Massachusetts and arguing its case on Digital's own turf. This form of lobbying paid off. Digital resumed the supply of J-11s. "That was our first lesson in dealing with Digital in the US and alerted us to the opportunity of doing business in the US," Peirce says.

The PDP-compatible single board computer business grew. In later years Mentec also developed Intel-based versions that ran Unix applications and a succession of high-speed processing boards for video-conferencing systems. The company built up a direct presence in the US, initially opening a sales office, then adding engineering and customer support functions. It continued to sell Digital-compatible boards up to the turn of the century.

Mike Peirce and his colleagues took advantage of the same fiscal incentives that the Irish government had put in place for Digital and other foreign investors. Mentec Computer Systems, the company that developed the single board computers, exported everything that it produced. Its revenues were never spectacular — by 1990 they had risen to approximately $8 million a year — but this was a profitable business and the profits were tax-free for both the company and its directors.

Digital Equipment entered the 1990s with plans for a new generation of processors and migration strategies for all of its existing computers and software. By then, however, it was struggling against structural changes in the information technology industry. The new leaders were focused companies that dominated specific product categories. Intel in microprocessors, Microsoft in operating systems, EMC in storage and Oracle in databases were the most prominent examples. Digital, meanwhile, remained an old-style vendor that tried to operate across the full product spectrum. It still sold everything from semiconductors to network management software to consulting services. The corporation began to clock up trading losses. Its founder, Ken Olsen, stepped down in 1992 after 35 years in charge of the business. By then Digital resembled the Austro-Hungarian empire in its twilight years — a far-flung but poorly co-ordinated entity that could take pride in its former glories but was no longer sure about its place in the world. In 1994 Mike Peirce saw and seized an opportunity to grab one of the old regime's best loved heirlooms.

Mentec bought the entire PDP-11 software business from Digital — the RSX and RSTS operating systems, related networking products and associated developers' tools. Digital would continue to sell these products, but it would do so as a Mentec distributor. The agreement required Mentec to invest in maintenance resources and to prepare the PDP software for the date change at the end of the millennium. It met these commitments.

According to Mike Peirce, the transaction had two main advantages for his company. It inherited a relationship with Siemens on which it could build more business in Europe. It also achieved an immediate and substantial increase in its activity in the US.

Digital Equipment no longer exists. Mentec, the OEM that bridged the divide between hardware and software development, has outlived the Massachusetts mammoth.

Small in Japan

The people in the trade board told Malachy Smith that he was making a big mistake. "All the agencies told me that the Japanese would not buy anything from a small technology company," he recalls. But he went to Tokyo anyway. The computing congress was already underway when he arrived. He missed the first day of the exhibition. And he spent the second day setting up the stand that he had brought with him. His tiny fold-up display looked out of place among the corporate showcases that huge Japanese firms had erected around it.

No one stepped onto Smith's stand for two days. On the final day of the fair, however, the man from Sony approached and said that the company had been monitoring him. It was important, he said, that Smith should postpone his planned departure from Tokyo at the weekend. Sony wanted him to attend a meeting on Monday. He kept the appointment. When he arrived at the Sony office, he was ushered into a room with an electronic blackboard — something that he had never seen before. His contact from the exhibition asked him to sketch the design of his product on the board. Smith started to draw a diagram that showed what the software did. As he did so, a wall panel slid away to reveal an audience of 300 Sony engineers. There was no need for a translator. The guys in the audience wanted to study his drawing and would discuss it afterwards among themselves.

Malachy Smith was a returned emigrant. He left Ireland as a student and attended Hamilton Institute of Technology and Waterloo Lutheran

University in Canada. He came back in 1981 after working on a broadband network project with Bell Canada. Smith was keen to continue
working in data communications, but found that the opportunities were
rather limited. The Guinness brewery in Dublin, however, had ambitious
plans to distribute purchasing information from an ICL mainframe
around its premises. Smith joined a team that designed a three-kilometre
broadband ring for Guinness, using technology from 3M. Des Cahill,
who co-founded Intelligence with Smith, worked on this project as well.
So did Alan Repko, whose company Bootstrap Datacomms was one of
the first in Dublin to specialise in data networking, and John Carolan,
who had already established his reputation as a formidable software developer. At that time, Carolan was employed by Rainsford Computing
Services, which was a subsidiary of Guinness.

The brewery project was supposed to open up new opportunities for
Rainsford to provide network design and installation services to other
companies. But the project team came up with alternative ideas. Personal
computers had arrived on the scene and it was obvious that new pieces of
software were required to connect them. The Guinness network team
debated how much demand there might be for emulation software that
made these new machines behave like the terminals attached to mainframes and minicomputers. They reckoned, Malachy Smith says, that
four products could meet most of the communications needs inside IBM
and ICL installations. Smith and Cahill formed Intelligence Ireland in
1982 to develop such software. The new venture got started with an office in Dublin and a consulting contract from Guinness. John Carolan did
not join the firm, but kept in touch.

Intelligence survived for just four years. But its evolution was fast and
furious and it did things that no one else in Ireland tried in the early
1980s. It wanted to grow fast by trading globally. It pitched for funds
from venture capitalists in Silicon Valley without success and then made
headlines when it secured external investment from Musgrave, a distribution group that had never been involved with a software company before.
Intelligence also declared that it would aim for a stock exchange listing. It

claimed world firsts in communications software development. And it won the trust of Sony when there were only 18 employees on its books.

In 1982, the term PC was not yet in widespread use. But there were many embryonic systems around. Different vendors promoted their own microcomputer designs and, as with minicomputers, the software developers still hitched up with specific hardware brands. Intelligence soon concluded that its target market lay among these system manufacturers rather than in user organisations.

Malachy Smith and Des Cahill also noticed that the economics of software production were changing fast. Minicomputer package developers could be successful by installing their products on dozens of systems, but PC software suppliers needed to cater for many thousands of computers. Products like the WordStar word processor and the VisiCalc spreadsheet had already shown that this was possible. Looking back, Malachy Smith says that the new breed of software companies were real risk-takers and that Intelligence wanted to be one of them. This strategy may have been acceptable in Silicon Valley, but the prevailing attitudes in Ireland were very different. Investors, he explains, wanted a predictable return and had no concept of risk. "Failure meant that you got a slap in the face," he says.

Intelligence Ireland hired a small group of programmers and set out to emulate the new breed of American software companies. It designed its own suite of desktop applications with built-in data communications functions. Other vendors sold word processors and spreadsheets and databases that could share the same data, but the user had to open and close these different pieces of software. Intelligence wanted its package to move data from application to application more easily than the other suites allowed. The users' data constituted an "information pie" and Intelligence would provide tools that cut into the pie in different ways. The diagram that Malachy Smith drew for Sony's engineers in Tokyo encapsulated this approach to desktop software.

The result of his presentation was Project Gemini. Sony awarded a $300,000 contract to Intelligence to develop a prototype package. It had to run on a new breed of microcomputers that several Japanese companies were preparing to launch. The consumer electronics industry there had followed the spread of PCs in the workplace and concluded that there would soon be a market for home computers as well. The big firms got together and laid down a common design specification for these products. They called it MSX.

In 1984 Project Gemini became an integral part of Sony's plan for MSX — the creation of a set of communicating software products. Sony coined the name Thinkman for the software and plotted a marketing campaign around this brand. The corporation sent eight engineers from Japan to inspect the Intelligence organisation. They found a small office in the Dublin suburbs whose occupants tried to behave like their role models in Silicon Valley. They worked long hours, subsisted on the beer and pizza that they brought into the premises and genuinely believed that they were capable of world domination. They were also well connected. For example, when Intelligence identified the need to add an extra circuit board to the MSX machines, the company tracked down two Irish engineers who could design one and then had it made in Taiwan.

Sony assigned Kozo Hiramatsu to oversee the work in Intelligence. He developed a good relationship with the company, partly because he was already familiar with Ireland. His new colleagues in Dublin, indeed, helped him to track two girls from Nenagh who had befriended him on his first visit to the country some years earlier. As the MSX initiative gathered momentum, the opportunities for Intelligence expanded. Epson, for example, contracted it to supply applications software for its MSX computers.

MSX, however, flopped. There was less demand for home computers in the mid-1980s than the manufacturers had forecast. The buyers, moreover, shied away from the Japanese system standard. As in the business computer trade, consumers soon started to ask for "IBM-compatible" machines instead. And Project Gemini died.

"The reason why Intelligence failed at the end of the day was that the home computer in Asia failed," Malachy Smith says, "And because we were so small there was nowhere else for us to turn." The company landed some consolation projects from Sony and took on other assignments for corporate clients like British Telecom and ICL. Without Project Gemini, however, Intelligence suffered acute cashflow problems. It needed to find new backers to survive. Smith and Cahill discovered that they would need to hand over 80 per cent of the equity to attract a new investor. They decided to sell the entire company instead.

In July 1986 the Dedeir Group, an investment company controlled by Dublin-based financier Dermot Desmond, acquired Intelligence. The transaction paid off the company's debts, but Musgrave, which had owned just over one quarter of the shares, could only recoup about 30 per cent of the money that it had put in. Dedeir already controlled a cluster of software ventures. These proceeded to integrate communications technology from Intelligence into software applications for financial services.

The Intelligence team scattered. Des Cahill and Sean Dunne — the first software designer that the company had hired — stayed on for a while. Dermot Desmond subsequently financed another software venture led by Cahill. Malachy Smith, on the other hand, made a quick exit. After a short spell as a consultant, Wang recruited him as managing director of its Irish sales subsidiary. He spent the next eight years moving up the US corporation's management ranks and later became head of Pitney Bowes' operations in Europe. He did not return to Ireland until 2001.

Just Having Fun with Computers

Working for Motorola was the safe option for software developers in Cork in the late 1980s. The risk takers joined SMC. This company was formed in 1985 and thundered along for six turbulent years. It had four directors at the beginning. Very quickly, though, SMC turned into a double act. After two of the founders left, the company was run by Shemas Eivers and Kevin Paul — engineering graduates with contrasting personalities. Eivers was an outstanding software engineer — a techie's techie who enjoyed trying out new tools and technologies. He took a masters degree in civil engineering, then worked at the Cork-based National Microelectronics Research Centre as a researcher. Kevin Paul was a fast-talking, hyper-energetic dealmaker, who loved the cut and thrust of selling. He made a point of attending industry conferences just so that he could make contacts among the other delegates. He always appeared to be on a permanent quest for the "wonder deal".

SMC was fuelled by passion, not built to a plan. "We were 24. We didn't see ourselves going anywhere. We were just having a bit of fun with computers," Eivers recalls. He remembers the late 1980s as a wild ride when the company tried its hand in one new business area after another.

The passion began at the engineering department in University College Cork (UCC), where second-year students were taught Fortran programming. Lecturer John Campbell, who is now an associate professor at the department of civil and environmental engineering, encouraged the undergraduates to take on computing projects. A hard core created their own subculture, coding together for long hours in their hang-out on the top floor. The regulars liked to get there early so they could grab the six swivel armchairs in the room. This clique stayed in contact after leaving college. Several members ended up working at SMC.

The company was formed at a time when PC sales were rising fast. The mainstream software industry was still focused on minicomputer applications. So the new venture concentrated instead on desktop machines and their ability to handle databases.

SMC initially followed the traditional strategy of the generation two start-up. It offered local development services in and around Cork. In practice, what happened was that Kevin Paul placed his sales talent behind Shemas Eivers' technical skills. SMC's first major project was a cost control reporting application for Angus Fine Chemicals. The fledgling firm hired its first employee to work on this job, training him at night. When Angus sent an executive from America to review its work, Eivers assumed that the customer had unmasked the makeshift nature of SMC's operation. The visitor had actually travelled over to offer more development work to the Cork outfit.

From then on most of SMC's projects came from manufacturing companies. In 1987 Kevin Paul, the consummate convention goer, organised a conference on computers in manufacturing. This made the SMC name better known outside Cork. The company had also come to the attention of IBM Ireland.

The systems maker was preparing to launch its AS/400 mid-range computer and wanted to ensure that its Irish customers could obtain suitable software for the new platform. IBM decided to develop Bicarsa — a suite of sales and marketing applications — and asked SMC to work on this project. The Cork crew signed up for the journey after IBM chief Tony Furlong indicated that the software might have international sales potential. Shemas Eivers, though, was puzzled that IBM wanted them. SMC had no experience with the System/3x minicomputers that the AS/400 would supersede. And it had never worked with the RPG programming language that IBM was using to write the new applications. "We never understood why they came to us and we didn't care," Eivers says. The terms of the deal were good and SMC stood to share the future revenues from the product. The company cemented its alliance with the computer giant in 1988 when IBM Ireland's chairman, John Donovan, agreed to chair its own board of directors.

Shemas Eivers and half a dozen other SMC developers were soon transported to an IBM building in Dublin's Mount Street. There they were provided with connections to a pre-release AS/400. This model's specifications were so confidential that the SMC team was never allowed into the room that contained the machine.

Back in Cork, meanwhile, SMC pushed out some products of its own. A drawing office management system, Cadman, sold well in the UK and was also shipped into the US. PlantCare and StockCare were complementary packages for plant maintenance and for production control and planning. The company also offered its package development environment for resale. SMC's best shot, though, was its MSS management information system for multi-location, multi-language accounting and distribution. This started as a custom project for Zenith, which had set up a computer assembly operation in Kells in 1983 and wanted financial software that could run on the PCs that it made. Zenith eventually implemented it in Britain, Germany and the Netherlands, as well as in Ireland. SMC set up a sales subsidiary in England for MSS and sold the software into other organisations.

The Bicarsa project, however, was a flop. The software never made it onto the market. It was not a financial failure for SMC. The fees that the company received from IBM were greater than its costs. But the affair sapped its strength. Other projects were under-resourced and went astray. The MSS initiative lost momentum. And SMC was suffering from a lack of strategic planning. It had evolved into a group of companies, spawning a dozen subsidiaries with complicated relationships. Its headcount kept increasing, but the employees were struggling with a rising workload.

The sales department kept pulling more work in, including exotic assignments with American companies that Kevin Paul had made contact with. "Kevin was a brilliant opportunity sniffer. He just did not like finishing things," Eivers says. His colleague, he adds, also appeared to be losing interest in the software business.

SMC became more focused in its later years. One side of the business, run by Paul, focused on computer-aided design, while Eivers concentrated on database development with the dBase product set. But the market was shifting away from dBase. "What caught us out in the end was that we were in the wrong technology, using dBase rather than SQL," Eivers says.

The wild ride came to an end in 1991. MF Kent Corporation, an international engineering, project management and construction company, acquired SMC and tried to redeploy its staff in project management services. It also cultivated a relationship with Perot Systems, which at that time was interested in stepping up its operations in Europe. But the former SMC premises in North Mall shed employees steadily and the business was finally wound up in 1994, after an examiner was appointed to its parent group.

By the early 1990s SMC had grown its workforce to 60 people. Most came from Cork and many had passed through the engineering department in UCC. Some had left the city to gain software experience and returned in order to join SMC. When it disintegrated, they fanned out and created a new cluster of Cork-based technology firms, including software developers like Cadco, Qumas and PM Centrix. SMC's legacy was an affinity between Cork and engineering applications. It is still discernible long after the company's demise.

Client Solutions, which Shemas Eivers co-founded in 1994, was another generation three heir to the SMC tradition. It grew bigger than SMC had ever been. Now part of a publicly quoted services company, Horizon Technology Group, Client Solutions employs 70 staff in Cork and Dublin. The company, though, is strictly in the software services camp. It does not build products. In contrast with SMC, moreover, Eivers has maintained a tight control over its financial performance. He is still a hard-core techie, but has gradually assumed the unofficial role of software industry leader in the southern region. Kevin Paul, meanwhile, left the software business and spent much of his subsequent career in the European telecommunications industry.

Both of the SMC chiefs, it appears, have followed their instincts. Shemas Eivers retained his passion for the intricacies of software engineering. Kevin Paul kept searching for the perfect deal.

Wearing Suits and Adding Value

The typical generation two software company started as a service provider to local customers, wrote its first code as a sideline, re-positioned itself as a product developer after a few years and ceased trading before its tenth birthday. Vision Consulting did the opposite at each stage in its development. It failed to make the grade in packaged applications, then re-emerged as a software services venture. Most of its contemporaries are long forgotten, but the Dublin company has survived into its third decade.

Vision was born in 1984. Led by founders Janet Howard and Gerald Adams, the start-up released Equifacs, a document management application for networked PCs. It catalogued and cross-referenced word processing and spreadsheet files. Equifacs was designed for export. By 1987 the company had localised its package for German-speaking countries and started to appoint distribution partners. In the following year it added a consulting department and recruited Billy Glennon, who had learned his craft at Arthur Andersen, to run this part of the business.

The soft-speaking, reflective Glennon reinvented Vision as a miniature and more agile version of Andersen. He believed that a small firm with fresh ideas should be able to win contracts from large enterprises, such as banks and insurance companies. Its costs would be lower than the multinational management services outfits, so its fees could be lower as well.

This business model, however, required Vision to act differently from a PC package developer. Working with Adams as the chief technology officer, Glennon fostered a distinctive company culture. He hired graduates and trained them in this style, favouring recruits from colleges whose curricula included work experience. Vision employees wore suits. Its software developers learned how to converse with bankers in their own language. They read books on customer services as well as programming manuals. Vision, despite its origins in PC software, gradually mastered the nuances of working in corporate computing departments with a mainframe heritage.

By 1990 Billy Glennon had officially assumed charge of the company. Vision, which had just five staff when he joined it, now had 40 employees. The group retained a product development division through the early 1990s, offering computer-based training packages that taught structured testing techniques to programmers and an administration system for large IT departments. But Vision described its core business as "value-added consulting".

The company took on another 100 people in the first half of the 1990s, including teams in Northern Ireland and Scotland, where it carried out a series of projects for energy company Scottish Hydro-Electric. It opened a London office in 1995 and another in New York three years later. The mini-Andersen model meant going after large contracts, so Vision expanded into the places where it could find those. In 2000 the company employed 400 staff and recorded sales of $65 million. Five big customers accounted for about three-quarters of these revenues.

Gradually, moreover, the consulting team reduced the computing content of its work and focused more on business process analysis and organisational change. Vision distanced itself from software product development, although it continued to attract some of Ireland's top technical talent. In the mid-1990s the company started to collaborate with Business Design Associates, a California firm that promoted management re-modelling as a means of overhauling business processes. Drawing on its partner's experience, it showed information technology managers how to present themselves as their companies' change agents. In 2000, Vision acquired its American partner and inherited its operations in San Francisco, Mexico and Chile.

Billy Glennon became one of the Irish software industry's intellectuals, a lateral thinker whose analyses often turned in unexpected directions. He enjoyed tracking new trends in technology, customer services and business organisation, speculating where they might lead and repositioning his company accordingly. He experimented, for example, with billing methods based on the business results of a project. His approach was reminiscent of Tom McGovern at System Dynamics, but he operated internationally, not just inside Ireland. Vision went looking for innovators and risk takers at global level and negotiated deals with those that liked its worldview.

Vision's progression from small-scale product development to multinational consultancy included several twists along the way. There were rapid ramp-ups followed by sudden scale-downs. Big initiatives collapsed and small ones took off in unanticipated directions. The Dublin company was also lucky. The rush to the internet in the late 1990s played to all its strengths — technology assessment, business re-modelling, customer relationships and project management. Concepts that had been bouncing around the Vision office for years came into vogue. Major corporations, moreover, came under pressure from their shareholders to address these issues.

At a time when every company needed to be seen to have an e-business strategy, Vision was ideally placed to formulate plans that stood out from the pack. New consulting firms and development service providers proliferated in those years. Most spent lavishly on their facades but had very little substance behind them and soon collapsed. Vision, in contrast, could draw on a decade of relevant experience.

Its customer list included heavyweight names like General Motors, BNP Paribas and Citibank. It landed substantial projects like the design of a "virtual banking" system for Dime Savings Bank of New York and a "global architecture" to promote Warner Music Group's artists and labels on the web. An American online financial news publication, TheStreet.com, sought its expertise in content management. Vision built Europe's first internet bank, Banking365, for Bank of Ireland, and then designed and established Intelligent Finance — a completely new online and telephone-based savings and loans bank in Britain — in less than one year. This led to a commission from the Mexican government to create a banking model and a technology strategy for a new institution that would offer financial services to millions of citizens who had never previously held bank accounts.

With this series of contracts under its belt, Vision was arguably the most successful e-business venture in Ireland. It not only grew rapidly in the boom years of the internet; it also knew how to adapt in the quiet spell that followed, advising customers that needed to retrench on how they could improve the bottom line. Speaking in 2002, Glennon said that he was driving the company to offer better business results, rather than better technologies, to its clients. "We need to be proactive in making offers and we need to bring a number of parties to the table to put together those offers," he elaborated.

Once an unsuccessful product developer, Vision had turned consulting services to its advantage. Throughout these years it also remained one of Ireland's biggest employers of software talent, but never made any fuss about the fact. By the time of its twentieth anniversary in 2004, indeed, the company's handiwork could be traced in systems and services from New York to Mexico City.

Chapter 3

COLLEGE CONNECTIONS

The Numbers Game

The government floated a plan to reform higher education in the late 1960s. But the academics saw it as a threat.

Dublin had two universities and the government — a Fianna Fáil administration — wanted to combine them. The normal practice in Europe was for each city to support one university. The duplication of resources in Dublin was an accident of history, rooted in political and religious divisions of little relevance in the second half of the twentieth century. The government drew up a merger plan. Some disciplines and departments would be assigned to Trinity College — the Dublin University campus in the city centre — while others were allocated to University College Dublin (UCD) in the suburbs.

The Trinity engineering school found these proposals particularly unpalatable. Engineering was supposed to be consolidated at UCD. The Trinity school not only resisted the overall strategy; it also introduced a measure that might enable some of its staff to remain in town. In 1969, the engineering school set up a department of computer science and allowed it to establish a separate identity. The school inherited a masters course in computing and started life with three academic staff. The head of the department, John Byrne, had brought the first IBM computer into the campus some years earlier. Neville Harris and Francis Neelamkavil completed the team. All three were still based in the department more than 30 years later.

Academic resistance to the university merger was widespread and the plan was soon abandoned. It had, however, helped computer science to emerge as a discipline in its own right. Trinity introduced a computing stream to its engineering curriculum and developed a range of diploma courses.

In the years that followed, both universities offered computing education. But their courses evolved in different ways. The association between software and engineering has continued to the present day at Trinity College Dublin; computer science is still a department of the school of engineering. At UCD the new discipline found a home in its science faculty and remained there. In later years, turf wars were fought in other colleges for stewardship of the new subject, with business schools sometimes presenting an alternative to the science and engineering factions.

The range of courses and qualifications increased in the 1970s as more third-level institutions were established around the country. The National Institutes of Higher Education and Regional Technical Colleges that opened in the 1970s were designed to meet changes in the industrial labour market. The European Social Fund provided subsidies to some of their computing students. The resources of the new institutions, though, were often thin. The Regional Technical College in Waterford introduced a two-year certificate in computing in 1975 and admitted 20 students. There was no computer on the campus that they could use. The college had only a teletypewriter link over a phone line into University College Cork. The certificate course students had to send batches of punched cards by train for processing on a civil service mainframe in Dublin. The situation improved when the college obtained a minicomputer with a paper tape reader. This machine was not provided by the Department of Education, but donated by a local company.

When the software development industry expanded in the early 1980s, most of its workforce were former mainframe and minicomputer minders, self-taught enthusiasts or graduates in other subjects who had begun programming in college. Only a couple of hundred people in the country held formal computing degrees, mostly from an evening course that Trinity College Dublin had introduced in the early 1970s.

As the number of degree, diploma and certificate courses increased, the entry routes into software development were formalised. The industry also differentiated between graduates from the older and the younger third-level colleges. The newer institutions designed their syllabi with an eye to employment trends. Most of their students spent blocks of time on placements in commercial firms. Employers assumed that these graduates would have more commercial awareness and would become productive more quickly when they joined the workforce. Some stated a strong preference for recruiting from the two National Institutes of Higher Education — the colleges that later changed their names to Dublin City University and University of Limerick.

Some of those graduates, however, discovered the limitations of their vocationally oriented education and concluded that the courses had prepared them to become software technicians rather than software engineers. Their education equipped them to write code, but lacked a theoretical underpinning. John Byrne at Trinity College tells a story of two software developers who went to work in a local government authority. When they were asked to take on a new task, the Trinity graduate said that he would need time to read up on the subject. The other recruit declared that he could not work on something that he had not been taught in college.

The divide was probably never as rigid as such anecdotes suggest. The lecturers on Trinity's evening courses held day jobs in industry. The university also ran computing diploma courses at various times for electrical engineers, librarians, linguists, financial services specialists, medical administrators and employees of Digital Equipment Corporation. Dublin City University (DCU) professor Michael Ryan contends, meanwhile, that the theoretical component of his college's degrees was always comparable with Trinity's. What DCU added, he says, was contextual material that graduates could utilise in the workplace. According to Ryan, this gave students a basic familiarity with accounting terminology and manufacturing processes. By the mid-1990s, he adds, DCU was awarding more higher degrees in computing than any other Irish university.

According to University of Limerick graduate Robert Baker, the Irish education system has always over-reacted to shifts in the labour market. The colleges, he argues, kept adjusting their courses to reflect the expected demand for different styles of programming and paid too little attention to the fundamentals of computer science. "We got paranoid about crises and produced people who were more interested in applying technology than in developing technology," Baker says.

The education system certainly became preoccupied with a numbers game. It tried to match the output of computer science graduates with the human inputs that the software development industry wanted. This locked it into a cycle.

When the industry complains that the colleges are not producing enough graduates, the government steps up investment on the campuses. It takes time, though, to build more lecture halls, to enlarge the libraries and to recruit additional lecturers. The labour market does not stand still during these preparations. By the time the additional students qualify, the employers have stopped hiring. Many of the graduates move into other lines of work or leave the country. Sooner or later, new technologies emerge and new markets open up. Industry representatives warn of skills shortages again. And the entire cycle is repeated.

The first major alarm was raised in the late 1970s, when minicomputer sales were increasing. At the start of the decade, a typical computer installation for accounting and payroll management cost hundreds of thousands of dollars. The price dropped steadily and computer shipments rose. More hands were needed to keep the systems running in user organisations, especially in the foreign-owned assembly plants. The colleges introduced additional qualifications, raised student intakes and launched "conversion" programmes for graduates from other disciplines. Advertisements in British computer magazines offered incentives for expatriate systems analysts and applications programmers to return home.

A group of industry associations and the Irish Computer Society set up a joint committee in 1979 to consider the country's future needs. This committee's recommendations led to a marked increase in student numbers and established an infrastructure for computing education in the following decade. No one anticipated, though, how quickly packaged software would displace in-house programmers. The under-supply scare was short-lived. The 1979 expansion plan was based on the generation one industry model. By the time it was implemented, generation two had arrived. The new product development firms failed to employ enough graduates to compensate for this shift.

Trinity College Dublin, meanwhile, had introduced a four-year BA course. The first graduates completed their degrees in 1983. The embryonic DCU awarded its first computing degrees in the following year. Both universities admit that there was a high emigration rate among their graduates for the first few years, but point out that many went on to successful careers in software development. College leavers with lower qualifications were usually less fortunate. Some of the two-year computing certificate courses, indeed, became predominantly female in the mid-1980s and were regarded as training schemes for technically adept secretaries.

The emigration of software developers remained high throughout the 1980s. A 1989 report commissioned by the Minister for Industry and Commerce noted that only four out of ten graduates with computing degrees or diplomas were obtaining employment in Ireland.

Generation three, in contrast, was characterised by more technically sophisticated products and by software firms that the universities regarded as suitable places for their graduates to work. The pool of coding skills within the country was soaked up in the early 1990s and shortages were feared again. This time the problem was international. The cycle proceeded as before, but the number of vacancies and the pressure for additional college places were both much greater this time around. Unfortunately, however, construction workers were also in short supply. "There was a push to build more accommodation. Then the Celtic Tiger came and ate up all the bricklayers," University of Limerick Vice President Kevin Ryan recalls.

A 1998 report by McIver Consulting tried to quantify the skills shortfall. It estimated that almost 20,000 people worked in the software industry, including nearly 7,000 in localisation and distribution roles. These figures included the employees of international companies. An additional 10,000 people were engaged in software-related work for user organisations and in the electronics industry. McIver presented three different growth scenarios and reckoned that the 20,000 jobs would increase to between 30,000 and 51,000 over the next five years. Most of the extra places would go to software developers. The consultants concluded that the supply of graduates was running far below demand.

The industry tackled this problem by recruiting staff in other countries, using the internet to support individual teleworkers and employing new teams of developers in satellite offices outside the main cities. Companies also lowered the academic qualifications required for specific jobs, opening more positions to people without degrees. These actions made it more difficult to maintain software quality.

Skills shortages hurt academia too. Kevin Ryan suggests that the computer science departments became lopsided. It was hard to find experienced software engineers who wanted to work as lecturers. It was much easier to recruit former mathematicians, physicists or psychologists. Their interest in software was genuine, but they knew more about the use of the technology than about its foundations. "I was always concerned that the core skills of how to build good software were underestimated — across all the colleges," Ryan says. By the turn of the century, 20 third-level institutions in Ireland offered computing qualifications. Northern Ireland had another 20, including colleges of further education, and many of their graduates crossed the border to seek employment.

As before, the shortage of software developers was temporary. The employment climate changed after the turn of the century. Corporate expenditure on information systems declined, particularly in the US. The software product developers soon felt the effect. By 2002 employers could find experienced software designers and programmers to fill vacancies and no longer needed to take graduates straight from the colleges. The pattern was familiar, but this time it affected more people than in the previous cycle.

One result was an increase in the number of postgraduate students. This was a welcome development, because the university research groups had been under-populated in the second half of the 1990s. Over in the admissions offices, however, the number of applications for places on computing courses declined. This fall, coupled with the increased capacity on the campuses, meant that school leavers required fewer Leaving Certificate points to enter the courses. Generation four software company chiefs complained that school leavers with good grades and aptitude were being turned away from the computer science courses. In generation five, the professors were worried that they were admitting too many students who lacked the ability to complete their degrees.

Fewer young people, it appeared, saw the software industry as a good place to seek a career. Some academics blamed popular mythologies about dotcom disasters. Others blamed poor public relations by the software industry. In 2001, when PC hardware vendor Gateway shut down a sales and distribution operation in north Dublin, there was a visible decline in school leavers' interest in information technology. At DCU, whose campus was near the facility, the number of applicants who listed computer applications as their first choice fell from 800 in 1997 to 243 in 2003. Gateway had run a call centre with computer assembly and packaging responsibilities. Its only relationship with software development was that the company put an information systems department into the premises.

The Irish Computer Society responded by running a special campaign to improve the image of software careers. Paradoxically, because of the cyclical nature of the industry, the negative perceptions of software development arose at an ideal time for students to begin a higher education course in computing science or software engineering. In the words of DCU professor Michael Ryan, "We have been through a bubble, but you have to remember that the bubble came on top of a wave."

From Esprit to SFI

"The way you get rewarded in academic life," former national software director Barry Murphy says, "is purely down to the number of papers you publish and the speeches that you give at conferences." Success in the universities, he concludes, has nothing to do with whether a researcher's work actually benefits anyone. Occasionally, Murphy adds, commercially aware individuals emerge from the university system. Some of them — he cites Michael Purser and Chris Horn as examples — have had an enormous influence on the Irish software industry. Few people cross the university–commerce divide successfully. So various programmes have tried to create mechanisms for ideas and inventions to do so.

The first schemes to have an impact in Ireland came out of the European Commission. "Esprit was a total mindbender," declares Kevin Ryan, who was based in the Trinity College Dublin department of computer science when the pre-competitive research programme was launched in the early 1980s. There had never been much funding within Ireland for software-related research. Commissions from industry were narrow and brief and the state always seemed to treat its research grants as charitable donations. Because money was only provided on a short-term basis, continuity was not an option for university research groups. The European Commission's information technology programme not only offered more finance for software research, but also offered it on a multi-year basis. This stimulated a significant increase in postgraduate numbers.

In addition, Kevin Ryan recalls, Irish academics made contacts for the first time with "blue sky" research units in large companies. "They were often further from reality than the university researchers were," he says. Ryan and his colleagues began to forge contacts in a community that they could never have accessed without Esprit.

Brian O'Donnell at the National Board for Science and Technology provided a link between the colleges and the Commission. Esprit began with a call for pilot proposals in 1983 and was expanded in size and scope in the following year. The early phases of the programme were heavily weighted towards the interests of a dozen large corporations that helped to draw up its workplan. The fortunes of the big twelve had little relevance to Ireland. O'Donnell, however, spotted openings for university-based researchers in several of the Esprit proposals and helped them to gain a foothold in the project teams.

Chris Horn was on the inside track as well. In 1984 he completed a PhD at Trinity College — Michael Purser was his supervisor — and spent a year at the European Commission in Brussels. His job there was to review computer networking projects in Esprit. Horn returned to Dublin in 1985 with contacts in major technology companies. These assisted Trinity to form partnerships of the type that the programme managers wanted to see in Esprit proposals.

At first, the Dublin-based academics joined projects that others had already established. Soon, though, they were formulating their own proposals and seeking industrial partners for new submissions to the programme. By the end of the 1980s, Trinity College Dublin was receiving more money from Esprit than any other European university. Ireland, indeed, received a disproportionately high share of the programme's budget — about four times the level that its population would suggest — because of the academic contributions.

As Esprit matured, the Commission permitted projects that were closer to commercialisation. It also introduced complementary programmes that focused on applications of information technology in telecommunications, medical services, transport and other domains. In the 1990s, the Commission encouraged user organisations to become more directly involved in the research and development efforts. Later still, software research was subsumed into a broader European Union programme on information society technologies.

Esprit and its successors were always supposed to strengthen European technology companies. Over the years, the focus moved from the big corporations — many of them no longer exist — to smaller and more specialist firms. In Ireland, however, Esprit had a lasting impact on the universities. International research became accepted as a normal activity for computer science departments. When academics saw their colleagues winning contracts and funds for research students, more joined in the submissions process. The momentum that developed in the early rounds of Esprit was never lost.

Ireland continued to lag behind other EU states, however, in the provision of national research funding. Support schemes did exist, but their budgets were low and the money flows into the colleges were inconsistent. The launch of Science Foundation Ireland (SFI) in 2000 promised a dramatic increase in expenditure. New measures would raise the calibre of Irish research in information technology and in biotechnology. Priority would be given to areas in which Ireland had the potential to achieve international leadership. The government allocated €635 million to a "technology foresight" fund that would operate until 2006. SFI was established to administer this fund.

The creation of the agency represented a radical break with the past. It brought new issues onto the research agenda, placed international experts in Irish colleges and paid for the construction of top-class laboratories. In many respects the initiative reworked the economic development strategies of an earlier age. The government was offering incentives for scientists to relocate to Ireland in the way that international manufacturers were attracted three or four decades earlier.

As the pieces of the new programme fell into place, however, it became apparent that SFI was less interested in software development than in the physical sciences behind electronic components and equipment. There was a striking shortage of software expertise on the original board of the foundation. This was rectified when SFI was placed on a statutory basis in 2003 and a new board was appointed. Its members included Baltimore Technologies and Euristix founder Jim Mountjoy and Jane Grimson, who had established a knowledge and data engineering group at Trinity College Dublin. By then, however, much of SFI's funding for information technology had already been allocated to disciplines like nanotechnology and optics.

The largest software-related initiative that Science Foundation Ireland has supported in its first four years is the Digital Enterprise Research Centre at National University of Ireland, Galway. SFI awarded €12 million over five years to this unit in 2003, following a long evaluation process. The choice was controversial. The Galway college had limited experience in its chosen field of semantic web technology. In the EU programmes Galway had been known for its expertise in computer integrated manufacturing. Its new research theme encompassed internet information retrieval and personalised web applications — areas where other Irish universities had long track records.

SFI subsequently allocated smaller sums to software engineering research in other colleges. But the computer science departments gained the impression that the research authority preferred other disciplines.

Software research is more open-ended and less goal-centred than, for example, biotechnology projects that set out to treat specific diseases.

The effectiveness of SFI will depend on the availability of the right people — researchers who can deepen the level at which academic research is conducted in Ireland and can interact with leaders in the international research community. In the medium term, the centres and projects that received investments must also produce work that is relevant to the software industry, particularly to Irish firms. The early evidence suggests that international corporations are taking more interest in the research plans. Jim Mountjoy believes that he was appointed to the SFI board because of his familiarity with software development companies. "The challenge for me," he says, "is to get ways of involving indigenous industry with the universities."

In monetary terms, Science Foundation Ireland represents as giant a step as Esprit in the 1980s. Whether the national initiative can bring permanent changes in attitudes and behaviour to the campuses, as the European programme did, should become evident by the end of the present decade.

Missing Linkages

National programmes that aimed to assist the Irish software industry have always highlighted the potential for better connections between commercial ventures and the colleges. They invariably predict, indeed, that the next generation of companies will be born in academia. Somehow, however, the next bunch of businesses has always come from somewhere else.

Most software start-ups in the early 1980s grew out of the computer systems trade. These were soon joined by companies run by former users who capitalised on their knowledge of a particular line of business. By generation three, experienced executives were splitting away from established development firms and founding new ones. The industry gradually became self-replicating. There was always talk at software conferences about improving linkages with the universities. But the level of action on the campuses never matched this rhetoric.

Apart from a few well-known exceptions, companies that originated in academic research have made a limited contribution to the growth of the software industry. Successful campus companies exist, mostly in and around Trinity College Dublin, although most move away from the university early in their careers. Iona's success as a spin-off from Trinity's distributed systems group is widely known. The founders of more recent start-ups, such as Havok, Prediction Dynamics and Wilde Technologies, also worked in its department of computer science. ChangingWorlds and WBT Systems came out of University College Dublin. Other colleges, including some of the Institutes of Technology outside the major cities, have also produced generation five start-ups, but these have still to achieve sustainability.

Overall, however, only a small minority of Ireland's software businesses have ever come from the higher education sector and these have not necessarily been the most technically oriented firms.

The European research programmes always involved commercial organisations as well as the universities. They transformed computer science in the colleges, but their impact on Irish industry was much harder to measure. The EU projects benefited individual researchers in development companies and enabled them to advance their careers. They also established inter-country business relationships. But it proved very difficult for software firms to turn their collaborative research into saleable products.

At the high point of Esprit in the late 1980s, a cluster of technically strong companies became regular participants in the programme and grew accustomed to collaboration with academic partners. Some firms, such as Captec and Generics, based their business plans around the European programmes. From generation three onwards, most software exporters targeted North America rather than Europe and looked for institutional investment instead of R&D money from the Commission. The collaborative programmes, with their complex financial rules and uncertain commercial returns, lost most of their earlier appeal.

"We all did Esprit projects, but the timescales were too long for us," Jim Mountjoy recalls, referring to his time at Baltimore Technologies. The dominant roles of the big corporations and the emphasis on pre-competitive topics seldom suited smaller companies, such as software firms. Esprit, Mountjoy argues, achieved little in Ireland outside the colleges.

Vector Software participated in an Esprit project called ToolUse, but the directors of its parent group objected to this involvement. "We pulled out of the project before it was over," former Vector leader Tony McGuire says, "It was a board level decision and it had nothing to do with the quality of the work." He regarded Esprit as an opportunity for "proper research" and never treated it as a means of earning money. But the directors could not see commercial sense in ToolUse and overruled him.

Captec was the most notable exception to the prevailing trend. Founded in 1979 by Fred Kennedy, who had been joint managing director of System Dynamics some years earlier, this Malahide company has made its living from research projects ever since. Its early work on machine-based vision and image analysis in Esprit led to the development of image compression tools. Captec also obtained a stream of contracts from the European Space Agency. These projects have spun off a couple of software products over the years, but the company has always appeared to be more comfortable as a research contractor than as a product vendor. It stayed small, employing engineers and scientists with postgraduate qualifications and frequently engaging in partnerships with university research units.

A succession of government programmes tried to deepen the university–industry connections, but failed to produce more companies in the Captec mould. One reason is that the schemes were usually devised to suit interests of foreign-owned, as well as Irish, companies. Sections of the civil service and the state agencies have always believed that linkage schemes should suit the interests of the international companies with branch plants in Ireland. In the 1980s this led them to assist American electronics companies to participate in Esprit, even though the programme was conceived to give competitive advantages to European vendors. Echoes of this episode could be heard during the Irish EU presidency in 2004, when members of the European Parliament accused the country of "playing lapdog for the US". This allegation arose when the presidency rolled back a parliament decision to limit patentability in a manner that large American software firms disliked.

Linkage schemes to support native software developers always lived in the shadow of the services for the multinationals. This was especially true when those schemes required campus-based teams to sell services. The foreign-owned factories were always more likely to pay than local outfits.

In the first half of the 1990s the main vehicles for transferring academic skills to industry were the programmes in advanced technology (PATs). Partly funded by the European Commission, these covered a broad range of disciplines from materials research to power electronics. In all cases, they involved the creation of campus-based research and advisory centres that were expected to become financially self-sufficient after a few years. A software PAT with three strands was launched in 1991. A development centre for executive information systems was set up at University College Cork, but soon moved off the campus after a bout of academic in-fighting. Twin centres at Trinity College Dublin and University of Limerick were given responsibility for multimedia technology. This arrangement proved unmanageable, partly because of rows between the managers of the two units and partly because of the need to supplement their research activities with commercial work.

The Centre for Software Engineering (CSE) at Dublin City University was the third and most successful strand of the software PAT. This started as a technology transfer agency, advising software companies on how to adopt good development practices and meet quality management targets. It grouped the client firms into clusters so that they could share the costs of training and consulting. Later on the CSE participated in European research projects and in standards development groups. For more than a decade it provided assistance to 40 or 50 companies a year, including user organisations with software staff. After 2000, however, many of the development firms had to reduce their costs and stopped sending their employees on training courses. The CSE's commercial income fell. The centre was reorganised in 2003 under a new chief executive officer, Michael O'Duffy, who reduced its headcount and switched more resources into international training and consultancy. It has continued to counsel and support young software ventures, but its advisers can only cater for a small percentage of the start-ups.

University of Limerick Vice President Kevin Ryan explains the shortcomings of the Irish linkage programmes by comparing them with the "research ecology" that exists in Sweden. There, he notes, research laboratories are allocated resources two years in advance and can always plan ahead. Programmes and schemes are able to expand and contract in a natural way as themes and issues change. Companies place key employees inside the universities on year-long assignments and pay the colleges for this privilege. "I saw how industry valued experience in research in a much more serious way than anywhere in Ireland," Ryan observes, "That brought home to me the difference between having your own multinationals and having someone else's."

The contrasts are clearly visible in the immediate neighbourhood of Kevin Ryan's office. A technology park was built beside the University of Limerick in its early years. Shannon Development, the regional economic development authority, set up this park as a prototype that other cities could learn from. By the mid-1980s the complex included an Innovation Centre — the first technology incubator in Ireland — where Shannon Development introduced an "entrepreneurship and high technology programme" to assist the formation of new companies. It based a business mentoring scheme on role models in the US. As the more successful start-ups grew, the park expanded its range of facilities to meet their requirements.

This infrastructure was intended to encourage interaction between the Innovation Centre's tenants and the academics across the road. The university, indeed, is represented on the board of the company that manages the technology park. The Innovation Centre and the surrounding buildings house several software development companies at any time. But these have never shown much interest in collaborating with the college. "That whole thing is talked up and most of it is just talk," argues Chris Byrne, who has managed a series of software companies on the park. The only merit in having a university as a neighbour, he says, is that it can be good for marketing.

Only one software start-up of note has crossed out of the campus and into the park. Piercom was launched in 1993 to commercialise software re-engineering tools based on research inside the university by Professor Tony Cahill and an information systems and engineering group. In its first five years the company won a Smithsonian medal for innovative technology and one its code inspection packages was added to the National Museum of American History's collection of significant information technology products. Digital Equipment selected Piercom's diagnostic software to enable users of its largest systems to make advance provision for the date change at the end of the millennium.

As the company matured, however, its ties to the university withered away. Piercom's business mix shifted from product development to software services. It introduced e-commerce integration services and became more dependent on Irish customers than on exports. It formed partnerships with middleware vendors and trained its staff to implement their products. Piercom shrugged off its academic origins and came to resemble the other software companies in the park.

Patricia Byrne, the director of knowledge enterprise in Shannon Development, is a former chief executive of the management company at the technology park. She points out that the level of interaction between its companies and the local university has been comparable with other parts of the country. The Limerick region, she adds, has had to catch up with others. Few technology-based companies were founded there before the park was established. "In one sense we could not have created a cluster if the university was not there," Byrne says, "But looking at it from another perspective, the software companies have not got much from the university. I believe that the links will happen organically. The university is still very young."

With more state funding for software research going into the colleges, the old excuses for the low interaction with industry do not sound as convincing as before. But no one has yet proved that they have a formula for linkages that last.

Chapter 4

ART OF THE STATE

Few Votes in Computing

Insight Software founder Matt Crotty started asking questions about corporation tax in the early 1980s. His company's international product sales were rising and he knew that the exporters of manufactured goods were taxed at a lower rate than other businesses. When Insight claimed the reliefs that applied to manufacturers, however, the authorities said that it was ineligible for these. Software companies, they insisted, belonged in the services sector. Insight's accountants responded that they could prove the firm's credentials as a manufacturer and suggested that the Revenue should inspect its operations.

Tony McGuire has vivid memories of the Revenue delegation that visited his offices in 1983. He had prepared a one-day seminar for them — a software-for-beginners course that would build up to a special climax. The lessons began in the developers' room, where he explained how Insight defined the requirements for each new piece of software and the processes that were needed to create the code. He explained the elements that made up a software product and the nature of the market. The standard format for delivering a package in those days was an eight-inch floppy diskette. He showed one to the tax officials. Then he introduced them to a duplication machine.

"I put the diskette into the slot, showed them how to type in the right command, transferred the software, packaged the disk and sent it out," he recalls. "Then I said, 'That looks like manufacturing to me'. They agreed!"

Insight was allowed to claim manufacturing relief after this demonstration. The software company was told that it qualified because it was not sending its developers into customers' premises to deliver a service there. In 1984 the tax law was amended to extend the lower rate to computer services companies that had received employment grants under the IDA's international services programme. This amendment explicitly included the online transmission of "computer-based material" as well as packaged diskettes. Other computer-related services became eligible in later years.

As this episode shows, communications between the Irish software industry and the apparatus of the state have frequently been hampered by their different perspectives. At various times, development companies or their industry associations have presented cases for tax concessions, employment grants or financial support for research and development. They usually confined their dealings to specific government departments or agencies and tried to identify officials who understood their causes.

Software developers do not engage in the cut-and-thrust of electoral politics in the same way as industries such as construction, agribusiness or telecommunications. They have seldom curried favour with ministers and other elected politicians. In fact, the Irish software industry is strikingly apolitical.

This probably explains why it has never featured in the tribunals of inquiry into political donations. No minister or Dáil deputy has ever been accused of unethical involvement with a software firm. On the other hand, no elected representative has ever tried to champion the interests of the code cutters. According to Irish Software Association (ISA) activist Donal Daly, most politicians lacked the passion to promote the industry or simply did not care about it at all. The political parties have never presented alternative strategies for supporting the software industry or debated Ireland's role in application and middleware development. No one wanted to be accused of pandering to an elite.

One junior minister achieved a degree of notoriety in 1995 when he told a joint conference of the ISA and the Massachusetts Software Council that software companies paid their staff too much. Most of the audience took this comment as evidence that he did not understand their industry or its concerns. The incident, however, did no harm to the minister's political career. Pat Rabbitte went on to become leader of the Labour Party.

Some suggest that the interests and concerns of development companies are global whereas Irish politics are inherently parochial. Iona's Chris Horn points out that successful software companies need to track worldwide trends, not local issues. In addition, he argues, software is a youthful industry and young people in general are less inclined than their elders to engage in politics.

Perhaps there is a more fundamental cultural phenomenon behind these observations. Electoral politics has seldom appealed to the sort of people who are attracted to programming languages and software engineering methodologies. Very few software developers have ever put themselves forward for political office. Names from the IT community crop up occasionally in elections to the university seats in the Seanad. But no one has made a career jump from the software industry into the Dáil.

Dennis Jennings was the first software community figure to seek election to the corridors of power. He had originally trained as a physicist, but developed an interest in computing when he needed to analyse data for his PhD in gamma-ray astronomy. He became an adviser at the University College Dublin computer centre. In 1972 he joined System Dynamics as a programmer, then transferred into the company's consulting group. He returned to UCD in 1977 and took charge of the campus computing service, installing one of Digital Equipment's largest machines there.

Five years later Jennings had his shot at the Seanad, equipped with a membership card from the Fine Gael party and public speaking skills that he had honed by chairing a residents' association. Fittingly, perhaps, his campaign is remembered for a technical innovation. He ran the first election mailshot without envelopes. His election message was printed onto A4 sheets of paper that could be folded over and sealed with address labels. This labour-saving innovation soon became the norm for electoral snail mail. It was also the biggest success of his campaign.

When the votes were counted, Jennings received less than two per cent of the poll — 500 first preferences in a constituency with a quota of about 5,500.

The lesson was clear. There are few votes in computing, even when the electorate is confined to university graduates. "You need to have a political constituency of people who know you," Jennings observes. Success in Irish software has never resulted in celebrity.

The mutual disinterest between software and politics has persisted since the 1980s. It appears to exist in other countries as well. Looking back at his electoral adventure after two decades, Dennis Jennings suggests that this is a cultural issue. "People in the technology business have no time for ass-kicking and arse-wiping," he concludes. To the technical mindset the clientelist aspects of getting elected are distasteful. After the Seanad contest Jennings concluded that his forte lay in international industry politics. He channelled his energies to this area and especially into the governance of the internet.

The early 1980s, when Dennis Jennings ran for the Seanad, was an important time for Irish software. The first packaged products reached the market and the leading development companies made their first forays abroad. This was also the time when the country's economic development agencies realised that they would have to grapple with the idiosyncrasies of the software industry. Jennings became a director of the National Software Centre, which attempted to address the producers' needs. The initiative, however, went hopelessly wrong.

A Muddled Mandate

Industrial Development Authority (IDA) executive Michael Wilson had sensed that a new business was taking shape some years earlier. In 1977, he convened a meeting of Irish computing service providers and floated the idea that they should seek contracts outside the country. He discovered that the companies were more preoccupied with untapped opportunities in Ireland. In particular, they resented the tendency of public sector organisations to look abroad for system analysts and software developers.

What this group of companies really wanted, Wilson discovered, was local recognition of their abilities.

Nonetheless, the concept of exporting software from Ireland had been placed on the national agenda. By the early 1980s Córas Tráchtála had extended its export promotion services to software developers. It was a significant departure for this state agency, which was more accustomed to assisting the producers of knitwear and craft goods. The National Board for Science and Technology (NBST) also factored the software industry into its policy analyses. The board was responsible for advising the government on trends in a variety of disciplines. In 1979, it appointed Robert Cochran, who had been a statistician and software developer at other public sector organisations, as its "data processing" expert. Within two weeks of joining the NBST he convinced his superiors that this job description was too broad. From then on he focused on the software developers.

The IDA, meanwhile, responded to the rising volume of enquiries from software companies by setting up a unit, led by Eamonn Ryan, that would provide grants to Irish-based "international services" companies. This initiative was also influenced by a critical report on the agency's performance by consulting firm Telesis, which highlighted the lack of key competitive activities in foreign-owned electronics facilities and called for more attention to building structurally strong Irish companies.

Former client companies speak positively about Ryan's team. Two of its members, Declan Murphy and Tom Weymes, maintained a long term engagement with the software industry and became closely identified with it. The IDA as a whole, however, appeared to be much less interested in the welfare of native software developers. The 1980s, after all, was a decade of high emigration and industrial progress was measured in crude workforce headcounts. One foreign-owned hardware assembly plant could train and employ several hundred production operatives. Ministers wanted to steer such projects towards their own constituencies or other locations that suited their governments' interests. The largest software firms, on the other hand, might provide a few dozen jobs. They were never going to excite the politicians. It was obvious where the IDA's priorities would lie.

Inside the agency, moreover, officials sought to advance their careers by becoming associated with successful companies and avoiding the riskier ones. When the first software package exporters appeared, the IDA acknowledged that it should address their needs. But few of its staff were attracted to this work. It involved dealing with small companies with products and markets that could be difficult to understand. Other posts were much more likely to lead to promotion.

Robert Cochran at the NBST took a very different perspective from his counterparts on the IDA career ladder. In his opinion the industrial development agency was wrongly preoccupied with hardware production, and especially with chip manufacturing, at a time when software companies were re-shaping the computer industry. "It was clear to me that there was an upsurge coming," he says. These expectations were confirmed when he joined an Organisation for Economic Co-operation and Development study group and observed what was happening internationally.

Irish software development companies, Cochran concluded, were immature — not just in a commercial sense, but also in the adoption of the newer technologies and processes. In the early 1980s he proposed the creation of a new organisation to address this weakness and drew up a three-year plan. The agency would promote technology transfer and provide advanced training to software staff. He examined institutions in other countries and recommended that one in Copenhagen might be an appropriate role model. "My view was that this was a public service and would need a fair amount of public money," he says. That meant that he had to convince one of the bigger state agencies to allocate part of its budget to the plan.

The national training agency, AnCO, and the Department of Labour were unwilling to get involved. They saw their function as "vocational training" for apprentices and operatives. Robert Cochran was proposing further education for people who already held qualifications. This was not vocational training. He was told that it might be a job for the universities.

The IDA was equally unenthusiastic about Cochran's idea — except for just one aspect. The agency could see some merit in establishing an entity with "software" in the title. It might fill a gap on its itineraries for visiting industrialists. When the IDA ran tours for potential investors from overseas semiconductor companies, it showed off the facilities at the National Microelectronics Research Centre in Cork. If the visitors came from electronic product firms, it wheeled them into the Microelectronics Applications Centre in Limerick, which had introduced a service to adapt equipment for compliance with European standards. It would suit the IDA to have an equivalent resource that it could show to executives from US software companies.

This role was never part of Cochran's plan. But the IDA had the finance to make something happen. It drew up its own proposal and obtained government approval to establish an organisation that would encourage more inward investment. In October 1983 Industry and Energy Minister John Bruton announced that the IDA was going to establish a National Software Centre (NSC) in Dublin "to support the continued growth of the electronics industry in Ireland". It would be run as a private company. The initial mandate for the new organisation was to develop software in co-operation with other firms and to take part in international research programmes. It would also offer technical assistance to software developers in areas like documentation and it would provide advanced training.

This was the first co-ordinated action in which the Irish state recognised the economic importance of software development. The brief that the IDA gave to the new centre was, however, hopelessly muddled. The NSC was supposed to become self-financing after three years by selling its employees' skills. This mandate meant that one part of the centre would assist clients in the software industry while another competed for business against such firms. The IDA never resolved this contradiction. It was never really interested in sorting it out.

When Robert Cochran drew up his original proposal, he had sounded out the Irish Computer Services Association (ICSA) — the precursor of the ISA — which had started operations in 1978. He got a lukewarm reception. Some of the association's members, after all, were making good money from software training services and argued against the introduction of state-funded courses.

The industry group was even more hostile to the IDA's concept of a centre that would solicit more inward investment by foreign software companies. Such projects, it presumed, would poach good staff and make it even harder for local firms to find and retain skilled developers. The description of the NSC in the Minister's announcement suggested that the centre would compete against ICSA members for software development contracts as well as for training fees. The association raised further objections in 1984, when the IDA named the directors of its new centre. None of the ICSA's leaders were included on the board. There were, however, two academic appointees — John Byrne from Trinity College Dublin and Dennis Jennings from University College Dublin.

"I had no idea what the National Software Centre was supposed to do." Jennings recalls. "The board meetings were very unhappy and confused. It was as if the IDA wanted to say, 'We have a National Software Centre'. That was the be-all and end-all of it." Ideas were floated and discussed, but it became clear to him that the IDA had no desire to pay the implementation costs.

IDA official Tom Weymes, who assessed software companies for grant support during the NSC years, is equally critical of the board. A stand-offish relationship developed between the centre and the IDA's international services group. "I am inclined to think that it was the fault of directors trying to carve out their own turf," he comments.

Robert Cochran, meanwhile, had decided on a career change. He set up a new venture, Generics Software, in 1984. Before his official departure from the NBST, however, he received a phone call from Brian Dugan, the American consultant that the IDA had headhunted to be the managing director of its centre. "I had lost the argument on the sort of organisation that it should be," Cochran says, "but Brian Dugan said he had been going through the files and come across a lot of stuff written by me. He liked my model and asked if I would join the NSC as technology director." Dugan convinced him that his original proposals for technology transfer could still be implemented and he accepted the offer. "I went in on the basis that there would be money flowing in from the IDA," Cochran says. "That never happened."

Brian Dugan understood how the software industry worked from his previous career at Standard and Poor's in New York. But he was ill-prepared for the power struggles and faction fights that he encountered in Ireland. Dugan had high standards. He was accustomed to conducting thorough research at the start of each new project and to ensuring that it was well resourced. He spent six months studying the brief for the NSC before he hired anyone. He installed an expensive minicomputer, because he wanted good information systems to back up the centre's services. Critics regarded this system as a wanton extravagance. Dugan's research convinced him that the National Software Centre had little to offer to inward investment projects, but could provide practical advice on exports to the growing band of indigenous software companies. This not only went against the IDA's agenda; it also opened up a conflict between the centre and Córas Tráchtála, which held the budget for state assistance to exporters.

In addition to persuading Robert Cochran to take charge of technical services, Dugan appointed Pat Divilly as commercial director of the NSC. Divilly, who had held international marketing posts at Cara and Digital Equipment, designed an international marketing assistance programme that would promote clients' products in selected countries. Córas Tráchtála objected to this scheme. Its attitude, Divilly says, was that the NSC should confine its attention to technical matters.

The National Software Centre lasted for four years. Brian Dugan quit before its final phase, leaving Pat Divilly in charge. The IDA eventually replaced the NSC board with a fresh team of directors chaired by Tony Kilduff from the ICSA. This new board served for only three months. It formally advised the IDA that the centre could not generate the funds required to maintain its operations. The NSC ceased trading in May 1988.

Generation two software companies were failing at an alarming rate in 1988 and the formation of start-ups was slower than at any time since the beginning of the decade. The shortage of work for software engineers had become an urgent issue. Record numbers of computing studies graduates were spilling out of the colleges. Many chose to emigrate. The closure of the NSC was thus part of a much bigger malaise. Its disappearance was just another software collapse.

In defence of the National Software Centre, Pat Divilly points out that the organisation gave struggling companies a half day of advice when they needed it and raised the industry's awareness of software quality and methodologies. But it could never hope to make a greater impact than these modest interventions. The NSC was always saddled with an impossible mission.

The Roll Call of '89

The shutdown of the National Software Centre did not happen in isolation. It was part of a larger process choreographed by the IDA and the outgoing NSC board. They tried to present the demise of the centre as a positive development — a fresh start in the awkward relationship between the software industry and the state.

The ICSA, led by Kindle Group founder Tony Kilduff, had been lobbying the government for support mechanisms that were closer to its members' tastes. Sympathetic officials in the IDA gave discreet assistance. Three months before the software centre was axed, the association commissioned a firm of management consultants, Coopers & Lybrand, to take stock of the condition of the industry and to assess its future prospects. It presented the consultants' report to the government towards the end of the year. The minister responsible for industrial policy promptly convened a working group and asked it to draw up specific recommendations in a matter of weeks.

This committee was chaired by civil servant Ronald Long. It had three members from private industry and one each from three state agencies — Córas Tráchtála, IDA and the NBST. Tom McGovern from System Dynamics, playing his customary role as industry statesman, and Tony Kilduff represented the software developers. The line-up was completed by Aidan McKenna from Memory Computer, a generation one computer services outfit that turned into a hardware reseller. McKenna had also been a member of the original NSC board.

In February 1989, the working group produced a report that made extensive use of the Coopers & Lybrand document. Some of the content was predictable. It stressed the potential to create employment through software development and set a medium-term target that was sure to appeal to the politicians. The report proposed the establishment of a National Software Directorate to provide advisory services and suggested that a consultative council could maintain dialogue among the industry, academia and the state agencies. It pointed out that these measures should be eligible for subsidies from the European Regional Development Fund. The introduction of the European single market was scheduled to remove all remaining constraints to cross-border trade at the start of 1993 and the committee argued that its proposals would help the software firms to prepare for this new world.

The most interesting aspect of this document, however, was that it contained a list of 101 companies that the committee regarded as potential beneficiaries of its recommendations. The working group explicitly advocated intervention in individual enterprises. Then it presented the companies' names.

This roll call included the bigger and better-known names from generation two. Most of the firms, however, were very small. The average headcount was twelve and their combined exports in 1988 were worth about $40 million. The committee set an employment growth target of 15 per cent for the selected companies by 1993.

Looking back after a decade and a half, the strategy of selecting and supporting individual companies seems reasonable. But the list of names compiled by the expert committee reads like a graveyard register. Most of the 101 firms disappeared during the 1990s.

Some underwent mergers or acquisitions or radical restructurings that created new entities. Virtually all of the larger companies on the 1989 list were taken over. System Dynamics, Kindle, Expert Edge, GC McKeown and Glockenspiel all passed into the hands of foreign owners. Other generation two companies ceased software development in the

1990s and turned to other lines of business, such as systems integration or implementing software suites from bigger vendors. Dillon Technology, a multi-currency accounting package developer, relocated to England. The company had previously transplanted itself from Cork to Dublin. Flite Software, which wrote applications for fluid engineers, also underwent a change of jurisdiction, although its move was only a short hop from Letterkenny to Derry in Northern Ireland.

Only 13 of the companies that the working group identified as the core of the industry in 1989 continued to develop software in Ireland into the twenty-first century. That number dropped to twelve in 2004, when SSAP, a tax return applications producer, was acquired by Sage.

Most of the survivors sell packaged software and would have been counted among the more specialised outfits in 1989. MCS, for example, writes engineering software for offshore oil and gas operations. Datacare Software Group sells corporate records management applications, while Compufast produces a suite for human resource managers. Financial Courseware, whose name was self-explanatory in 1989, lives on as Intuition. The survivors also include Delphi Technologies, Vision Consulting and Codec — three companies that preferred international services to product development.

The software industry has always been volatile. It is hardly surprising that so few firms from the late 1980s are still alive. The native companies on the roll call, indeed, fared better than their foreign-owned contemporaries. The 1989 report also listed more than 50 software groups with international parents. Microsoft, Motorola and Kerridge are the only unreconstructed survivors.

In retrospect, the expert committee placed its faith in the wrong companies. The explanation may lie in the composition of the working group. It failed to notice that a new type of software company was evolving — a breed that was not represented in the inner circle of the ICSA. The report to the government championed generation two, the purveyors of safe but unoriginal products, at a time when innovators like Glockenspiel and Generics were laying the groundwork for generation three. Remarkably, the 101 names excluded research-centred companies like

Captec and Broadcom Eireann Research. Even Aldiscon, which subsequently became one of the industry's superstars, was left off the list.

The software development industry achieved and exceeded the growth projections set down by the minister's working group. Some of the measures that came out of its report contributed to this success. The creation of the National Software Directorate, which went ahead in line with the committee's recommendations, was particularly helpful. The policymakers, however, had backed the wrong talent.

In 1993, four years after the roll-call report, Iona submitted a request for investment with the IDA. This was the year when the middleware company released Corba, the product that became a market leader. The development agency, however, told Iona that its business plan was not good enough. The IDA turned down the company because it did not understand its vision. It subsequently made amends and assisted Iona to source funding in the US. But the IDA was clearly out of touch with what was happening in object technology.

Perhaps the agency was reluctant to support a project that seemed to pose a challenge to Microsoft, which was its largest client from the software industry. Or was it, like the authors of the 1989 report, still looking for companies that conformed with the generation two business model? Could government agencies ever learn how to pick real winners?

The High Potential Filter

The angel investor is a key figure for many young companies. This is usually a wealthy individual who finances the design of a new product or service and introduces the firm to institutions that can provide more money as it grows. The angel investor thus plays the role of talent spotter, picking out business proposals and enabling the better companies to advance to their next stage of development. Some of Ireland's software industry veterans act in this way. Most development firms, however, expect Enterprise Ireland to do the angel's job.

The state agency is less susceptible to the whims of fashion than individual angels. Reports from the US in the late 1990s suggested that the early-stage investors had abandoned developers that were not writing software for the web. Later on the angels appeared to cease support for software firms in general. The number of American start-ups certainly dipped in the early years of the new century. Enterprise Ireland, in contrast, started 2002 by introducing a dedicated unit to counsel new software ventures.

Enterprise Ireland commenced operations in its present form in 1998. It inherited the support services that IDA and Córas Tráchtála had provided to Irish firms in earlier times. It also inherited the National Software Directorate, which was originally established inside the IDA. Insight veteran Barry Murphy was its director from 1991 to 1996. His brief was to monitor the software industry and to provide management support and advisory services. The job description pointedly excluded the requirement to generate revenue that had brought down the National Software Centre.

Barry Murphy describes the early 1990s as a transition period for Irish software. His new organisation conducted a series of surveys to map the industry and to measure its presence in different product sectors and export markets. The IDA kept pressing for job creation figures. Government policy still placed quantity ahead of quality. "If people created wealth, that was fine. But creating jobs was everything," Murphy recalls. "To my mind the IDA did a tremendous amount for industry, but the instruments that it used were very blunt."

Paul O'Dea chaired the Irish Software Association in the mid-1990s. He says that, in general, the government agencies have paid only lip service to the software industry. But the relationship improved enormously when Murphy, with his development company background, became head of the directorate. The industry, he says, was able to interact effectively with the state "at Barry level".

The National Software Directorate — or National Informatics Directorate as it is known today — has an unconventional role. It undertakes industry analyses. It monitors academic research for commercialisation opportunities. The organisation also liaises with administrations in other countries and responds to their enquiries about the environment that produced Ireland's software successes.

Generation three was on the rise when the directorate carried out its first industry survey in 1992. It published a strategic review that counted 291 companies, including 183 active exporters. Their combined headcount was 3,800, compared with about 1,200 for the 101 firms listed in the February 1989 report. Barry Murphy clashed with his superiors over the growth target that he set in the review. He believed that it was realistic to aim for 20,000 jobs by 2000. The IDA management rubbished this figure. In hindsight his estimate was conservative.

The 1989 report and the 1992 study both comment on the small size of the exporting firms and portray this as a weakness. The earlier document found that only 13 employed more than 20 people. The Directorate's review counted 60 companies in this bracket, but the average number of employees had not increased since 1989. More significantly, however, the type of software that Ireland was producing changed in the years that separated the reports. Generation three firms had given up on accounting and production planning software and moved into specialised applications, development tools and middleware.

The services provided by the government agencies had to adapt as well. Traditional IDA grants for Irish firms were tied to job creation or to research and development projects. Enterprise Ireland, in its angel investor role, acts rather differently. First it acquires shareholdings in companies. Then it assigns advisers who refer them to other departments of the agency as their requirements change. Forbairt, which held responsibility for supporting indigenous companies between 1994 and 1997, was the stepping stone between the old model and the new. Forbairt selected software development as the pilot industry in which it would introduce a combination of seed capital and hands-on assistance. The National Software Directorate devised the rules.

Filtering companies is a distinctive art. The form that has evolved at Enterprise Ireland distinguishes certain software companies as "high potential" start-ups. These are deemed capable of achieving annual sales of €2 million or more within a few years and they are offered services that improve their chances of making this target. The designation is reserved for a limited number of firms, some of which come from areas other than software development. It not only brings financial support from the agency itself. Institutional investors offer matching funds. Venture capitalists prefer to deal with firms that have already passed through the Enterprise Ireland filter. As the high potential companies grow, they also become eligible for subsidies to exhibit at international congresses and are entitled to tap into the resources of the agency's worldwide office network.

In recent years the "high potential" tag has become almost as important to a young software company as landing the first sale of a new product. And there are never enough tags to go around. Enterprise Ireland's internationally traded services division has limited resources and often struggles to keep up with all the business proposals that it receives. In the filtering process there are losers as well as winners. Companies that gain access to the support system often give high praise to Enterprise Ireland programmes and executives. Those that are not accepted into the club are seldom complimentary. Critics suggest that the agency follows outdated business models and may not understand the circumstances of companies from the latest generation.

Whatever strengths and weaknesses exist in the support structures for the software industry, it has to be acknowledged that Ireland has done things differently from other countries. Mike Peirce, who led Mentec for many years, thinks that the state agencies are distinctive because they are "worldly wise". The equivalent bodies in other countries, he suggests, function like branches of the civil service. Enterprise Ireland, meanwhile, attracts comparisons with angels.

Chapter 5

FOREIGN AFFAIRS

Lotus Blossoms

Lotus Development was the world's coolest company in 1985. Two years earlier it had launched 1-2-3, a software product that integrated spreadsheet, graphics and database applications. The package appeared at a time when the first personal computers were arriving in many workplaces. PC dealers loved 1-2-3 because it enabled them to win new customers. Lotus Development's sales rocketed to $157 million in 1984. The company expanded its repertoire with Symphony, which added word processing and communications to the mix, and Jazz, a suite of applications for the Apple Macintosh. Personal productivity software was still a fresh concept. It made computing seem more relevant to end users. These products gave them a sense of control over their work. No one felt that way about accounting ledgers on a minicomputer.

The arrival of Lotus in Ireland was a major event. The company set up a facility in Santry and held an official opening in June 1985.

This was an elaborate production. The Minister for the Public Service presided. National and local politicians attended in force, along with the top brass of the Industrial Development Authority (IDA), business leaders, community representatives and an ecumenical delegation from the Christian churches. Lotus had only 30 employees in Ireland, so the company sent a team from its headquarters in Cambridge, Massachusetts to boost the numbers. Most of the Americans were wearing "Jazz" badges that had been issued for the recent launch of the Macintosh product. These apparent declarations of musical taste puzzled the local dignitaries.

Lotus offered to explain its business by providing tours of its new premises. After the formal opening ceremony the guests were organised into small groups and escorted around the building. But there was not much for them to see. The facility was really just a warehouse. Its production process was based around a floppy disk duplicator. An operator fed in a master disk and this machine copied its content onto a batch of blanks. There were no robots or conveyor belts or technicians with sophisticated tools. The duplicator looked more like a stray component from someone's home entertainment system.

Quite simply, this was not a photogenic factory. Convention dictated, though, that the visiting VIPs should have their pictures taken on the production floor, preferably at the controls of some exciting piece of technology. Fortunately for Lotus, it had installed a shrink-wrapping machine to put layers of plastic around boxes of disks. On the opening day this device provided a focal point where the politicians could pose and the photographers could capture the ambience of the event.

It did not matter that the same technology could be found at the meat counter of the nearest supermarket. That shrink-wrapping machine became a symbol of Ireland's participation in the shiny new world of packaged software.

Lotus, it was clear, was not a software company in the same sense as Insight or RTS — or even Intelligence Ireland, which liked to present itself as a direct competitor to the Cambridge firm. Lotus had a real manufacturing process. It had not leased a city centre office. It had fitted out a factory in an industrial estate close to the airport. Its employees were production operatives and they worked machines. One part of the building took in materials. Another shipped out cartons of finished goods. Here was a software company that behaved like the electronics hardware manufacturers that the IDA and its political masters knew and understood. From the agency's perspective, furthermore, Lotus was the leader of a wave of PC package companies and could influence other American firms to come into the country.

Lotus was not the first US software company to invest in Ireland. It was not even the first to duplicate and package PC applications. The

Santry project, however, launched a series of logistics management operations. These expanded software packaging and distribution to a massive scale that swelled the national export figures. They also helped the IDA to distance itself from a recent debacle involving another sort of software service and US company Informatics.

The agency kept a constant watch on American business to identify companies on the rise. It contacted these firms when their sales reached a certain threshold, asked them to consider Ireland as their springboard into Europe and introduced its line-up of incentives. Computer vendors like Digital Equipment, Apple and Wang were among the companies that the agency persuaded to assemble products in Ireland. By the start of the 1980s, the IDA had supported about 80 electronics manufacturers and these had a combined workforce of 14,000 employees.

To the promoters of inward investment, writing software looked similar to building hardware products. The IDA tried, therefore, to build an offshore development capability, not unlike the services industry that evolved much later in places like India, Egypt and South Africa. In the jargon of the time, the agency promoted Ireland as a base for "bodyshops". By 1977, its software client list included Samsom Automation, Zeus-Hermes, Comtech and Holland Automation. None survived for long. Altergo Ireland, which was British-owned, outlived the rest of this bunch. It operated for nine years and eventually closed in 1984. Altergo Ireland ran computer training courses, mainly for Libyan students, and later became a software contractor for companies in the Middle East. The main asset of this operation was its address. Ireland had a more acceptable image in the Arab world than the European states that had tried to colonise it.

The pitfalls of the bodyshop became uncomfortably apparent in the Informatics incident. This US corporation had a software pedigree that stretched back to the early 1960s. One of its divisions sold programming services to American computer installations. Informatics employees worked on assignments at the customers' premises. In 1981 the professional services provider began to hire staff in Ireland — as well as in other European countries and India — because it wanted to build up its

New York office. The company was offering careers in America and programmers liked the idea of working on large systems. Informatics was active at the mainframe end of the computing spectrum, where the software pay rates were highest.

Informatics became a key target for the IDA. In 1982 the agency announced that the company would establish a "software consultancy" in Ireland with an employment target of 180. The IDA was planning a dedicated business park for software companies in south Dublin and it hinted that Informatics could become the anchor tenant. There were also suggestions that the company would repatriate its Irish employees in the US to form the core of this new operation.

Soon, however, complaints about Informatics began to circulate among Dublin's tight-knit band of mainframe users. The US company was holding regular hiring fairs in the city and targeting their employees. The local installations reported that experienced staff were being drawn away by the bright lights of America. The IDA's proposal to subsidise an Informatics bodyshop in Leopardstown added insult to injury,

Then hard luck stories started trickling back across the Atlantic. Some of the Informatics' recruits, especially those who had not previously worked on IBM mainframes, found themselves without work assignments for long spells. Promises of technical training failed to materialise. The employees were told to read programming manuals instead of taking courses. Housing and transport problems were common. In one case four Informatics recruits were crammed into an apartment with a single bedroom and the company charged them above-average rents for this accommodation.

Some Informatics employees discovered that the contracts they had signed with the company contained punitive clauses on the reimbursement of expenses. Others alleged that their employer had not complied with US immigration regulations and had brought them into America on visas that were meant for short-term business visitors. The programmers also sent word home that Informatics paid less than the going rates for software workers in New York.

According to the Irish recruits in the US, moreover, Informatics had no interest in re-assigning them to Ireland. Those who asked about this possibility were told that the company had no operating unit in Dublin, even though the IDA had already provided it with training subsidies. Informatics, in turn, complained to the IDA that the Irish programmers lacked maturity, had no respect for authority and did not understand how the software industry operated in the real world. By 1984 relationships in the New York office had deteriorated to the point that the employees dredged up as much of the Irish language that they could remember from their school days. They wanted to speak to one another in a language that their bosses could not understand.

IDA officials admitted that the "software consultancy" in Dublin had fallen behind schedule, but continued to assert that Informatics would establish an Irish base. Even after Sterling Software acquired the company in 1985, the agency insisted that the project was not dead, but still represented an opportunity to expand the country's pool of IBM mainframe expertise. This never happened. The affair increased the pressure on the development authority to come up with a successful software project.

This is why the arrival of Lotus and its introduction of a new business model were so significant. Close behind came Microsoft and Ashton-Tate. Oracle, Symantec, Corel, Claris, Frame Technology and Novell followed in the early 1990s. They packaged their software, printed user manuals and shipped the boxes to distributors in different countries. As this activity grew, the IDA assisted a supporting cast of subcontractors, starting with disk duplicators and printers, then followed by document authoring services, translators and testing specialists. These companies did not develop software. They constituted a new industry. Software localisation became a support service for software developers.

Localisation began in MicroPro, a California company that opened a development office in Dun Laoghaire in 1981. MicroPro's WordStar product was the first volume-selling word processor for desktop computers. The package played a major role in killing off the single-purpose text editing computer. MicroPro initially wanted the Irish subsidiary to modify its existing products, while more important work on the next generation was done in the States. By late 1982 it employed nine people in Dun Laoghaire. These included Mike Brady, who had previously worked for Altergo. MicroPro's company culture was unlike anything that he had encountered before.

MicroPro had been financed by venture capital and had gone through an initial public offering. Brady's American colleagues were obsessed by quarterly results and talked constantly about their stock options. Short-term performance was all-important. The company hired and fired staff every quarter as part of the effort to make its figures look better. Mike Brady and his colleagues in Dun Laoghaire found this behaviour utterly irrational. MicroPro, though, provided them with technically challenging work. Its programmers required strong engineering skills. The Dun Laoghaire team planned and produced the first version of WordStar for computers based on Intel's x86 architecture. Compared with other opportunities in Ireland, this was high-level work.

The MicroPro operation expanded when the company hired a second group in Dun Laoghaire. Its task was to translate the software into nine European languages. The linguists soon outnumbered the programmers. At its peak the MicroPro office employed 28 people, but the bubble burst in 1984 when a recession hit the PC trade. By the end of 1985 there were only five people left. They concentrated on disk duplication and packaging and took on more language-related tasks. Much of the work was outsourced to subcontractors. The company finally closed its Irish office in 1990.

When Lotus landed in Santry, it introduced the same type of localisation process as MicroPro, but did everything on a much bigger scale. The facility soon became the cockpit of the software localisation industry. David MacDonald, its general manager from 1985 to 1987, had previously worked for Technicon, Amdahl and Trilogy Systems. He knew how to play company politics in US corporations. MacDonald persuaded Lotus to assign more responsibilities to Santry and to employ a more skilled workforce there. At the end of 1986, the company announced that it would develop French, German, Italian, Spanish, Swedish and Dutch editions of its products in Ireland. In later years it also addressed the linguistic needs of Eastern Europe, South East Asia, South America and the Middle East. And in the early 1990s the facility was finally allowed to develop a Lotus product — the Domino Global Workbench. This was a computing environment in which other developers could create multilingual applications.

"Lotus was like a school for localisation. That's where the standard approaches were developed," explains Reinhard Schaeler, who worked there in the late 1980s and is now chief executive officer of the Institute for Localisation Professionals. The Lotus team produced the future leaders of the software localisation industry. Schaeler, for example, headed the Localisation Research Centre at the University of Limerick and pioneered an education and professional development structure for practitioners. Ian Dunlop moved to the US and took on senior management positions at Novell and MessageLabs. Another Lotus veteran, Tony O'Dowd, runs Alchemy Software Development, which produces visual development platforms for translators. David MacDonald chairs Alchemy's board of developers.

According to Schaeler, another Dublin company, Softrans, was the first to define its business as "localisation". He thinks that the word might have originated in Apple, where Softrans founder Brian Kelly previously worked. It soon caught on as a term that not only covered the translation of products into different languages, but also the modifications that ensured compliance with the legislation in different countries.

This service industry passed through two rounds of rationalisation. In the early 1990s the smaller localisation service companies, including most of the Irish-owned operations, were acquired by international firms. Later in the decade there was a series of mergers and acquisitions among these big players. The survivors, such as Bowne Global Services and Lionbridge, offered a full spectrum of consulting, translating, engineering and testing services for software products and websites. The largest players are US-owned, but they run facilities across the globe. Reinhard Schaeler reckons that the industry reached its peak size in the late 1990s and slowed down thereafter. Most of the growth since the turn of the century has been in India, China and eastern Europe.

Ireland has retained its pre-eminence in localisation services, but the requirement for packaging and documentation services has shrunk. Labour intensive translation and testing have gone to low-wage economies. Dublin, the site of the first localisation hub, has become the place where new processes and technologies are conceived. Industry standards, such as the XML Localisation Interchange File Format and web services that automate recurring processes, originated in the city. The value chain began with software manufacturing, evolved through independent service providers and has now led to a cluster of "languageware" expertise. The transition from low-skill warehousing to a highly specialised community of language engineers has taken just two decades.

When Lotus blossomed, a new industry was born in Dublin. Software localisation, indeed, is arguably the only industry in which the rest of the world looks to Ireland for leadership and new concepts. It will always be a backroom activity that attracts attention only when it is done badly. But it has come a long way since the photo session at the shrink-wrapping machine.

Hot Stuff from Ovens

EMC's international operations complex lies on the westbound road out of Cork city. The data storage company has grown steadily since it came into Ireland in 1988 and its facility now sprawls across the townland of Ovens. There is nothing at the location to commemorate its history before EMC arrived. But it holds a special place in the Irish software story. In the mid-1980s this site housed a sort of finishing school for software entrepreneurs.

Ovens started the 1980s with an abandoned electronics factory. The previous occupant, Data 100, had pulled out and the IDA had gone looking for a new tenant. In 1981 the agency announced that Minnesota-based CPT Corporation had agreed to assemble hardware products there. This company produced word processing systems. Its name, indeed, was originally an acronym for "cassette powered typing".

CPT spent just five years in Ovens, but it provided a wild ride for the software developers that it attracted there. At first its set-up was just another assembly plant. Operations like this, however, came under critical scrutiny in the early 1980s. Consulting firm Telesis had highlighted their low skill levels and the limited contributions that they made to the competitiveness of their parent firms. Ireland's political establishment wanted to be seen to respond to the Telesis analysis. The IDA lobbied its clients to add development functions to their facilities. The Irish managers in US-owned factories knew how vulnerable these operations were and gladly accepted the challenge. Some moved into process engineering research. Others sought a bigger role in corporate information management. Here and there a new software application got written or a new circuit board was designed.

CPT placed more trust in its Irish subsidiary than any of the others. The company staked its whole future on a development project at Ovens.

In the early 1980s the suppliers of word processing systems knew that they needed to diversify. Personal computers built on Intel and Microsoft technologies were eating into their market and the major PC makers were bigger and better resourced than the likes of CPT. The Minnesota firm launched two programmes to develop new types of product. One was a network-based office automation system. This was entrusted to a project team in the US. The second involved a much more radical concept — shrinking down the ultimate office workstation to fit into a portable device.

The product, Workmate, aimed to establish a new category of business equipment. Ten years later it might have been labelled a personal digital assistant, but there was nothing else like it in the 1980s. Workmate required an original hardware design and extensive software development. The product would ship with built-in word processing, spreadsheet and electronic mail applications. CPT assigned the entire mission to its Irish subsidiary.

The Workmate project attracted dozens of top-notch engineers to Ovens. About 100 people, many of them working as contractors, contributed to the design of the system. Robert Ardill was placed in charge of the overall project. Fergus O'Connell, a mathematical physics graduate from University College Cork, became leader of the software developers. The star of the team, however, was John Carolan. Robert Ardill persuaded the software guru to act as the technical visionary for Workmate. Carolan fleshed out the initial product concept and advised CPT to license the MTOS operating system to drive the handheld computer. The company agreed and its software group proceeded to write applications that sat on top of MTOS.

Mike Brady was one of the software developers. He left MicroPro in Dublin, moved south and signed on at CPT as a contractor. The company, he says, was offering "outrageous money" to attract a strong project team. Even though he was never a CPT employee, Brady became head of a six-person group that would develop the word processing application. It had to start from scratch and deliver the software in 14 months.

Raomal Perera was another recruit. Born in Sri Lanka, he had studied electronics at University College Swansea and joined BL Systems in England, where he worked on a file transfer system. He and his Irish girlfriend decided that they would rather live in Ireland, but the employment opportunities for a file transfer specialist were rather limited. Both were delighted when CPT's recruitment agency approached Perera and invited him to apply for a position in its new R&D group. They married just before he joined the company, which immediately whisked him off to Minneapolis without his partner. He spent three months there learning the company's ways before taking up a post at Ovens.

"Looking back on it, we had really bitten off more than we could chew," Raomal Perera recalls. When he joined CPT in 1983 it was a $100 million company that flew its own private jet. Its headquarters were so large that it installed a robotic transport system to carry documents around. But its core business was shrinking and its revenues fell every quarter. CPT underestimated the speed at which the commodity PC would displace its word processing systems. The Workmate team likewise failed to anticipate how quickly PC packages would sweep other software products aside. Its MTOS-based applications were not only incompatible with the new desktop suites. They were also unable to interoperate with the products that CPT had sold in the past.

By the end of 1985 CPT was struggling to stay afloat. The hardware elements of Workmate were complete, but there were still gaps in the software. The senior management in the US concluded that Workmate was not going to rescue the company. The Irish operation attempted to raise external funding in early 1986 to keep its project alive. This bid failed and the Ovens facility shut down in the summer. CPT itself ceased trading a few years later.

The failure of Workmate could be explained by issues specific to CPT. In general, however, the Telesis-inspired policy of deepening the skills in foreign-owned factories was not producing the desired results. Declan McCarthy was a recruitment consultant to a number of US companies in Ireland. He thinks that they looked at the country in the same way that Americans saw India in later years. They had no reason to stay in Ireland after a development project was complete. "Companies were attracted in by the grants, then found that the marketing could be done better somewhere else," he says. A branch plant with development engineers was consequently no more secure than one with operatives who screwed components together on an assembly line.

CPT's effort to create a new computer category in Ovens had, however, raised the ambitions of its software developers. Mike Brady moved to Océ in the Netherlands in 1985 and assisted half a dozen of his former CPT colleagues to join a development project there. Fourteen years later, back in Ireland, he founded mobile gateway development firm Anam. Looking back, he observes that international companies invariably regarded their Irish developers as backroom guys. "We were always at the back end of the chain", he says. "What we didn't learn at the breast of the multinationals was how to sell."

CPT had not been the only US word processing system firm with a presence in Cork. California-based Compucorp had also set up a research and development unit at its base in Little Island, which is on the opposite side of the city to Ovens. This was on a smaller scale to CPT's group and was no more successful at bringing a new product to market. Compucorp ended up in receivership in 1987. The California firm, however, had followed the ups and downs of the Workmate project. Its head of engineering, Andy DeMari, was impressed by the calibre of the team that his rivals in CPT had assembled. He concluded that high-grade software development could be done in Ireland.

Born in Italy and resident in California, Andy DeMari was an unlikely champion for the Irish software industry. But he founded three of the companies that gave the country an international profile in software development. DeMari is a classic example of the serial entrepreneur who creates businesses with venture capital support, builds them up and sells them off at a premium price. He harnessed Irish software talent and made it part of his formula.

Retix was his first attempt. Andy DeMari established this communications software company in 1985 in Santa Monica, California. Two years later Retix opened a European development and support centre in Dun Laoghaire. Its first recruits included Fergus O'Connell, who became general manager, and Raomal Perera. Both were chosen on the strength of their contributions to the Workmate project at CPT. Retix was a US company with a technical office in Ireland. DeMari's next start-up, Isocor, was a California firm whose entire development division was initially located in Ireland. Isocor was always headquartered in the US, but the business was driven from Dublin and the bulk of its revenues came from Europe.

Network365 was DeMari's third project in Ireland, but the first software corporation that he based inside the country. Raomal Perera was its co-founder. In 2003 Network365 merged with a Silicon Valley company, iPin, to form Valista. Andy DeMari became chairman of the enlarged entity and Raomal Perera was named chief executive officer. One of the crew members on the Workmate voyage had joined the captains of the industry.

Servant of Three Masters

The September 2001 announcement that Hewlett-Packard and Compaq had agreed to merge sent shock waves through rank-and-file employees in both organisations. It was obvious that the deal would result in widespread rationalisation and lay-offs. The Compaq software centre in Galway, however, had few reservations about being acquired by HP. In fact, its management was rather keen to become part of a bigger corporation.

All the business units in the centre were slotted into the international HP organisation before the merger was completed in May 2002. Some groups gained additional responsibilities. Rory O'Connor, the centre's managing director, declared that it was great to be competing at the top of the market again. He believed the new owner, unlike Compaq, was big enough to compete head to head against IBM. "The HP merger feels like a merger. It does not feel like a takeover," he insisted.

HP, it was said, regarded Compaq's high-performance computing group in Galway as one of the key assets that it had acquired. It was the third American corporation in four years to place its logo on the front of the centre. The building previously belonged to Digital Equipment, which was the largest employer in the western city for many years. Compaq bought Digital in 1998 and retained the Galway operation as part of its services organisation.

Digital ran the biggest computer assembly operation in the country for two decades. The Galway facility configured and delivered the company's most powerful computers, contributed to product design and participated in research projects on computer integrated manufacturing. It started to develop and distribute software in the mid-1970s. A sister operation in Clonmel employed another team of design engineers.

Digital was renowned for allowing its staff to try out new ideas and its Irish organisation made full use of these opportunities. Managers like John Giblin, the company's director of European technical support, knew that configuring computer systems would not always be a viable activity for Galway. Groups at the facility therefore investigated new ways of licensing and delivering software. They studied the software needs of major customers and devised support services, not only for Digital products but also for other vendors' applications. The Galway organisation enjoyed closer links with Digital's headquarters in Massachusetts than other US-owned computer factories in Ireland had with their head offices. These relationships enabled it to get approval for more software-related projects.

The software side of the operation employed 350 people in 1993, when Digital finally phased out computer assembly in Galway. Hardware production had always had a high profile in the city and many locals saw the software centre as a minor remnant. The Galway organisation, however, had matured into one of the few successful US-owned concentrations of Irish development talent. It had created Digital's system management support assessment tool, an application that identified computer configuration problems and suggested actions to improve performance. It had written a unique software asset management system for large customers. It had set up a laboratory where people were observed interacting with software and the usability of products could be assessed.

The high-performance technical computing group was added to this mix in 1993. Its role was to support scientific and engineering customers that used the company's "workstation farms" and to assist them to exploit the parallel processing capabilities of these systems. The group also interacted on behalf of Digital with independent software vendors and open source software consortia. Its leader, Mark Gantly, hired a multi-disciplinary team that included specialists in chemistry, applied mathematics and engineering.

As the group's experience grew, so did the scale of its customers' applications. Gantly's team collaborated with Quadrics Supercomputer World to obtain memory channel technology for massive supercomputers. In 1999, the group enabled the French Atomic Energy Commission to install the most powerful computer in Europe, containing 2,560 processors. It soon advanced to delivering a 12,000-processor monster to the US Department of Energy. The Galway group also supplied software advisers to Celera Genomics, when it needed to ramp up its computing power to map the human genome.

Projects like these raised the profile of the high-performance technical computing group in a rarefied subset of the international software community. The asset management group in Galway, meanwhile, became a leader in another subset, automating software installation processes in large, geographically dispersed organisations.

These activities looked out of place inside Compaq, a company that had grown up as a PC box shifter and always measured its success in terms of unit shipments. Nonetheless, the software centre kept expanding under Compaq. When the company was merged into HP, the headcount in Galway stood at about 500, including more than 200 software engineers.

Since Digital Equipment's time, the computer systems trade has consolidated into a small set of large competitors. As Rory O'Connor implies, both HP and IBM can supply wide portfolios of products and services to corporate accounts. The Galway software centre makes direct contributions to these customers' operations. IBM's Dublin Software Laboratory, in contrast, has a much narrower brief.

A Little Piece of Big Blue

IBM was the dominant force in global computing. At the start of the 1980s Big Blue's annual sales were greater than the sum of all the other vendors in the industry's top ten. If the IDA had published a wish list in that era, it would probably have placed an IBM computer factory at the top. But the corporation had a policy of rewarding its biggest markets with strategic investments. Its European production units were strategically distributed among the biggest countries. The Irish computer market was puny and offered few opportunities for IBM to sell the mainframes whose blue cabinets explained the company's nickname. IBM Ireland was the biggest system supplier in the country, but its share of the business was lower than the corporation was accustomed to elsewhere in Europe. Most of its revenues in Ireland came from minicomputer shipments to IDA-backed manufacturing plants. Digital Equipment had prevailed in the public sector.

The IBM Ireland sales organisation did its best to be a good corporate citizen, developing relationships with the universities and telling anyone who would listen about its policies to source computer components and subassemblies in Ireland. The local management was as keen as the IDA to pull investment money into the country. It knew that it could not land a major project, so it pitched for a small software centre whose set-up costs would be relatively trivial. The strategy worked.

IBM Ireland Information Services Ltd (IISL) was established in Dublin in 1983. The centre's mission was to design, development, test and maintain bespoke software. Other IDA clients, such as Digital, Ericsson, Nixdorf and Prime, had come to Ireland to assemble equipment and added software groups at a later date. IBM was important as a role model for standalone software projects.

The company had a policy of hiring graduates and training them in its ways. Few IBMers worked for other firms before joining the corporation. The rare examples were known internally as "vitality hires". According to the IBM tradition, its people served from birth to death — or at least from graduation to retirement. The IISL workplan reflected this culture. The software centre was initially given fairly undemanding tasks, mainly in technical support, and had to earn the right to take on more important projects. Despite these modest beginnings, the new operation reported export revenues of almost $2 million in 1984.

In the following years IISL developed new software for internal use by the IBM organisation in Europe, Middle East and Africa. The centre scored a significant success with one of its first applications — a data warehouse. This catalogued and stored company information in a format that allowed it to be accessed for different purposes. IISL's work sparked IBM's "information warehouse" strategy of later years and one Dublin-based employee, Barry Devlin, acquired a corporation-wide reputation for his expertise in this area.

By the start of the 1990s, IISL was developing products for sale to customers as well as for its fellow IBMers to use. First came the Systems Application Architecture Delivery Manager, which co-ordinated the installation of specific pieces of software onto specific workstations. This was followed by a succession of "electronic forms" products and banking applications built on its own financial services data model. By 1991 IISL's revenues had risen to approximately $18 million and its headcount was close to 100. In the following year the organisation was formally accredited as an IBM development laboratory. This designation meant additional responsibilities in worldwide business management and marketing for its products. IISL also began to report directly to the US.

Here, it seemed, was a textbook example of software development expanding in Ireland through inward investment. The IISL structure, however, turned out to be rather fragile.

The crunch came in November 1994. IBM described it as a "remissioning" of IISL. But this was actually a severe demotion. It was not prompted by anything that the Dublin-based crew had done — or failed to do. The centre was stripped of its "laboratory" status by a corporate decision to reduce the number of IBM software laboratories outside the United States. Other units in Europe and Canada met the same fate. These things happen when large corporations shuffle around their senior executives.

IISL lost responsibility for the FormTalk forms processing software and the data replication technology that it had created. The corporation reassigned them to American software units. IBM Ireland managed to redeploy IISL's employees, offering their talents to other IBM Europe subsidiaries. The banking software group thus managed to remain intact for a few years.

Nonetheless, the ease with which IBM dismantled IISL rammed home the message that Ireland would need to create its own software companies if it wanted to play in the major league.

In the second half of the 1990s the IDA finally persuaded IBM to set up component manufacturing operations in Ireland. On the software side of the corporation, meanwhile, new policies were introduced after it acquired Lotus Development in 1995. IBM retained the Lotus software product unit in Santry, which continued to upgrade the Domino Global Workbench. This group was working in an area that suited IBM's primary focus on middleware and infrastructure management software. In

1999, indeed, the corporation decided to phase out its remaining line-of-business applications so that it could concentrate on the underlying technologies. This strategy also improved its relationships with independent software developers.

Today, once again, IBM runs a software laboratory in Dublin. But its origins lie in the localisation research at Lotus, not in the old IISL. IBM has created a language technology architecture that embeds support for multi-lingual computing into its software development process. The Dublin group took over the management of this architecture in 2000. It now directs an international team of engineers who understand the intricate trade-offs between software performance and linguistic diversity.

In 2003 the Dublin laboratory was given new responsibilities. It began developing components for a new generation of IBM middleware that combines e-mail, instant messaging, document management and team collaboration. Twenty years after the first IBM Ireland software project, company employees were finally working on a core product. A long-standing objective had been achieved. But IBM had reached this destination by the most circuitous of routes.

Neighbours and Strangers

The first exit from Cork's ring road on the south side of the Jack Lynch Tunnel leads into Mahon. This district has two large concentrations of software activity. Each one studiously ignores the other.

The NSC Campus houses a cluster of development companies. NSC stands for National Software Centre, but this one has nothing to do with the ill-conceived centre that the IDA set up in the 1980s. The title displays a Corkonian assertiveness that the second largest city in the state wants its share of national institutions. In fact, the NSC was conceived in the late 1990s by the Cork Business and Innovation Centre and some of the city's software industry veterans. They wanted to overcome a shortage of good office accommodation with high-speed communications links.

To date, there is only one building on the campus, but the land is zoned to accommodate up to eight additional blocks, each housing between 300 and 500 software developers. The founders of the NSC not only wanted to create a conducive environment for cutting code, but also aimed to provide all the ancillary services that a growing software business might require. One of the rooms off the entrance hall was therefore reserved for an internet service provider. Another was earmarked for a venture capital firm. The tenant companies are a mixture of start-ups and established names and their staff are encouraged to meet and interact in the public areas of the building.

Mahon's second software hub lies down the road and around a couple of corners from the NSC Campus. Motorola's software centre is one of the longest-running development operations in the country. The US corporation came to Cork in 1984, when it took over Four Phase Systems and inherited the company's subsidiary in Ireland. By 1990 the centre employed 27 people, producing management applications for analogue mobile networks. Motorola described the Mahon building as the only facility in the world that it had dedicated entirely to software development. It expanded steadily in the 1990s, supplying software for the digital GSM mobile standard and supporting network operators around Europe. In 2000 Motorola employed some 400 people in Cork and had set up a semiconductor design group beside the software developers.

In theory there could be many sorts of collaboration between the two development centres in Mahon. The buildings are close enough for employees to meet during coffee breaks. In practice, however, Motorola and the NSC Campus might as well be located on different planets. They do not engage in subcontracting or staff exchanges or skills transfer projects. They do not communicate. John Phillips, Motorola Ireland's country manager, says that he has never visited the NSC and has never been invited. When asked what impact the centre has had on Cork, he replies that he is not aware of any.

The roots of this divide can be traced back to the 1980s when Motorola and local company SMC hired different types of software developers. SMC lived hard and died young. Motorola attracted a more conservative breed, including programmers who had previously worked for other international corporations. Most software firms in Cork today are descended from one group or the other.

The histories of the two camps unfolded along different lines. Shemas Eivers, the former SMC leader who later became one of the founders of the NSC, says that software development in Cork passed through two growth spurts — a PC-related surge in the 1980s and a web-led rush at the turn of the century. He describes the interim period in the early 1990s as the "death and destruction" phase. These years, in contrast, were the boom times for the Motorola operation in Mahon. It embarked on an expansion plan in 1990, when it took on responsibility for GSM development. It produced an operations management system for GSM networks that started, in John Phillips's words, as "a white sheet of paper". In 1994 the Cork centre won a corporate accolade in a Motorola quality management programme based on the Software Engineering Institute's capability maturity model.

John Phillips says that Motorola assisted the IDA to attract other international companies into the Cork area, especially CMG, Logica and S3, which all shared its interest in mobile communications. His company made a point of following how these investments fared. With the exception of S3, their residencies in Cork were brief. In contrast, Motorola's managers paid little attention to the 40-odd locally owned software companies that were limbering up in the nearby NSC building.

This phenomenon is not unique to Motorola or to Cork. The subsidiaries of international companies maintain contact with each other. Irish-owned software firms move in different circles. The two groups have few reasons to meet. They seldom buy products from each other and, when they do, the transactions may take place through intermediaries. Occasionally an applications firm might run a joint promotion with a middleware vendor, but these partnerships are usually arranged through offices abroad. Since 1994 the two camps have dealt with the state through different agencies. People usually follow a career path on one side of the fence or the other. When crossovers occur, it is usually because an Irish firm has been taken over by an overseas company and its staff want to return to the native side.

Twenty years ago the software development community was considerably smaller and the dividing line was much less rigid. There was more interaction between Irish- and foreign-owned companies and the state agencies ran linkage programmes to identify areas where they could collaborate.

Generation two software companies often got off the ground by finding an IDA-backed factory that was willing to test their new applications and to act as a reference site. PC package vendors like MicroPro and Multimate and local software engineering firms sought similar skills. CPT's Workmate project attracted personnel from all over the country and most of its developers subsequently worked in indigenous companies. Ericsson, which was the largest software employer in Ireland in the mid-1980s, shared interests with small computer-based training companies. Relationships like these faded in generation three and no longer existed by generation four.

The Connect Ireland database project at Córas Tráchtála showed how the ties were unravelling. Its primary aim was to encourage exports. But it was also supposed to assist technology companies to supply goods to the foreign firms in Ireland, on the assumption that these deals were stepping stones to international sales.

Córas Tráchtála — or Bord Tráchtála as it became known in the 1990s — had always found it easier to understand the electronics hardware trade than the software industry. Software, however, was something that it had to address, especially after the National Software Centre closed down. Peter Bennett, who held a PhD in organic chemistry, was one of the agency's specialists in services for technology-based industries. In the late 1980s he set out to show how information technology could promote their capabilities. He envisaged a master catalogue of all the electronics and software companies on the agency's books, incorporating a classified guide to their products and services. The project attempted to index the industry, to place search routines in front of all the company information and to add features that automatically generated requests for further information. The whole work was condensed to fit on a floppy disk that could be duplicated easily and distributed as widely as possible.

The first version of Connect Ireland was released in 1990, but had only a limited circulation. It was built on a proprietary template from Polydata, an information management specialist that targeted the plastics industry. Peter Bennett decided to produce a Microsoft-based edition before proceeding with a major launch. He found consultants and contractors to assist with different aspects of the database and its graphical user interface. Connect Ireland mark two shipped in 2002. It listed all the firms that electronics companies might consider as suppliers — metal frame makers, plastic component moulders and cable assemblers as well as all the software businesses in Ireland. Mark three, which followed in early 2003, zeroed in on the software developers, providing details of more than 400 companies on a single disk. Copies of "Connect Ireland Software" were sent to corporations all over Europe and offered to visitors at the CeBIT fair in Hannover.

According to Peter Bennett, Bord Tráchtála was never able to measure the effectiveness of the project. At first, the agency wanted to be notified whenever the system generated an enquiry and sent it to one of the featured companies via fax. This idea was opposed by its clients and had to be abandoned. It also struggled to establish where the limits of the software industry lay and to keep up with companies that changed their product plans and business models. Some recipients of the disk tried to use it as a resource for selling to the listed companies instead of buying from them. In the end Bennett got more feedback on the database application itself than on the number of leads that it generated. He says that Bord Tráchtála could actually have sold its software abroad if it had chosen to do so!

The Connect Ireland exercise indicated that few IDA clients were sourcing applications from local software developers any more. The World Wide Web appeared shortly after the Bord Tráchtála project. Prospective trading partners went online to find information about one another. Internet communications, indeed, played an important part in the rise of Irish software exports to the US. As the case of Motorola illustrates, though, foreign-owned software units in Ireland have had little inclination to inspect their neighbours' websites.

Is There a Future for Inward Investment?

Professor John Byrne can only recall one occasion when an inward investment project from the US took on a group of his Trinity College Dublin graduates. Oracle, he says, employed some for software debugging. These, he adds, had been the weaker students in their year. In general, the university's computer science graduates did not regard the foreign-owned software operations in Ireland as appropriate places to seek jobs.

Compare this observation with the advertisements that the IDA placed in the arrivals section of Dublin airport for many years, promoting the capabilities of Ireland's youthful workforce. The agency frequently depicted graduates in its marketing campaigns. Local companies complained about its advertisements whenever the software labour market was tight. Some would gladly have replaced the airport posters for corporate visitors with "turn back" signs.

Since localisation evolved into a service industry in its own right, the overseas software corporations in Ireland have sought skills other than software design and development. As the localisation business matured in the 1990s, the IDA focused instead on call centres and customer support services. These were even less likely to appeal to ambitious graduates with computing degrees. More recently, the US corporations have tried to evolve into "command and control" centres that co-ordinate international supply chains. Companies like Microsoft, Oracle and SAP will probably continue to locate back-office functions in Ireland, but they will never bet their future on Irish engineers in the way that CPT once did.

Inward investment projects became less and less relevant to the careers of software developers in the 1990s. Barry Murphy tracked this transition during his time as National Software Director. "Right through the 1990s," he says, "the number of jobs created by the indigenous companies was about the same as by the multinationals. But they were significantly better jobs."

This was a watershed for the Irish economy. Technology-based industries had been imported for decades and sustaining the flow of foreign corporations was regarded as a political imperative. Software development was the first industry where native firms overshadowed the multinationals. The good jobs, the most challenging work and the best opportunities to associate with industry leaders were all in Irish-owned companies. People who worked for the multinationals were more likely to wind up dealing with freight forwarders or keeping records of which customers held licences for which products.

There was a new sense of self-confidence in the country. Ireland's macroeconomic success was becoming internationally known and the software industry proved that this was not merely the result of foreign investment.

Some international companies, it is true, continued to develop software in Ireland, usually in provincial centres, after the localisation business took off. The IDA's incentives convinced a small set of American corporations from manufacturing industries and financial services to open in-house software groups. This bunch started with projects like the "strategic remote programming centre" that Travelers Corporation opened in Limerick in 1987 and a Boeing Computer Services unit that lasted for five years in Cork. The trend has continued into the twenty-first century in towns such as Letterkenny, the home of Prudential Financial's Prumerica Systems Ireland subsidiary, and Mullingar, where General Motors set up GMAC Commercial to write financial software.

The vulnerability of this cluster was shown, however, when Honeywell shut its long-established application software business in Waterford. This operation ran from 1987 until 2003, when Honeywell transferred most of its work to a sister company in India. User organisations with internal software development projects can choose among a growing range of low-cost locations.

The same economic reality applies, though perhaps to a lesser extent, to computer systems vendors. The case of Software and Systems Engineering (SSE) is especially instructive. SSE originated at the start of the 1980s as a backroom networking software project at Nixdorf Computer's Dublin office. Later on the group won Esprit contracts and started to win development assignments from its parent organisation in Germany. After Siemens took over Nixdorf in 1990 SSE became an autonomous software services company. Over the years it made some unfortunate technology choices, specialising in non-internet communications standards and developing office applications that were unable to compete successfully against Microsoft.

By the mid-1990s, when its headcount had risen to more than 100, the Dublin development group appeared to have found a good niche. It offered a suite of security software that controlled access to corporate networks and protected confidential e-mail. SSE's problem was that its parent never really thought of it as a product development centre. Its German bosses saw the business as a bunch of offshore programmers. By the end of the 1990s Siemens knew that it could hire software developers in India for less than a tenth of the hourly rate in Dublin and it lost interest in maintaining the Irish subsidiary. A Munich-based security software firm, Guardeonic Solutions, took over the security products in 2002.

SSE was one of the foreign-owned operations whose technology interests overlapped with the more technically inclined Irish companies in generations two and three. ICL was another company that co-operated with the locals. Iona's Chris Horn taught object-oriented programming to the employees at its information technology centre in Leopardstown. The first copy of Iona's Orbix product was supplied to this centre, which developed a graphics development system called GraphicsPower. The companies ran a joint demonstration of their technologies at the Object World show in San Francisco in 1993. Sun, whose computers were sold through ICL, noticed this partnership and took an interest in Iona. By the end of the year Sun had invested $600,000 in the Dublin firm in exchange for a minority shareholding.

Sun had recently set up a software subsidiary of its own in Dublin — partly because an earthquake in California had alerted it to the risks of concentrating too many of its software engineers in one place. This office eventually took charge of the corporation's desktop software strategy and managed some of its open source initiatives. When Sun and Iona teamed up, they discovered how the state agencies were providing vastly superior support deals for foreign companies than for Irish firms. "When the Sun people sat down and read through the agreements, they were astounded by the difference in the grants and incentives that the IDA had given them," Chris Horn recalls.

According to Barry Murphy, this discrimination was justified by the competition for US investment from other countries. But it became less easy to defend in the second half of the 1990s when software engineers were in short supply and the industry had to encourage immigration to relieve the skills shortage. The IDA's grants were blamed for fuelling a rise in wage costs. The launch of Enterprise Ireland in 1998 was welcomed as an effort to address some of the anomalies. The new agency focused on the needs of Irish-owned companies. But these firms continued to feel like the poor relations of the multinationals.

Is there a case, then, for dismantling the support infrastructure for inward investments that involve software development? There is certainly an argument for overhauling it to reflect the changing nature of these projects. Ireland has come a long way since the years when international companies were offered low-tax packages and other inducements to provide work for software engineers. Such companies have continued to enter the country, however, through merger and acquisition deals. In the past these usually involved foreign-owned operations that changed hands. Today, and for the foreseeable future, foreign software companies are more likely to come into Ireland by taking over Irish firms. As Chris Byrne at Narragansett Technologies puts it, Ireland's opportunity to work for US companies is gone, but America has accepted the country as a place that good software comes from.

Byrne's previous company, Limerick-based Software Architects International, was acquired by US corporation Clarus. E-learning vendor Thomson Netg also established a presence in Limerick through an acquisition deal. Logica and Marconi and Siebel Systems came into Dublin via high profile takeovers. General Electric bought Office Integrated Solutions. Sita Information Networking Computing snapped up airline application developer Eland Technologies. Acotel Group acquired wireless internet specialist Jinny Software. BeTrusted purchased Baltimore Technologies' UniCert business. Torex, which later became part of the iSoft Group, took over McKeown Software and MoreMagic acquired Agile.

Deals like these have created a template for inward investment in the twenty-first century and present the IDA with an agenda that is far removed from what it did in the last century. Once again, the software developers may be setting precedents for other manufacturing and service industries in Ireland. There are, however, two radically different policy positions that the state authorities can adopt in relation to acquisitions and trade sales. Should they develop a set of mechanisms to ensure that the new owner retains a presence in Ireland and, perhaps, embeds itself into the country in the way that Motorola has done? Or should they assume that technology takeovers are usually asset-stripping exercises and expect the Irish entities to disappear after a year or two? If so, new measures should be introduced to accelerate skill transfers to other companies and to assist displaced employees to launch new ventures or buy back elements of the acquired businesses.

This is what happened through a management buy-out at Clarus in Limerick, when a start-up called SAI New Technologies took over the Cashbook products originally created by Chris Byrne and his colleagues. Something similar occurred after General Electric acquired Office Integrated Solutions in 1999. The American corporation was keen to enhance Purchasing Expert, the Dublin company's requisition and order management package, and assigned 80 people in Ireland and India to this work. Two years later it decided to withdraw from the information services business. Document Centric Solutions, a new outfit set up by the founders of Office Integrated Solutions, took control of Purchasing Expert in 2002. They recovered the intellectual property rights to the software in return for agreeing to manage the customer contracts.

There are credible arguments for and against shoring up acquired businesses, for and against pulling them apart and for and against supporting buy-backs. These arguments are seldom voiced. Political discourse in Ireland still harks back to 1970s-style industrialisation and foreign-owned branch plants. The software industry, meanwhile, requires an economic development model in which fiscal incentives for international corporations may not matter any more.

Chapter 6

THE MIDDLEWARE STORY

An Object-oriented Original — 1

If John Carolan had chosen another line of work, he would have been a household name. But he made his career in software development, where his talents were quite extraordinary. One former colleague describes Carolan as "the James Joyce of the last 25 years", because of the creativity that he applied to writing code. Like the famous novelist — a fellow Dubliner — Carolan's achievements received more recognition outside Ireland than at home. He attained celebrity of a sort, especially in the software architecture hubs of the US and among the inventors of advanced programming languages. He missed the boom years of the Irish software industry, spending most of the 1990s in America. He died in Dublin in 2001.

Other software developers have benefited from Carolan's stellar reputation. He did more than anyone else to convince the outside world that Ireland could produce cool software. He was not only a brilliant thinker, but also attracted a following of younger developers and inspired them to aim high.

John Carolan was never a conventional ambassador. A bulky figure, heavily bearded with flowing grey hair, he became known at an early stage in his career for his disdain for dress codes. One acquaintance memorably summarised his appearance as a cross between Santa Claus and the Buddha. As a committed environmentalist he was known to refuse on principle when invited to travel in a car. Originally known as John McDowell, he and his partner Ann O'Brien both changed their name to Carolan shortly before the birth of their first child. It was a way of formalising their relationship and avoiding unwanted attention from the bureaucrats in the maternity hospital. Legend has it, indeed, that John and Ann met each other after he set himself a challenge to date as many Ann O'Briens as possible and worked his way through all the leads in the telephone directory.

When no one else could trace the cause of a software problem at the Bank of Ireland, Carolan shut himself into its computer centre with a supply of beer and sandwiches and worked non-stop for three days until he found the solution. When Trinity College Dublin set up its first full-time undergraduate course in computer science, he provided advice on the curriculum. He was the behind-the-scenes visionary on CPT's Workmate project. His involvement in broadband networking at Guinness led to the formation of Intelligence Ireland. In 1984, at a time when lookalike outfits were popping up in every neighbourhood to develop lookalike products, he created a software company unlike any that the country had seen before.

Even after two decades, there are two opposing schools of thought on Glockenspiel. To its admirers, this was the company that caused Irish software developers to stop producing stodgy, unoriginal applications for end users and proved that they could export advanced enabling technologies. Glockenspiel sold products from a run-down building in Dominick Street — an area of Dublin's inner city that well-heeled citizens avoided — to blue-chip research laboratories. This version of the company's history blames its demise in 1992 on a dark conspiracy among US corporations and their Irish associates or on the incompetence of various institutions that never appreciated the genius of Carolan and his acolytes.

The detractors' version of the story presents John Carolan as a sort of geek messiah, who led his followers down a false trail. They highlight a lack of basic business skills inside his company and his unwillingness to share management responsibilities with others. They argue that Glockenspiel failed because Carolan picked inappropriate partners, including a US distributor that led the company into financial difficulties. On paper, Glockenspiel achieved exports worth millions of dollars. In practice, its liquidator was unable to put a meaningful valuation on its remains. Its collapse, the critics say, made it difficult for more deserving software companies to obtain public or private investment in the early 1990s.

John Carolan became a software developer in the mid-1960s after undertaking numerical analysis for plasma physics research. ICL hired him as a systems software specialist, working on its proprietary mainframes. By the start of the 1980s he was employed by Rainsford Computing Services, which was part of the Guinness Group. But his knowledge was frequently sought by other companies that wanted to stretch the boundaries of their software. He maintained regular contacts, for example, with Bell Labs' Computing Science Research Center in the US. Software theorists were questioning the dependence of software environments on specific vendors and their hardware designs. Bell Labs created the Unix operating system, which could be licensed to a variety of computer manufacturers, and the C programming language. Carolan was aware that the research centre planned to develop a new language that would extend the capabilities of C and contributed his ideas to the project.

When Bell Labs produced a beta version of its new C++ compiler, it sent out two evaluation copies. One went to Stanford University and the other to John Carolan.

Glockenspiel was formed to build a business around Carolan's knowledge of C++ and the new object-oriented style of software development that the language facilitated. Clive Lee, Declan McCarthy and John Pierce — former colleagues who knew of his abilities — put money into the start-up business. Carolan's first choice name for the company was not available. Having recently returned to Dublin from a project in Austria, he chose Glockenspiel for its Viennese connotations. Under this brand name he got the C++ compiler to run on PCs before anyone else, then launched it as a commercial product.

All Glockenspiel products were primarily John Carolan's handiwork. Gradually, though, the company attracted a workforce of like-minded software engineers, who wanted to learn from the master. At its peak the company had about 30 staff. Applicants for employment had to submit themselves to a "torture test" that Carolan devised to sort out the true techies from the pseudo-geeks. It took less than half an hour. He handed the candidate a piece of code and asked "What does this program do?" Those who gave a satisfactory reply got into Glockenspiel. But Carolan never revealed the complete answer to anyone.

"The torture test was a geek thing. John developed a culture around it," recalls Declan McCarthy, one of Glockenspiel's original backers and a non-executive director of the company. Stories about the test started to circulate in other Dublin workplaces. McCarthy ran a recruitment agency for software staff and referred promising candidates to Carolan. The block of code, he says, could be used for a variety of purposes. Anyone who said that it was written for one specific task failed the test. Those who recognised, and could discuss, its adaptability scored well.

In its early years Glockenspiel was primarily a services company — a provider of consulting and training services and a contract developer specialising in C++, C and Unix. It boasted that all of its employees had at least two years' experience of system software development in C. Glockenspiel promoted its "C by Satellite" service on the basis that software developers in Ireland would work for lower pay rates than Americans. It offered "fixed-price fixed-time contracts at a price no one in the US can match" and regular contact with clients through e-mail. Messages were sent via the European Unix Users Group (EUUG), which had noticed the potential of inter-company e-mail when most of the industry still treated it as an internal communications medium. John Carolan sat on the governing board of the EUUG and obtained an internet e-mail address half a decade before the first internet services provider opened in Ireland.

Glockenspiel's services, however, were soon overshadowed by its products. By 1986 the company was selling a collection of development tools to other Unix loyalists. Pride of place went to its version of C++. Other Glockenspiel products assisted developers to design applications on graphic user interfaces or to work with information inside database files. Carolan worked hard to ensure that his C++ compiler ran on a wider range of system platforms than anyone else's and won orders from major corporations within and beyond the IT industry. At the end of

1988 Glockenspiel claimed that it had sold more than 5,000 copies of the compiler. Some 70 per cent of these deliveries went to the US.

Coming at a time when other prominent exporters were collapsing or selling out, this success carried a potent message for the Irish software industry as a whole. Glockenspiel had shown that software engineers in Ireland could sell tools to software engineers around the world without setting up a sales and support subsidiary in every country. Technical products could be sent out in a box and did not require any implementation services. Most line-of-business software had to be translated into foreign languages and localised to suit national standards, currencies and legislation. Geek software, in contrast, could be sold worldwide without modifications. If the customers had problems, they were more likely to send an e-mail to the development group than to harass the sales manager.

Here was a new strategy for software development in Ireland. It required networking with the leading players in the industry. It depended on early access to emerging software technologies — particularly the type that sat between the operating system and the application and later became known as middleware. Above all it needed celebrity geeks — individuals like John Carolan whose technical reputations could sell products. At the end of the 1980s the industry establishment, as represented on the government's software strategy committee, was backing mundane applications based on proven technologies and steered by conservative managers. Carolan personified an alternative model, based on untested technologies, volatile markets and the culture of the torture test.

It was not hard to marginalise the geeks. The mainstream software industry in the late 1980s paid little attention to advanced development concepts. Most developers wanted to get a minicomputer or PC package to market as quickly as possible and to sign up customers who would pay regular fees for upgrades, training and support. Most users still thought in terms of investing in an accounting system or planning and control software for their own lines of business. The payback from development tools and methodologies was much less predictable. It might take years to commercialise these technologies and they might never sell. Glockenspiel's activities were so obscure and its modus operandi was so alien that few people in Ireland noticed its progress. The company never curried favour with politicians. It was ignored by most of the media. John Carolan did not take part in the debates about the condition of the Irish software industry. He was passionate about technologies, not about national plans. He did not belong in the conservative consensus that treated the guys with crumpled jeans and funny haircuts with disdain and believed that successful software firms were built by men in suits.

In March 1989 Glockenspiel launched its flagship product — a toolkit called CommonView — at an exhibition in San Francisco. This introduced a range of additional options for the programmers who used its C++ compiler. Object-oriented programming differed from other types of software development by offering data structures — or classes — that could be re-used in one application after another. CommonView was a collection of C++ classes — a framework that enabled developers to make their applications run on different operating systems and under different graphical user interfaces. CommonView offered software portability between platforms without disturbing the look and feel of an application. Each of its classes was pre-tested for optimum performance with as few computing resources as possible. Carolan claimed that the object technology toolkit could reduce dramatically the cost of software production. All for a fixed price of $400.

It was not long before CommonView accounted for most of Glockenspiel's revenues. The company made arrangements to supply the product in volume by contracting out the packaging and distribution work to a software publisher in New York.

By now, powerful forces were following John Carolan's movements very closely. Borland and Symantec, two well-financed suppliers of development tools, entered the C++ arena. Microsoft took a close interest in CommonView. When Glockenspiel released the toolkit, Microsoft ran a mailshot campaign to promote it, encouraging C++ developers to port their applications to run in its Windows environments. In 1990 IBM forged a joint marketing agreement with the company to sell an updated edition of the C++ compiler in conjunction with its new RS/6000 computers. CommonView 2 appeared later that year, adding support for other suppliers' implementations of C++. An American trade magazine, *Computer Language*, gave the product its annual award for making the greatest contribution to the productivity of software developers. In 1991 Glockenspiel announced a development alliance with Coopers & Lybrand, promising to deliver new programming products and to deliver them through the consulting firm's global operations.

By then, however, the industry environment for object-oriented software had changed. The software business had suffered from the "Unix wars" of the late 1980s, when rival groups of vendors, including all the big system makers, had pushed alternative visions for the operating system. This led to fragmentation in the market and hampered the overall uptake of Unix-based computers. These players were concerned that object technology could be Balkanised in the same way, with different factions adopting different frameworks and components. Microsoft, in particular, was gearing up for competition, not collaboration, in this field.

In 1989 Hewlett-Packard, which had tried to drum up support for its NewWave application environment, and American Airlines orchestrated the establishment of a new industry association. The Object Management Group (OMG) would seek consensus-based standards for class libraries and other manifestations of object technology. By the middle of 1991 more than 150 software developers and hardware vendors had signed up to the OMG and Glockenspiel's customers were starting to ask if CommonView had a future under the emerging regime. Glockenspiel's marketing manager Adam Winkelmann informed the doubters that, despite the OMG's promises, the consortium's members were still peddling incompatible programming tools and that developers still needed his company's tools.

The CommonView business peaked in 1991, when Glockenspiel claimed annual revenues of more than $3 million. Only one other Irish-owned software company, CBT Systems, reported higher international sales that year. In the months that followed, however, Glockenspiel ran out of money. Its American distributor, Imagesoft, collapsed, owing $250,000 to the Dublin company. Then Glockenspiel's bank put Carolan under pressure to deal with its overdraft. The IDA had never liked the way that he ran the company, explaining its difficulties to all the staff and confiding in his techie pals rather than professional advisers. Takeover rumours started to circulate. And it was obvious that the development agency would much prefer to deal with another US multinational than to haggle with the geeks in Dominick Street.

John Carolan applied for an examinership — the Irish equivalent of filing for Chapter 11 protection. The High Court in Dublin appointed an examiner to take charge of Glockenspiel's affairs in June 1992 and gave the company three months to find a "white knight" that could sort out its finances. Examinership was a fairly new procedure and this was the first time that it had been applied to a software firm. In the weeks that followed, the examiner negotiated a deal with Computer Associates (CA), the second largest software company in the world. CA agreed to give Glockenspiel enough cash to pay its debts and keep trading for another year. At that point it would have the first option to buy the company outright.

Computer Associates appears to have been thinking defensively. It was rumoured that Microsoft wanted to get its hands on Glockenspiel's technology and CA's investment would hold its rival at bay. The deal would cost the corporation about $5 million. From Carolan's perspective the terms were quite favourable. Glockenspiel would have a breathing space to find another supply channel for North America, make money out of its partnership with Coopers & Lybrand and choose a strategy compatible with the changes that the OMG was plotting for object technology. The benign agreement, however, soon unravelled.

Computer Associates thrived on acquisitions. The company understood how to take control of assets and extract as much money as possible out of them. That was how it had ramped up its revenues to more than $1.4 billion a year. John Carolan was ill-prepared and, as usual, reluctant to accept advice from outside Glockenspiel, when one of CA's top executives, Sanjay Kumar, swept into town with his team of lawyers. CA saw Carolan as a prize trophy and it was obvious how vulnerable he was.

The initial agreement collapsed when a newspaper article stated — incorrectly — that Glockenspiel had ended up in the hands of a receiver. It was still in the middle of the examinership process. Computer Associates took advantage of the change in circumstances and presented the examiner with a much tougher set of proposals. It now wanted to buy Glockenspiel outright and to lock Carolan into a five-year service contract. In return CA would pay off all the company's debts. The acquisition went through on these terms and was announced in September without disclosure of the price. In reality, however, CA had secured the asset it wanted for next to nothing. Carolan and his colleagues had nothing to show for their years of effort. The IDA added insult to injury by claiming back every grant that Glockenspiel had ever received.

At first CA declared that it would continue to market Glockenspiel's products and to employ the company's depleted workforce of 27, but the Dominick Street team soon drifted apart. Microsoft ended up with a consolation prize of sorts when it hired one of Carolan's most experienced deputies to write a C++ compiler of its own. CA whisked Carolan off to Long Island — he reportedly settled in a place called Hicksville — and made him the chief architect of its Jasmine object database.

He returned to Dublin in 2000 and joined a content management and portal development company, International Information Management Corporation, as chief technology officer. He kept a low profile in the months before his unexpected death in December 2001. John Carolan was 55 years old.

A Technical Elite?

Glockenspiel flew higher than any of the other technically oriented software firms of the time, but it was not the only geek-friendly employer in the mid-to-late 1980s. Carolan's company was the brightest star in a cluster that sprang up in and around Dublin in generation two and offered work to the new breed of graduates with primary degrees in computer science.

The first batch from the full-time degree course at Trinity College Dublin left the university in 1983. Most left the country too. They were eminently employable, but not in Ireland, despite the existence of more than 200 software companies. These firms competed to attract the employees of photocopier firms, who were renowned for their sales abilities, but showed little interest in hiring software engineers straight from college. The graduates' employment prospects improved, however, when companies like Glockenspiel emerged. Merrion Gates Software and Generics Software recruited from this pool as well and are also remembered as companies that were ahead of their time.

"Generics was like an extension of Trinity," recalls Chris Chedgey, a graduate of the college's computer science department. He found his second job there. The first was at Transtec Technology, a short-lived computer systems maker that employed software staff to write device drivers. At Generics, in contrast, he discovered that research could be open-ended. The company was technology-driven, not customer-driven — just like a university. Its employees interacted with the research teams in large corporations and gained the sort of grounding that prepared them to be technical leaders at other software companies. Years later, indeed, Chedgey founded Headway Software.

Robert Cochran set up Generics Software in June 1984, as the first round of the European Commission's Esprit research programme was ramping up. At the time Cochran was still working at the National Board for Science and Technology and he did not join Generics on a full-time basis until his stint at the National Software Centre had ended. Hans-Juergen Kugler took charge of day-to-day operations. From the start the company focused on international opportunities that involved software engineering, expert systems or the Ada development language. It soon secured a role in a five-year Esprit project, ToolUse. This aimed to construct an advanced support environment for software developers, providing them with expert assistance in the design, implementation and evolution of applications. Trinity College Dublin and Vector Software also joined ToolUse as subcontractors.

Robert Cochran believed that R&D work could sustain Generics while it evolved into a producer of software development tools — packages that would encapsulate the best methodologies for requirements planning and applications design, while guiding software authors towards better code quality. The company kept its hand in Esprit and also won development contracts from the European Space Agency. By the late 1980s it had more than 20 employees at an office in Sandyford and annual revenues of more than $2 million. But Cochran's desire to package Generics' knowledge of development methods proved over-optimistic. It lacked the business development expertise required to turn the output of the ToolUse project into a product with customer appeal. Chris Chedgey reckons that Generics' technical strength was also a commercial weakness.

Robert Cochran also learned how difficult it was for a tiny Irish firm to establish international credibility. In 1989 he went looking for a strategic partner for Generics — a big player that might integrate the Sandyford team into its software development operations and thus ensure its survival. Cochran talked to Boeing. Then he talked with Rational Software — the software vendor that eventually dominated the market niche where Generics had hoped to sell its packages. He suggested that Generics could act as the European wing of Rational. The US firm did not seem to have much interest in Europe. A Motorola group in Chicago, however, took the bait.

Over the next two years Generics and Motorola edged closer and closer to each other. The American corporation bought the rights to Generics' technology. The Sandyford group provided consultancy on how to improve Motorola's software quality and productivity. Then the US firm gave it the status of a preferred supplier. Both sides expected that the relationship would lead to a full takeover. In 1991 Cochran signed an agreement for Generics to be acquired. The terms included a 30-day transition period to complete formalities such as the integration of salary scales and pension schemes.

"Unfortunately in those 30 days their quarterly figures came out. The profits were below expectations, the share price took a dive and any deals that could be got out of were got out of," he says. "When that happened, we were already a *de facto* part of Motorola. It was just the *de jure* element that had not worked out." When the deal fell through Generics was mothballed. Robert Cochran transplanted his crusade for software quality to Dublin City University, where he set up the Centre for Software Engineering. Hans-Juergen Kugler became director of process improvement at the European Software Institute.

Merrion Gates Software, meanwhile, had a brief but eventful existence. The company tried to create a new paradigm for software development. Its mission was to integrate the Prolog language — designed for artificial intelligence and much hyped in the mid-1980s — with the commercial computing mainstream represented by Cobol programming. The brainchild of British software entrepreneur Bernard Panton and three computer scientists from Hungary, Merrion Gates settled in Ireland as the result of two coincidences.

When Bernard Panton could not obtain work permits in Britain for his Hungarian colleagues, he started to make enquiries in Dublin. Not only were the Irish authorities willing to admit the Hungarians; he also discovered a ready-made team of developers that could support them. Some years earlier, when the IDA prodded its electronics industry clients to undertake development, Prime Computer had set up a software unit at its premises on the north side of the city. The corporation had to cut its costs in late 1985 and decided that it did not need an Irish software group. Panton offered work to most of the Prime employees, including the group's leader Pat O'Connell. They moved as a team to Merrion Gates, which took its name from a level crossing near its office.

Dave Miller, a Trinity graduate who had spent three years working in the Netherlands, joined Prime just weeks before it axed the software unit. He moved to Merrion Gates and found it a great learning environment. "The Hungarians did the core work and we did the stuff around the edges," he recalls. But he got the impression that Panton did not know what to do with Merrion Gates once the product was written. There did not seem to be a realistic business plan for this Hiberno-Hungarian curio. The Dublin outfit won some contract work from customers of Panton's previous company, Telecomputing. But Merrion Gates was wound up after less than four years.

Episodes like this dented the image of the technical subset that appeared among the generation two software companies. But the cluster included firms with staying power, such as Baltimore Technologies,

Captec and Peregrine Systems. Towards the end of the decade these were joined by Broadcom Eireann Research and Irish Medical Systems. None of these companies was content to ape end user applications that were already on the market. They were confident that their software engineers were as skilled as any others. Chris Chedgey says that they had a real sense that they were inventing a new discipline.

This whiff of geek superiority — or snobbery — often put their work beyond the comprehension of outsiders and complicated the companies' dealings with, for example, bank managers. They usually sought international projects and seldom engaged with user organisations in Ireland. Most participated in Esprit or other European research programmes. And the employees came to constitute a distinctive labour force with an increasing range of experience that they could draw on.

When the me-too applications developers of generation two collapsed, this cluster evolved into the leaders of generation three. One firm, more than any other, inherited the best characteristics of the 1980s elite and avoided their weaknesses. Iona Technologies took on the mantle of Glockenspiel and raised the horizons of Irish software onto a higher plane.

An Object-oriented Original — 2

By the late 1980s computer science department at Trinity College Dublin was earning between $1.5 million and $3 million a year from Esprit projects. The distributed systems group (DSG) was the heart of the department's research capability. At peak, the group assigned 15 lecturers and postgraduate students to work on projects. It also employed Annraí O'Toole as its only full-time paid researcher. The DSG was an obvious candidate for Eoin O'Neill to inspect when Trinity appointed him as its first director of innovation services.

The college had already seen a number of commercial spin-offs, but it had received very little in return from these ventures. O'Neill introduced new structures for campus companies. He also surveyed the college, department by department, to identify research with commercial potential. The DSG, he found, had impressive industry contacts and a good relationship with the European Commission. Officials in Brussels could cite the group as evidence that their programmes had unleashed previously hidden development talent. The DSG's most notable achievement was the two-stage "construction and management of distributed office systems" (Comandos) project. The initial idea came from Neville Harris. He had recently returned to Trinity after a sabbatical in California, where he had encountered new approaches to distributed systems, and persuaded some of the large European companies to join a research project in this field. Comandos became an influential demonstration of integration among software modules from different sources.

If the DSG had attempted to create a campus company in the 1980s it might have looked a lot like Glockenspiel. The Trinity group became involved with C++ technology almost as early as John Carolan's company. Its work reinforced Glockenspiel's efforts to establish Dublin as a home of C++ expertise. There was no obvious way, however, to build a commercial business on its success with Comandos. Distributed computing was still considered rather futuristic.

The Trinity group had good insights into software industry politics, especially in the object technology area. DSG member Chris Horn tracked the creation of the Object Management Group and saw that the luminaries of the Esprit programme had little input to its deliberations on future standards. The OMG, Horn recalls, was born at the height of the competition among different versions of the Unix operating system. The OMG aimed to put an end to such battles. It wanted to establish consensus-based standards and it was focusing on the next generation of software tools and methods. "The OMG," Horn says, "was formed in the context of the industry coming together to discuss technologies that would not be commercial for several years."

In November 1990 the OMG issued a request for proposals for an Object Request Broker (ORB) — a communications mechanism for different pieces of software written in C++. The aim was to achieve interoperability among different applications on different systems in different computing environments in a way that would hide all the joins from the ordinary software user. The OMG received 18 submissions — 16 from the US and two from Europe. ICL and Bull based their proposals on the output of different Esprit projects. Bull drew on Comandos. Both were tossed out on the first inspection. Six American submissions went forward to the next stage of the selection process. "At the end of the day," Chris Horn suggests, "it was not just about technologies, but also about commercial weight in the US."

This realisation did not stop the Distributed Systems Group from joining the OMG. It also invited Richard Soley, chief technology officer at the industry body, to give a public lecture at Trinity. The academic team began to add more US contacts to its network. It was, in fact, preparing to launch a commercial vehicle for its work. Iona Technologies began operations as a campus company in March 1991. The start-up had three staff — Chris Horn, Sean Baker and Annraí O'Toole. But it had no bank balance, no marketing budget and no physical assets.

According to Chris Horn, the innovation services department in Trinity College operated and enforced strict rules for campus companies. Iona paid commercial rates to rent an office and to use the university's equipment. When it ran commercial training courses, it could not use any lecture notes or other materials from the department of computer science. Trinity took equity in the company and would be entitled to a share of any intellectual property that it created. On the other hand, the founders of Iona did not need to make a complete break from academic life or from their incomes as lecturers. They could reduce their teaching time over three years, while they built up the company.

The formation of Iona was preceded by long discussions about which members of the DSG would join the new outfit. Chris Horn says that it all came down to personal ambitions. Some of the academic researchers were comfortable about pursuing careers in the commercial world and expected that they would move that way sooner or later. Others were not interested. DSG founder Neville Harris and Brendan Tangney, who went on to become Junior Dean at the university, chose to stay on the academic career path.

Chris Horn had experienced life outside higher education during a stint at the European Commission. He also sat on the board of Baltimore Technologies. Horn was initially the chairman and chief architect of Iona, but he soon took on the role of chief executive officer. The company's first year, he says, was spent putting together a business plan and trying to raise capital. Its training courses pulled in some money. ICL became its biggest customer after it decided to stop developing software in C and retrain all its programmers in C++. Iona ran more than 30 courses for ICL. The Lotus operation in Santry also availed of the start-up's training services. Small roles in two European Commission projects enabled Iona to hire two full-time researchers.

Over on the other side of the Atlantic, meanwhile, the OMG was still seeking a common ORB. By the middle of 1991 it had narrowed down the six submissions on its shortlist to just two, both based on product prototypes from big computer corporations. One faction, led by Digital Equipment, advocated a dynamic approach to inter-object connectivity, using database technology to link components as the connections were needed. The alternative, promoted by Hewlett-Packard, Sun, NCR and Object Design, was a static process with more pre-set rules. OMG persuaded the two groups to combine their resources and produce an ORB specification with the strongest features of both proposals. In November the consortium announced version one of Corba, describing it as the heart of its object management architecture.

Those computer manufacturers were also the market makers. They participated in the creation of the Corba standard and declared their support for the new technology. In practice, though, they kept promoting non-standard software engineering products or introduced new releases that incorporated elements of the OMG specification, but also retained their proprietary technologies. The first commercial implementation of Corba did not come from any of these giants. It came out of HyperDesk Corporation, a little-known developer in Westborough, Massachusetts. HyperDesk had been set up just a few months earlier than Iona as a spin-off from Data General. The company had been a partner to Digital Equipment in the ORB contest and it had financial backing from Japan's

ASCII Corporation. Its mission was to get Corba to market before any of the big guys and it achieved this goal with the 1992 release of the HD Distributed Object Management System. This product, however, did not support C++, only the earlier C language that developers were already phasing out. HyperDesk's success was short-lived and the company was acquired three years later.

Iona knew that Corba would need to support C++ and set out to produce its own implementation of the Object Management Group's specification. The company's founders regarded this as an extension of the work that the DSG had done in Esprit projects like Comandos. Iona was thus ready to respond when the OMG issued another request for proposals in January 1993. It asked its members to provide a language mapping so that applications written in C++ could avail of Corba's distributed capabilities. HP and Sun joined forces to make a submission that looked very similar to Iona's. The OMG did not consider that any of the proposals were good enough and did not adopt any C++ mapping until the end of 1994. But Iona's participation in the process was noticed by the major corporations and generated goodwill towards the firm.

In June 1993 Iona launched its Orbix version of Corba at the Object World trade show in San Francisco. The company did not have enough money for a conventional marketing campaign, so it unveiled this middleware product at a gathering of Corba believers, preaching to the converted. The first edition of Orbix incorporated a C++ mapping that was very close to the standard that the OMG eventually approved. Orbix leapfrogged over the HyperDesk system. Iona described it, indeed, as "the first full implementation" of Corba. In mid-1993, according to the OMG, there were at least 58 different Corbas at various stages of development by its member firms. The industry body declined to endorse any of these as the first or the best. Nonetheless, when asked to comment on the release of Iona's package, the OMG welcomed the new arrival as a very complete implementation of its standard. It was evident that the consortium's senior management in Massachusetts had been monitoring the progress of the campus company in Dublin and were familiar with its capabilities.

Iona was now a company on a crusade. It was determined to prove that C++ was better than C, to show that commercial products could come out of the Esprit research community, and to demonstrate to the world that an Irish company could be built on high-level technical work. Iona was still a tiny operation with just eight employees. But it could network with the big corporations. Their techies respected the expertise of its techies.

Viewed from an Irish industry perspective, Iona had absorbed all the lessons learned in generation two. Chris Horn says that he viewed Mentec and Baltimore Technologies as role models. The biggest influences on Iona's strategy, however, were Glockenspiel, which had shown how to innovate around industry standards, and Chorus Systèmes, a Paris-based developer of systems software that had worked on Comandos. Michel Gien, the founder of Chorus, persuaded Horn that it was vital for Iona to succeed in the US before targeting any other markets. Glockenspiel's misfortunes convinced him that Iona would never sign an exclusive distribution agreement with an American partner. "We focused on the US but in a different way to Glockenspiel," he says, "We felt that we could sell into the US without having a distributor there."

Internet services had advanced considerably in the four years since Glockenspiel released CommonView. By 1993 the internet had became part of the basic working environment for the C++ developers that Iona wanted to reach. The company knew that it could distribute Orbix over the internet using FTP — a standard file transfer protocol — and that it could communicate with customers through e-mail. It used low-cost telesales to generate orders, pitched its prices at a level where individual developers could pay for the software with their credit cards and offered trial versions that were disabled by a built-in timebomb if the user failed to pay. Once Orbix started to ship, Iona quickly became the biggest user of internet bandwidth in Ireland.

It also made sales that were much bigger than credit card purchases. Orders worth tens of thousands of dollars were followed by orders worth hundreds of thousands. In 1994, Motorola picked Orbix as the middleware to underpin its control systems for a global satellite network. Then

Boeing invested $750,000 in Orbix licences and related consulting and technical services for its commercial aircraft business. This was said to be the biggest business processing re-engineering project in the world. Other big ticket deals followed in banking and telecommunications, initiating long-term relationships between Iona and large customer organisations.

The middleware vendor soon attracted many of Ireland's top-flight software engineers. The company went on a recruitment drive in early 1994, after Sun bought a minority stake in the firm and provided it with a cash injection. Iona hired ten former Glockenspiel employees. It cherry-picked the best developers from the ICL group that it had trained in C++. By the start of 1996 its headcount had climbed over 100 and the total doubled again during that year. Iona began to build an international network of distributors in 1994 and opened its first overseas subsidiary in Massachusetts a year later. A training centre in the heart of San Francisco followed in 1996. A regional sales office in Perth, Australia was charged with developing business throughout the Pacific Rim. By then the original Orbix package had grown into a suite of software integration products and Iona's brand accounted for more than half of the world's Corba licences.

According to Dave Miller, who moved to Iona in 1996, the result of this rapid growth was "controlled chaos with supreme arrogance". Annraí O'Toole asked Miller to introduce discipline into the engineering groups, where too many coders were behaving like prima donnas. The prevailing attitude in Iona was that the company could keep expanding indefinitely and was heading into the same stratosphere as Oracle or Sun. "They tended to look down on nearly everyone, to be quite frank," recalls Miller, who later became Iona's head of engineering and product development. On his arrival at the company he found incompatible versions of Orbix running on 20 separate computing platforms and a messaging product, OrbixTalk, that did not conform with OMG specifications. In addition, Iona had not put sufficient resources into customer services and its support department was under strain. On his first day on the job Miller suggested to Horn that he did not know how to organise his workforce. The chairman accepted this criticism. He also pointed out that he had never worked in a commercial company before setting up Iona.

Hiring Mick Prokopis, a former vice president of Digital Equipment, as chief operating officer was another attempt to impose order on Iona's chaos. Prokopis was based in the Massachusetts office which gradually came to house more and more of the senior management. By the end of 1996 the company looked less like an inflated replica of Glockenspiel and more like an American start-up en route to the Nasdaq exchange. Sure enough, Iona was listed on Nasdaq in 1997. Its initial public offering raised $60 million in cash. The company's revenues leaped by 129 per cent and reached $48.6 million in the year when it went public. From then on, however, it was under a permanent spotlight. Iona had become the flagship of Irish software and its performance was interpreted as a pointer to the overall health of the industry.

One of Iona's strengths was the speed at which it turned industry standards into saleable products. More important, perhaps, was its ability to network. Iona has maintained its prominence in the OMG, hosting the consortium's technical meetings and inserting its engineers into OMG working groups. Chris Horn and Sean Baker have both served on the OMG's board of directors. The Dublin firm also became an active contributor to other industry bodies, including the Java Community Process, the World Wide Web Consortium, the Web Services Interoperability Organisation, the SoapBuilders Forum and the Organisation for the Advancement of Structured Information Standards. This engagement with technical decision-making became a hallmark of the Irish software industry in generation three. People from smaller companies and countries are often elected to chair technical groups because the big corporations accept them as neutrals.

Iona never hid its Irish identity, even when it transferred more responsibilities to its international offices and more of its senior management were based in the US. At one stage it assigned the development of a major Orbix upgrade to Massachusetts. This followed the recruitment of John Giblin, who had previously built up the software development capability at Digital Equipment in Galway. Iona wanted an experienced manager of international engineering teams.

Iona also showed non-American characteristics when it attempted to bridge rival industry factions. As early as 1996, it balanced its OMG affiliation with a relationship with Microsoft, which was pushing its own object management technologies in opposition to the consortium. Iona tried to distance itself from this battle, claiming that its location in Ireland afforded a measure of neutrality. Ever since then the company has represented itself as the integration software vendor that bridges the gaps between rival camps as well as between alternative technologies. In practice, this meant being an upholder of industry standards that also stays friendly with Microsoft — a tricky diplomatic act at the best of times, but one that it has performed consistently.

Despite this stance, however, Iona's close identification with Corba held back the efforts to broaden its product portfolio. In the late 1990s Sun's Java became the preferred working environment for many application developers, but Iona's allegiance to C++ made it a relative latecomer to Java. When the company went out looking for acquisitions, it was attracted to other firms with Corba tools instead of developers from different backgrounds. A series of deals fleshed out its Corba offerings, but brought few significant benefits. Iona was slow to recognise the importance of the Java-based application server. In 1998 it turned down an opportunity to buy a San Francisco company called WebLogic. BEA Systems, which was only slightly larger than Iona at the time, snapped up this organisation instead. WebLogic had developed an application server whose sales rocketed after the change of ownership. Within a few years, BEA's revenues had soared close to $1 billion. Iona's peaked in 2001 at $180 million and declined thereafter.

Chris Horn's personal evolution was no less interesting than that of the company. The Iona chief became the public face of Irish software in the 1990s, much like Tom McGovern in earlier times. Horn worked the lecture circuit, briefed financial analysts, chaired expert committees and was appointed to advisory groups. He started to articulate development strategies for the industry as a whole. At a public lecture in late 1997, for example, he threw down a challenge to Irish software engineers to break the American monopoly on major innovations. All of the quantum leaps and discontinuities in the history of software, he argued, had come out of the United States. Iona had merely implemented an existing set of standards. Ireland's developers would really prove their worth, he declared, when they produced something as innovative as the graphical user interface or the Java platform.

Iona did not separate the positions of chief executive and chairman until May 2000, when the company promoted one of its US-based managers to chief executive. Barry Morris was born in South Africa and had long experience in the US. He had worked on software products and business development for Digital Equipment and Lotus Development before joining Iona in 1994 as product manager. Morris went on to become Iona's executive vice president of operations and chief operating officer before taking over the CEO's role. Chris Horn retained the chairman's job after Morris became CEO, saying that he wanted to give himself more time to work on Iona's partnerships and acquisitions.

Barry Morris led a drive by the company to establish itself as a front-runner in web services integration — a new breed of middleware based on the XML data format. The next generation of enterprise software, he argued, would be held together by a web services architecture. Other developers were introducing piecemeal solutions based on this technology. Iona promised to deliver a complete implementation.

According to Morris, web services integration was the sort of disruptive technology that would change the nature of software development, automating much of the integration effort. Corporations could solve integration problems by installing software products instead of creating work for large teams of developers. This revolution, furthermore, would create an opportunity for one middleware developer to establish itself as the dominant supplier in the same way that the relational database had made Oracle massive. Iona aimed to be that dominant force.

The company, however, suffered heavy losses in 2001 and 2002. Iona still claimed a stream of licence sales to large corporations and published reports on major projects based on its technologies. But the prices that software engineering tools could command spiralled downwards. The open source movement, where clubs of volunteers develop code, changed customers' expectations of software engineering products. They could download free code from web sites and tweak it to meet their specific needs. Iona argues that the open source movement has been far more active in development kits than in the software integration area that its products occupy. Nonetheless, the company became increasingly dependent on revenue from customer services.

Iona's stated policy was to maximise its sales of software licences and to refer opportunities for service contracts to specialist firms. These service providers, it hoped, would then choose Iona tools for big system integration projects. In practice, though, the company had to sell more services to pay its staff. Customer services accounted for just 30 per cent of its revenues in 2000, but almost twice as much in 2003.

In mid-2001 Iona had about 1,000 personnel on its payroll. Two years later it had only 450 employees. Barry Morris resigned in May 2003 and Chris Horn became chief executive once again. Shortly afterwards the company shipped its Artix family of enterprise software integration products.

Iona has positioned Artix as an equivalent to Orbix for the era of web services and expects that it will determine the future of the company. The drift towards services suggests another possibility. The software industry is restructuring around its customers' lines of business and much of Iona's revenues are coming from the telecommunications industry. Should the company narrow its horizons and specialise in integration tools and services for telcos?

Followers and Fellow Travellers

The fourth generation of Irish software companies — the start-ups of the mid-to-late 1990s — inherited the business model established by Glockenspiel and Iona and applied it to other product categories. They aimed their wares at software engineers so that they would not need to supply and support end users. They became active in the industry organisations that set or promoted software standards. Their business development efforts were primarily directed to the US. By the turn of the century the middleware clique had grown into an Irish middleware industry. The coders who had started their careers in the companies that were the technical elite of the 1980s were now entrepreneurs and managers.

In the words of Robert Baker, whose start-ups included middleware developers Xiam and PolarLake, Iona provided "the template that showed how an Irish company could be a player on the world stage".

Unlike Iona, though, its successors did not need to run training courses or sell consulting services while they developed their first products. Generation four companies were able to raise money from external sources, often at an early stage in their formation. By the mid-1990s, moreover, the linkages between the software development industry in Ireland and the local market for information technology products and services had all withered away. In the era of the minicomputer package, the developers' strategies were shaped by the needs of computer users inside Ireland. In contrast, when Iona became the world Corba champion in the 1990s, the technology was generally ignored by its compatriots in user organisations. Irish developers were obviously clued in to emerging technologies, but Irish users looked more conservative than ever. Unix — the computing platform with the greatest geek appeal — was less widely adopted than in other countries. Later on, when Linux took on this role, it was slow to make any impact in Ireland. Microsoft's server products, on the other hand, achieved higher than average sales. Microsoft Ireland deserves the credit here. It invested more in market research and business development than its major competitors, which often ran their Irish sales offices as branches of their British subsidiaries. But the way the market evolved also illustrates how the software exporters moved in different circles to their neighbours in the local trade.

In many cases the followers of Iona in generation four were literally its heirs and offspring. The middleware maker often assisted newer Irish companies by giving them space on its exhibition stands or allowing them to make presentations at its user conferences. It helped Cunav Technologies to promote object-oriented modelling software. It encouraged Orbism by making it a subsupplier to the Iona professional services group. Former Iona managers moved into software tool companies like Bind Systems, PolarLake, Rococo Software, West Global and eSpatial.

Iona also established a tradition of naming Irish software companies after islands. Perhaps the founders of the Trinity campus company felt an affinity with the monastic island of Iona, whose handcrafted Christian manuscripts represented the high technology of the ninth century. Its followers were less sensitive to historic signifiers. They just picked names from around the coast. The industry directory soon read like a maritime chart. Aran Technologies offered simulation software for mobile networks. Rockall Technologies developed loan management software for financial institutions. Shenick started as a software contractor to the makers of advanced communications systems. And Sherkin Communications wrote applications for network service providers.

Iona co-founder Annraí O'Toole took charge of another company that had borrowed its name from an island. Cape Clear Software started in 1999 when three Iona executives broke away to develop XML connectivity tools. O'Toole became its executive chairman in the following year, but remained a director of Iona. The separation was shown to be less than amicable in 2002, when Iona tried to prevent one of its American managers from moving to Cape Clear. The row ended in a Massachusetts courtroom, where Iona was refused an injunction to prevent the appointment. It also provoked the resignation of O'Toole from the Iona board.

More start-ups — including offshoots from the offspring of Iona — kept surfacing after 2000. Some, indeed, popped up in unexpected places. Epionet and SteelTrace emerged from failed e-business service ventures. Exaltec Software started life with a customer relationship management product. A legal dispute in 2000 cost the company its employees and its premises. But the near-death experience convinced the company that it should pursue the development of Java tools instead of applications and by 2003 its Java application generator had gained accreditation from IBM. Propylon, whose chief technology officer Sean McGrath had been a member of the World Wide Web Consortium working group that set the XML standard, divided its development operations between Ireland and India. Headway Software established a development base in Waterford and created an original code visualisation technology that revealed dependencies within existing software. Barry Morris joined Headway as chief executive officer after he parted company with Iona.

Seen from an industry-wide perspective, however, the middleware strand peaked at the turn of the century and its momentum flagged in the following years. One reason was the open source squeeze on the commercial developers of development tools. Another was that buyers consolidated the number of software products in their organisations. Established middleware vendors reported revenue declines, while start-ups found it harder than ever to penetrate the big accounts. "If you are selling something, you have to have a clear justification for selling it for a fee," Chris Horn advises Iona's followers.

At about the same time that Iona's revenues peaked, mobile applications displaced middleware as the most popular field for new Irish development companies. It was evident that companies in other product categories had adopted the strategies that worked for middleware in the 1990s.

Headway Software had curious similarities with Iona in the early years of Orbix. Even before Barry Morris took charge of the company, the parallels were strong. Headway's roots lay in an Esprit project. Like Iona, its products were designed for software architects and for engineers in large corporations. Its early adopters came from aerospace and financial services. And, like its predecessor, Headway networked assiduously in the US, especially with the gurus of Java and C++. It even hired Larry Mone, a former IDA representative in Silicon Valley, to act as its agent on the west coast of the US.

Chris Chedgey left Generics in the late 1980s and took his Esprit experience to Canada. "I got reasonably sexy jobs because of the Ada connection in Generics," he says, "I was one of the few people in the world with five years of Ada experience." The Canadian Space Agency employed him for five years on projects related to the international space station. He then spent four years at a Calgary company that worked on military communications projects. He changed his status there from employee to contractor so that he could give time to a product idea of his own and returned to Ireland in 1998 to set up a company. His technology concept for a code inspection and visualisation product was already in place. But Chedgey's participation in an enterprise development programme in Waterford highlighted shortcomings in his business plan. In October 1999 he showed a prototype to Brendan O'Reilly, who had run one of the more technically oriented software services firms in Dublin. They joined forces and Headway Software launched Refactory, its first inspection tool, in January 2000.

The company's first offerings analyzed existing code in the C++ language and assisted software engineers to reduce the complexity of these applications. Java and Ada products followed.

Headway Software reworked the Glockenspiel/Iona formula, targeting companies that employed expensive American programmers and offering them a better understanding of the designs that they already owned. Its tools went on sale, however, at a time when global spending on software engineering tools was depressed. The company initially saw telecommunications as its primary market, but the telcos had stopped buying software. A major financial services company in New York, meanwhile, told O'Reilly that it could not spend $20,000 without applying for approval by a vice president. In the end Headway found most of its reference sites in the IT divisions of large aerospace firms.

"We ended up chasing the market as it changed direction," Chris Chedgey admits. The company kept working on its implementations of his ideas and designed a flagship product, Headway Server, that would apply his complexity control processes across entire software development teams. After Barry Morris joined, it drew up an aggressive expansion plan that centred on North America.

This required a large infusion of venture capital. The blue-chip names on Headway's list of pilot customers enabled the company to establish contact with suitable investors in the US and these partners worked on its business plan. In 2004, however, the venture capitalists decided that the expansion project was too risky and pulled out. The company was placed in receivership. Three of its executives, including

Chris Chedgey, formed a new business called Headway Software Technology and bought the assets. Headway Server has attracted plenty of technical endorsements, but the new firm has to find new ways of bringing it to market.

Ireland's middleware developers have had a rough ride in generation five. The sector has lost its former pre-eminence and looks set for further decline. According to Brendan O'Reilly, however, US corporations have grown accustomed to sourcing software engineering products from Irish firms. When some of Headway's prospective customers heard where the company came from, he says, they started reminiscing about John Carolan. More than a decade after the demise of Glockenspiel, Carolan's name could still open doors in America for Irish products.

Chapter 7

THE E-LEARNING STORY

The Software Tycoon without a Computer

Pat McDonagh does not run a web log. He does not even have an e-mail address. In fact, he has never used a PC and gives the impression that he is rather proud of the fact. This attitude, however, has not impeded his success. The software industry has made McDonagh rich and his career has been punctuated by a series of multi-million dollar transactions.

Back in the late 1970s, selling computers was his job. When system maker ICL acquired Singer, it inherited a family of computers whose price tags had just five digits instead of the usual six or seven. ICL Ireland hired three former Rank Xerox sales staff to sell these machines. The company reckoned that hawking photocopiers was good preparation for shifting baby computers.

Pat McDonagh was one of these three recruits. He changed his job again in 1981, when an American company called Deltak chose him to set up an Irish sales office. It claimed to be a world leader in structured training for computer staff. Deltak had created a library of training books and tapes and rented these out to its customers. The founders had come out of IBM and its courses were slanted towards learners in mainframe installations.

Deltak did not yet use computers to deliver its lessons. Pat McDonagh left the company after two years to set up CBT Systems, a new venture that would put training material onto PC screens. CBT stood for "computer based training". It was 1983 and courseware —

software products that contained education and training content — had arrived on the scene.

CBT Systems — later known as SmartForce — was the first of three technology-based training start-ups that McDonagh founded. He likes to spot emerging trends and to time his entry to a market as it is starting to take off. He formed Riverdeep in 1995 to produce courses for school classrooms in the way that CBT had catered for the workplace. In 2003 he launched ThirdForce to develop self-study e-learning materials for sale to individuals instead of institutions. In each case, he put together an overall strategy and got other people to implement it.

Pat McDonagh is the type of entrepreneur who steers clear of trade associations and what he calls "the social scene". At the start of his career he qualified as a teacher and taught in a Dublin school. He likes to refer back to this classroom experience and says that he drew inspiration from it in later years. At the same time, though, his instincts are clearly commercial and the predominant non-commercial mindset in mainstream education seems to annoy him. Riverdeep, he says, tried to develop courseware in collaboration with two Dublin colleges, but soon concluded that it was more practical to work without academics.

According to McDonagh, the stock market valuations of CBT Systems and Riverdeep at their peak were the highest that the Irish software business has seen. "Only six companies ever got to Nasdaq," he points out, "and I started two of them."

These companies, however, followed very different routes to the stock market. CBT Systems grew organically, straying down blind trails on occasion. Its path from inception to initial public offering took 12 years. Riverdeep was built to a plan and accelerated like a rocket.

The first CBT Systems package, Intuition, offered screen-based training for money market dealers. Financial institutions were willing to pay high sums for this subject matter and the price of Intuition was pitched at about $1,500. The financial expertise for this product came from stockbroking firm National and City Brokers, whose chairman Dermot Desmond backed the formation of CBT Systems. Dedeir, a private investment company that Desmond controlled, subsequently bought the rights to Intuition. It set up a separate firm, Financial Courseware, which sold the package into dealing rooms from New York to Hong Kong. This business still exists today under the Intuition name. CBT Systems, meanwhile, launched Money Matters, which explained financial concepts to non-financial executives, in 1986. This was followed in the same year by Bankrole, which dealt with foreign trade and in 1987 by Protocol 90, CBT's first telecommunications training product.

Pricing these packages was never easy. "Money Matters almost sucked me into a boghole," McDonagh says. CBT Systems hoped that this eight-disk set could be a best seller and reckoned that it should sell for $800 — a figure chosen to suit the budgets of line managers. It promoted the product in Ireland through a business magazine and a computer magazine, attracting 600 leads. When it tried to close sales, though, only the biggest organisations paid up — at the price that was supposed to appeal to small firms. Some customers trained dozens of people on a single copy of the package. Pat McDonagh believes that the early buyers of Money Matters would have been willing to pay 20 times more than the fixed price. CBT Systems got a better return, however, when it opened a direct marketing office in England and won volume orders from the London Stock Exchange, UDT Bank and Tesco.

Following these successes, the British-based Hoskyns Group bought CBT Systems in late 1987. By this time the company had annual sales of approximately $4 million and 25 employees. Pat McDonagh, who owned more than 80 per cent of CBT, describes the transaction as "a creative deal". "I gave it away. We could not come to an agreement on what it was worth. So I said, 'If it makes these targets, here is what you pay me.'" If CBT had performed to plan, Hoskyns would have forked out over $9 million. The UK computer services group had a catalogue-based approach to selling software, but it had little flair for international package sales. When the deal was done, the majority owner of Hoskyns was an American corporation, Martin Marietta. McDonagh hoped to meet the sales targets by selling CBT's courseware into the US. Hoskyns, however, seemed content to concentrate on its home market in Britain and made little effort elsewhere. CBT Systems retained its separate identity, but its revenues remained static.

Pat McDonagh, meanwhile, was exploring other lines of business. He set up an investment vehicle, Thornton Group, that bought shares in Irish electronics and software ventures — Datacode, Intrepid, CRT and PS Squared. He even tried to establish a brand name for handbags. The tail-end of the 1980s, though, was a crisis period for Irish software developers and Thornton lost money. Its largest investment went to modem maker Datacode. This turned sour when the Dublin company went into receivership and offloaded its product rights to a Hong Kong firm. Looking back, McDonagh says that he made too many investments in those years. Thornton's fifth acquisition, however, was a success. The investment company bought back CBT Systems in September 1991.

Cap Gemini had assumed control of Hoskyns in the previous year. This software services company regarded product development as an unwelcome distraction. It inherited the CBT Systems portfolio which, under Hoskyns, had addressed computing skills and now included courses on local area networks and open systems software. It suited Cap Gemini's agenda to offload these packages. Pat McDonagh, on the other hand, was convinced that there was an untapped market in the US for the training products. He announced that he would target large American accounts through a new entity called Computer Based Training USA. He also arranged for system manufacturer Amdahl to resell its products.

Thornton changed its name to CBT Group and dropped all of its other activities. It also changed the sales model for its products from straightforward sales to library rentals — the way that Deltak had operated years earlier. Customers would pay a monthly fee based on the number of units that they used. CBT moved into vendor-specific courses in 1992, when it introduced a package for Lotus Notes users. It hired American salespeople to target Lotus installations and found that the product met a real need in those organisations.

The new-look CBT sold about $6.4 million worth of training software in 1992 and pushed up the total to $18 million in 1994. By then three-quarters of the company's revenues came from the US and all the major business decisions were taken there. Pat McDonagh was no longer involved in day-to-day operations. Bill McCabe, who had been managing director of CBT's UK subsidiary before the takeover by Hoskyns, was the company's chairman and chief executive until 1996. According to McDonagh, CBT Group moved into a higher gear after McCabe had a chance encounter on a plane. A conversation with a Lotus executive alerted him to the company's problems with end user training for its Notes software.

This phase of CBT's development culminated in April 1995 with an initial public offering on the Nasdaq exchange. Robert Stevenson, a California-based investment bank, had been advising the company on its financial options. CBT came close to selling a minority stake to the Gartner Group, but the consulting firm withdrew from the deal. Robert Stevenson then assisted CBT to accelerate the process of going public. "We were virtually at the finishing line before anyone in Ireland knew," McDonagh says.

Designed by a Committee

Other courseware start-ups appeared around Ireland at the same time as the first incarnation of CBT Systems. In the early 1980s, indeed, it was widely accepted that technology-based training would grow into a major industry, but no one knew which business models would succeed.

Consultancy firm Arthur D. Little delivered a report to the IDA in 1984. The development agency had asked the firm to identify opportunities for job creation in Ireland in internationally traded services. The answer, according to Little, was computer services in general and courseware in particular. Brian Dugan, who was putting together a workplan for the new National Software Centre at the time, supported this analysis. "I have had previous contact with the education system here and I know that its product is excellent," he said.

The courseware recommendation struck a chord in several parts of the public service. It coincided with the country's first initiatives in distance education. These aimed to reach sections of the population that had never previously benefited from higher education. AnCO, the agency responsible for industrial training, set up a showcase for computer assisted learning at its training centre at Loughlinstown in south Dublin. At first it talked about selecting the best screen-based training products on the market and distributing them to all of its training centres. Then it did a deal with Digital Equipment to develop video courses on Digital's proprietary training systems and to market these internationally.

AnCO's mandate was to provide training for traditional trades and for the operatives in IDA-backed assembly plants. Experiments with training software gave it an opportunity to move up the skills hierarchy. The agency established courseware scripting and development courses in Loughlinstown, instructing some groups on how to produce training packages for personal computers and others on how to use a new breed of interactive videodisc equipment that stored audio-visual lessons on an oversized precursor of the DVD.

Government Minister John Bruton took a more holistic view. If courseware development was going to be a national strategy, the full resources of the nation should be harnessed to build the new industry. This mission was too big to be left to the IDA and AnCO and the National Software Centre. Officials from his Department also conferred with the Department of Education on the viability of computer-based learning in schools and colleges. They drew the export board and the National Board for Science and Technology into the discussions. They pulled in broadcasting company RTÉ on the assumption that someone would need to produce video material for courseware packages.

By 1985, the discussions had created a national "courseware committee" on which all of these organisations and interest groups had representatives. The committee aspired to build a library of computer-based learning courses that would raise the standards of Irish education and package Irish expertise for sale abroad — perhaps into developing countries. The dividing line between the developers and users of learning products was always vague. There was an underlying assumption that the nation was good at teaching and that this competence should be channelled into new formats. Was the PC just another tool for the educationalist? Or was it a means of making profits out of pedagogy?

The committee requested submissions from courseware developers, from the big computer companies and from the major education and training institutions. It weighed up the responses and released its findings in May 1986. It estimated that the courseware industry already employed almost 100 people in 16 firms, including Courseware Ireland, Eureka Knowledge Systems and a recently established Ericsson subsidiary in Dublin. The total courseware workforce, the commission reckoned, could be trebled over the next two years. It also suggested that Irish courseware companies had the potential to achieve export sales of $10 million in 1988.

By the mid-1990s a large share of the world's library of computer-based training material was produced in Ireland. But this did not happen in the way that the courseware committee prescribed. Several aspects of its report already looked rather dated in 1986. The committee's understanding of courseware technology was coloured by its expectations for the interactive video medium. Most of the action had already moved to text and graphics presentations on regular PC screens. The report dwelt too long on the consulting aspects of courseware creation, despite plentiful evidence that the future belonged to inexpensive generic packages. It also skipped lightly over the problem of raising money for product development.

The sharpest criticisms of the courseware committee report came from the founder of CBT Systems. When the document appeared, Pat McDonagh dismissed its lack of commercial focus, its emphasis on custom applications and its failure to grasp the significance of packaged training products. "The key for this country," he asserted at the time, "is to develop high-quality generic products that are pitched for a particular audience and then sell them internationally." Looking back after two decades, he suggests that the expert committee never believed that Irish companies could achieve this.

An Insider at Work

Nothing about the premises of CBT Systems at Menlo Park in California suggested that the company had originated in Ireland. In 1997, moreover, a consummate Silicon Valley insider held the post of chief executive officer. Jim Buckley had risen through the ranks at Apple Computer until he became president of the computer-maker's sales and marketing organisation for the Americas. He left Apple in September 1996 to join CBT as president and chief operating officer and moved into the top job three months later.

Menlo Park — named, incidentally, after Menlo in Galway — lies at the north end of the cluster of business parks that make up Silicon Valley. According to Jim Buckley, CBT needed a presence in the area because seven of its ten strategic partners were headquartered nearby. By the mid-1990s the company had discovered that learners preferred courseware titles on specific software packages and networking equipment. It partnered with the larger software and hardware development firms and sold its training products to their customers.

The company measured its progress according to the number of titles that it shipped — around 40 each quarter — and by the number of vendors that it could identify as partners. Namedropping was part of its strategy. CBT had to keep a close eye on the big suppliers. The trick was to decide which of the products that they were developing would not only achieve volume sales, but would also be sufficiently complex for the buyers to spend money training their employees.

Jim Buckley spent just two years with CBT Systems. He quit in 1998 after a drop in the share value of the publicly quoted company and a below-forecast sales performance. CBT's business model existed before he joined the company. Buckley's method deserves attention, however, as an illustration of how to become a market leader in the US. He understood personal networking. In the same way that Iona built a middleware business through its membership of OMG technical committees, Buckley networked his way around the Valley. All of CBT's developers were based in Dublin. But the financial performance of the company depended on its industry contacts in America.

Commercial partnerships are probably more important for e-learning companies than for any other type of software product vendor. There are few opportunities for courseware developers to differentiate themselves through technology — everyone uses the same authoring applications to build their products — and there is limited scope to gain advantages through instructional design. Getting access to the subject matter is all-important. In technology training, that meant hobnobbing with California-based corporations like Cisco, Oracle, Sun and Informix. It was vital to get early information on forthcoming releases and to launch the training software as soon as their new products shipped. Whenever possible, Buckley sought exclusive rights to launch a learning package. In other cases, such as training for Microsoft users, CBT had to compete against rival courseware developers like Gartner and Netg.

Building relationships was also the top priority for the sales arm of the company. It targeted large organisations that spent loads of money on their information systems and needed to ensure that the technology was used properly. CBT employed a direct salesforce to manage the major accounts, renting out its products under one- or two- or three-year contracts. Most of these deals were done in the US, although the contracts could cover global workforces. The salespeople got these customers to make spending commitments in advance. CBT was a publicly quoted company at this time and institutional investors liked to see a big backlog of orders.

The market for packaged IT training software peaked during Jim Buckley's spell at CBT Systems. In the following years the focus moved to the delivery and management of courses through the internet and the computer-based training business evolved into the e-learning industry. In 1997, on the eve of this transition, CBT was riding high.

Infrastructures for Learning

Apple Computer wanted to prove a point in June 1995. The company believed that its Macintosh systems were capable of supporting large-scale applications, but few customers employed its machines in this manner. The computer maker convened an awards ceremony in New York to spotlight software developers that had used the Macintosh in innovative ways. The top prize for a client-server application in education and government went to a team from University College Dublin (UCD). Its project drew on the educational experience of computer science lecturer Henry McLoughlin and the development skills of research students Duncan Lennox and Eamonn Webster. Their system distributed courseware over the internet, allowing anyone with a web browser to view it. The UCD trio had also built an administrative toolset around this service, so that students could communicate with tutors and submit their course work electronically.

Here was an approach to computer-based learning that addressed the management of education instead of trying to package training documents for display on PC screens. The internet provided the distribution capability, while the HTML language enabled users with different computers and operating systems to access the same information on the World Wide Web. This concept was not limited to universities. It could also be applied in distance learning, community education and on-the-job training in companies with dispersed workforces.

The UCD group formed a company called Web Educational Support Tools. It was chaired by Dennis Jennings, the one-time Seanad candidate and internet pioneer, who was the director of computing services at the college. One day the founders walked into his office and asked if he could assist them to form a campus company. Jennings said yes. "I carried that company on my credit card for 18 months," he recalls. The system, he contends, was way ahead of its time. It converted lecturers' material, including PowerPoint slides and Word text files, into web pages. Then it managed the distribution process.

Web Educational Support Tools was not the only venture that aimed to deliver courseware through the internet. Other development teams with greater financial backing and better resources were also designing online infrastructures for learning. By 1997 American start-ups like Blackboard, Docent and Saba had moved into the field. Gartner Group created its own Internet Learning Center to deliver online training to its clients. CBT Systems launched CBTWeb, a product that enabled organisations to store a library of training courses on a web server for internal distribution. This was closely followed by CBTCampus, a training management and course delivery system, which the company described as the biggest development project that its Dublin office had undertaken.

The UCD outfit laid down a marker that it wanted to take on these heavyweights. The company changed the company name to WBT Systems, paying tribute to CBT Systems while highlighting its web-centred strategy. It branded its system as TopClass. It opened a sales office in San Francisco and recruited an American sales force. In early 1997 it raised about $800,000 in a first round of venture capital. Former Kindle chief Tony Kilduff participated in this process as an angel investor and joined the WBT board of directors.

At first the company targeted American universities through long-distance selling. It supplied and supported its software from UCD. In 1997 it landed a flagship order from the State University of New York, an institution with 13,500 faculty members and some 400,000 students. As its better-endowed competitors in the US ramped up, however, WBT found it difficult to make further sales to the colleges. Other companies were offering similar software free of charge to early adopters. The Dublin company switched its emphasis to corporate training. Here again it made a landmark sale. Dow Chemical chose TopClass as the foundation for a new support system for training and certifying its employees. It took more effort to scale up and customise the system than WBT expected, but Dow said that it had saved tens of millions of dollars a year by reducing the movements of trainers and materials.

According to Dennis Jennings, WBT threw itself into the private sector without proper market evaluation. "The move into the commercial market was a dotcom enthusiasm," he says. Web enthusiasts believed that they should offer highly favourable terms to their customers, arguing that they could charge more substantial fees at some point in the future, after the users had grown dependent on their technology. Companies with "web" in their names believed that they could raise as much cash as they needed while their business evolved towards sustainability. WBT was certainly not averse to accepting large infusions of institutional investment. The company netted a second round of venture capital worth

$6 million in 1999, followed by a further $20 million in the following year. By then WBT claimed to hold the biggest user base in e-learning content management with over 600 customer sites. The company also began to describe itself as headquartered in Massachusetts, where its American CEO, Peter Zotto, resided.

There were no rules to follow in the administration of e-learning. The idea was still too new. WBT Systems focused on the "learning object". This proposed that all the materials used in training could be embedded in a software architecture that enabled the same information to be re-worked in many different courses and delivered in a personalised form to every learner.

This was a more holistic vision than the other e-learning developers offered. Blackboard from Washington, DC concentrated on course ad-ministration in the universities and stayed out of commercial organisa-tions. It won out on the campuses because it understood how they worked and knew exactly what features would appeal to the average American professor. California-based Saba was more attuned to per-formance management and certification in large corporations. It spoke the same language as their human resource departments and sold its Saba Learning Enterprise to large employers. Many of its customers, indeed, came from the IT industry. Docent, meanwhile, defined its business as "education commerce" and worked hard to attract a network of partners whose training courses could be plugged into its online methodology.

The demand for e-learning management systems was never as sub-stantial as the vendors, or the investors that bankrolled them, had as-sumed. As usual, the more successful players were the ones with the good contacts, not necessarily the best concepts. Dennis Jennings says that WBT lost money and momentum between 1999 and 2001. Peter Zotto had no previous management experience in a small firm. He had been a successful line manager at Digital Equipment, where all the resources he needed were readily available. This background did not equip him to meet WBT's requirements and he departed in 2001. WBT laid off more than 20 per cent of its workforce and announced a shift of emphasis towards content management in "just-in-time" and "just-enough" learning environments.

Another scaling-down exercise followed in 2002, when WBT Systems offloaded its American sales and distribution operations to an independently owned partner firm. It also appointed a new chief executive officer, Declan Kelly, who believed that there were untapped opportunities for the company to pursue in Europe.

WBT Systems has had a series of chief executives but only one chief technology officer. Co-founder Duncan Lennox has held this post through all of the company's ups and downs. Lennox has always been the effective driver of the company, adapting TopClass to changes in the technology and shifts in the market. By the latter part of 2003 he was claiming unique capabilities for the company in regulated industries whose training needs are shaped by compliance with official standards and procedures. TopClass, he argued, could assist companies to plan the certification and re-certification of employees to meet the rules of the US Securities and Exchange Commission, the US Patriot Act and the Financial Services Authority in the UK. Most compliance management systems are built on document management, workflow control or business process automation software. According to Lennox, WBT had pioneered a different, but complementary, approach.

His company has always been something of a chameleon, switching its focus from sector to sector and modifying TopClass accordingly. The company's survival is no mean feat. In the early years of the twenty-first century, the e-learning industry as a whole endured quite a battering.

Backlash and Shake-out

E-learning specialists sometimes try to distance themselves from the rest of the software industry. It is more accurate, they suggest, to treat their business as a subset of education and training. E-learning needs expertise in general learning. On the other hand, it is also obvious that e-government software vendors have to be familiar with government and the suppliers of e-banking applications must understand how banks work. Computer-based learning requires line-of-business knowledge just like other vertical market software.

The development processes for software and courseware are basically the same — code writing, code integration and code testing. The tools of the trade are authoring languages rather than programming toolsets. And industry standards have been slow to materialise, although the Sharable Courseware Object Reference Model — a technical specification for the interworking and re-use of learning content — is becoming important.

The case for considering e-learning as something different was strongest in the late 1990s. The stock market flotation of CBT Systems influenced the venture capital operations that got moving in those years. In generation four it was easier to obtain finance in Ireland for e-learning projects than for other software plans. More developers mastered the tools of courseware construction. By the end of the decade a distinctive cluster of e-learning companies was active.

These contenders included Interactive Services, whose products trained engineers and technicians to work on telecommunications equipment, Ossidian Technologies which focused on wireless telecommunications standards, and Educational Multimedia Group, which revisited the software training category where CBT had been successful, but added audio-visual bells and whistles. Neville Technology Group, a Limerick company later known as PrimeLearning, produced training packages for generic business skills in sales, customer service, project management and inter-personal communications.

Riverdeep Interactive Learning, Pat McDonagh's second venture, was another of the start-ups in this wave. Founded in 1995, the company set out to examine what multimedia technology could do for mathematics. Riverdeep, co-located in Dublin and in Cambridge, Massachusetts, began at time when it became viable for companies to sell low-cost applications on PCs into educational institutions. It developed a full maths curriculum from kindergarten level to high schools in the US. Courseware vendors had been trying to sell into American classrooms for more than a decade. According to McDonagh, Riverdeep was different because its applications could be integrated into mainstream teaching.

The company introduced its first product — a complete mathematics curriculum for US middle-school grades — at a teachers conference in April 1998. It launched a sales drive in Texas, Florida, California and New York, trying to tap into a concern about declining mathematics standards in the American school system. Riverdeep, however, took to juggling numbers in a different way. The company expanded through a series of acquisitions, mostly in the US, and built up its market share at a rapid pace.

In 1999 it agreed to pay $5.25 million for the assets of an Israeli company, Logal Educational Software & Systems, which had developed a library of science and mathematics titles and had a customer base of 4,000 US high schools. This was followed by ED-Vantage Software, Teacher Universe, The Learning Company and Broderbund. From a tactical perspective, the key transaction was Riverdeep's purchase of the educational assets of an IBM subsidiary, Edmark Corporation, in an all stock deal. This not only added a range of early learning software to its product set, but also made the company a preferred provider of e-learning content to IBM. These transactions added up to a massive revenue stream. Riverdeep recorded sales of more than $200 million in calendar year 2002.

As with CBT, Pat McDonagh took a non-executive role in Riverdeep. Barry O'Callaghan, whose background was in investment banking, not software development, was the chief executive. In March 2000, as the acquisition binge accelerated, Riverdeep listed its shares on Nasdaq and the Irish Stock Exchange. It returned to private ownership three years later through a management buy-out led by McDonagh and O'Callaghan.

When the going got rough for the software industry after the turn of the century, the e-learning cluster suffered more than others. Customer corporations trimmed their overall IT spending in 2001 and 2002. But they hacked much deeper into their technology-based training budgets. The resulting slump undermined the business model that CBT Systems had pioneered — the combination of consultancy, courseware delivery and administration for an annual fee. The e-learning vendors found that their key customers were no longer signing multi-year contracts and were demanding lower prices.

Training is an easy target when cutbacks start. When companies stop hiring, they do not need to train new employees, while courses for existing staff can be deferred. Some organisations introduced programmes to reduce the number of suppliers from which they would source information technology. Others studied the return on their investments in technology-based training and concluded that it had not delivered tangible benefits. The courseware developers bore the brunt of the backlash. The formula that had served them well in the 1990s was no longer working.

According to Jim Breen, the founder of one of the newer ventures, the severity of this contraction was apparent to all by the start of 2002. His company, PulseLearning, had started operations just over two years earlier. It set up a team of developers in Tralee and took on projects as a subcontractor. SmartForce referred clients with special needs to the start-up. Philips became a PulseLearning customer through this connection. In 2002, Breen says, the subcontracting business evaporated and Pulse-Learning was forced to change its strategy. He argues, indeed, that all of the e-learning developers had to revise their business models. The time had come to scrap top-down training systems and programmes and to re-think e-learning from the bottom-up.

The big firms responded by axing jobs and merging with their peers. Interactive Services, which had received one of the last of the big venture capital investments in 2001, expanded and contracted in quick succession. Thomson Netg, which had a large courseware development operation in Limerick, announced that it would close it down in early 2002. Two years earlier Netg had employed 300 people in Ireland. SmartForce scaled down its base in Dublin, acquired a Massachusetts developer, Centra Software, and then merged with SkillSoft, another New England courseware vendor, under the SkillSoft name.

At the turn of the century respected industry analysts were projecting massive growth for the e-learning developers. By 2003 their business had shrunk instead. The analysts' forecasts were discredited and ignored.

And tens of millions of euro worth of venture capital had disappeared in Ireland alone.

It was still possible, nonetheless, to build new e-learning businesses, if they stayed very lean and very focused. The rise of PulseLearning, which is now targeting the US pharmaceutical industry, illustrates this point. Jim Breen says that the company made its transition almost by accident. But it was able to turn the accident to its advantage because of previous decisions.

PulseLearning always kept its headcount very low, employing no more than a dozen people. Instead it put together a structure to manage scattered groups of contractors — up to 50 at a time — around Ireland and further afield. It opted out of services in 2002 because the climate was so difficult. The company positioned itself between the packaged product trade and custom development projects, using these assignments to study the standard operating procedures in customer organisations. One of these projects gave rise to a set of scripts that assessed learners, selected materials for them to study and produced management reports. These added up to an authoring toolset that it branded as PulseAssess. The company realised that it could deliver the key functions of a learning management system at a fraction of the prices charged by WBT Systems and the other learning management system suppliers.

When the corporate e-learning market contracted, Jim Breen says, regulated industries such as financial services and life sciences kept seeking new solutions. PulseLearning modified PulseAssess to suit these industries and hired a sales team in New York with experience in the regulatory regimes. Very quickly the Tralee company had a multi-million dollar business in the US. The big break came in September 2003, when the National Aeronautics and Space Administration selected PulseAssess to train staff and contractors to comply with internal policies and external rules. The initial roll-out covered 1,500 people.

PulseLearning's transition was exceptional among the companies in the e-learning cluster. Most of the firms chose to re-channel their energies in a very different direction.

This Time It's Personal

The consolidation among e-learning developers in 2002 and 2003 was not confined to the big names on the stock exchanges. Some of Ireland's smaller developers also featured in the mergers and acquisitions. Intuition, for example, bought the assets of two Dublin companies, Educational Multimedia and Unlimited, and announced that it was forming a new computer literacy division. Rapid Technology Group, a supplier of "screenkey" devices for data input on point-of-sale equipment, took over Electric Paper, a long-established multimedia applications company that had evolved into a supplier of computer literacy education products. Pat McDonagh was the non-executive chairman of Rapid Technology. Chief executive officer Brendan O'Sullivan had previously been director of education for Apple Europe. They had quietly transformed the company into another e-learning venture. They sold off the screenkey technology and relaunched the business under a new name, ThirdForce.

Intuition and ThirdForce made these investments so that they could address a new constituency for e-learning — the individual in the home, rather than the employee in the workplace or the student in the college. Other Irish companies, like Advance Learning in Galway and Addoceo Digital Media, which was linked with the Centre for Learning Technology in Trinity College Dublin, also pegged their hopes on self-improvers.

This strategy draws on a long-term perspective. Technology-based training started in the 1980s with rudimentary graphics. The usual format was a set of floppy disks. The subject matter was technical, designed for users such as telecommunications engineers and currency traders. And the buyers tended to be large companies. As the visual quality improved and the CD-ROM replaced the floppy, the market expanded to a broader population of office workers. Information technology training was the main focus. After all, corporate IT departments were investing in more systems and needed to ensure that the employees knew how to avail of them. More powerful and more intuitive multimedia development tools came along in the 1990s, raising the presentation of content to a higher level of sophistication. When it became possible to deliver training courses across the internet, the potential market widened again. This history suggests that the next chapter in the e-learning story will see the emergence of a mass market.

Pat McDonagh points out that the e-learning business is still in its infancy. "It is still a small industry. Even though it is global, everyone in it knows what the others are doing," he says, comparing its 20-year track record with the slow evolution of pedagogy over thousands of years.

He believes that computer-based learning has only recently matured to a point where it can deliver education to 11-year-olds and that the content development industry is just getting to a point where it can really evaluate the effectiveness of its products. The learning management infrastructure, meanwhile, is expanding beyond corporations and colleges so that service providers can track the progress of individual learners, test their competence and provide them with accreditation. All these trends imply that personal e-learning is going to grow.

Pat McDonagh also argues that the next big opportunity for educational technology will be based around a new category of hardware. The PC, he argues, will never get into every home. An alternative device is needed so that e-learning can become all-pervasive. The enabling technology, he says, already exists, but it may take five or more years for the new category to establish itself. "If we could get into ten million homes in the US, we could have a $10 billion business," he reflects. Then he adds that least half a dozen competitors are pursuing the same goal.

The corollary of this progression is that courseware development may now become a commodity business, requiring the delivery and administration of large numbers of courses to large numbers of people at low cost. It is much more expensive to build a commodity application than a niche product. And the risks for developers and service providers are correspondingly higher. "As a nation, if we are going to be successful, [our companies] are going to have to be much bigger," McDonagh argues. He sees the present crop as too small, lacking management depth and failing to come up with original product ideas.

Free information is another risk factor. Will learners in the home want to pay for tuition when any web search engine can locate similar material without charging a fee? Commercial developers will need to concentrate on must-know subjects instead of less essential content. They will have to convince the users that their courses are better designed and easier to use than the free stuff. In particular, they will need to link up with certification authorities and collaborate on products that enable learners to attain recognised standards.

There is another, specifically Irish, phenomenon that underpins the new focus on personal e-learning. The Irish Computer Society (ICS) has promoted the international adoption of the European computer driving licence (ECDL), a scheme that tests and certifies end users' knowledge of everyday computer applications. This originated in Finland in the 1980s, but had a rather narrow reach until an ICS project team set up an ECDL Foundation in Dublin. The European Commission and the Irish government contributed funds. The chief instigator was Dudley Dolan, a senior lecturer in the department of computer science at Trinity College with a research interest in the pedagogical aspects of e-learning. When he brought the European Computer Driving Licence into Trinity, he ran up the highest phone bills on the campus as he tried to drum up national and international interest in the qualification.

By 2001 Ireland had the highest per capita participation rate in the ECDL programme and the Foundation was extending the scheme into the Americas, south-east Asia and the Arab world. The local e-learning developers took notice and designed courseware around the ECDL curriculum. Electric Paper was the most ambitious of the bunch, rolling out an Arabic version of a training product that included automated tests.

The ECDL movement showed that e-learning products could be sold in languages other than English and in places other than the US. The big vendors generate about 80 per cent of their revenues in the US and have always treated the rest of the world as somewhat peripheral. There is no reason to assume that the personal study market will be led by American users. It could be driven by demand from countries like China and India. The e-learning developers may need to grapple with localisation and accreditation issues to a much greater extent than ever before.

Another issue for the cluster is the convergence of content development with learning management and online service delivery. Jim Breen at PulseLearning argues that it is futile to continue to segment the e-learning industry into these three groups. The vendors like to break down the market in that way, he says, but it does not make much sense to their customers.

Some advocates of personal e-learning believe that it will flourish when anyone can plug into online libraries of training courses and identify the ones with high-quality content. What the users are waiting for, they suggest, is the equivalent of a dial tone — a universal infrastructure for content and service providers. Here again there is an assumption that education and training are turning into commodities.

Maybe, after all these years, the next generation of e-learning technology might actually be used in Ireland. Long ago the government courseware committee wanted to implement new learning systems across all the educational establishments and training centres. This never happened. By the peak years for e-learning exports, the failure to cultivate a local market was a dirty little secret that no one mentioned in polite company. Ireland, Dudley Dolan says, "has a reputation for prowess in e-learning, but the amount of e-learning that is done in Ireland is very small. Our knowledge of its use is very small."

He recalls a European Union initiative to designate a small number of "e-learning cities" and compare their experiences. Dublin — the birthplace of CBT Systems, Riverdeep and WBT Systems — was not accepted into this project because it had not learned how to use the technology.

Chapter 8

THE FINANCIAL SERVICES STORY

Conservative in the 1980s

Two Dublin companies won contracts to develop retail banking systems on minicomputers at around the same time in the late 1970s. System Dynamics took on a project for the Irish subsidiary of Barclays Bank in association with computer vendor Nixdorf. Always the quintessential software services company, System Dynamics treated this as a once-off assignment, delivered the goods and moved on its next job. The second contract went to Triple A Systems, a company affiliated with ICL. The customer was a precursor of Ansbacher Bank. In this case, however, the software provided the foundation for a packaged application, Bankmaster, that would literally spread throughout the world as the flagship product of the Kindle Group.

One strand of the Irish software industry has always been concerned with banking, insurance and financial trading. There was never a homogeneous cluster of companies. Most focused on a specific category of financial services and they seldom competed against each other. The majority of financial software comes from global trading centres such as London and New York. Irish companies have always been outsiders. Nonetheless, for two and a half decades, there has always been at least one financial applications developer among the large exporters — companies like Cognotec and Quay Financial Software, Trintech and Card-Base Technologies, Eontec and Fineos.

Kindle Group came first. It was Ireland's biggest software exporter for most of the 1980s. Its products, however, scored low on originality and its business models were consistently conservative.

The company was admired by the state agencies and institutional investors that could never make sense of class libraries or protocol stacks. They knew what went on inside a bank branch and why a copy of Kindle's Bankmaster might be useful there. The company's managing director and majority shareholder, Tony Kilduff, spoke their language. He sometimes boasted, indeed, that he could not recognise a single line of the code in Kindle's products. Tall and dapper, Kilduff was the antithesis of the techie stereotype and became the software chief that the establishment preferred to deal with.

Kindle was also admired by many of its peers. "They had hunters as sales people," remarks consultant Paul O'Dea, who regarded Kindle as a role model when he worked at Credo Group. The company, he says, took pride in its sales ability in the way that others took pride in their products. He remembers Kindle as a bunch of tough business people.

On the other hand, Kindle was disliked and shunned by most of the young developers who came out of the universities in the 1980s. They saw outmoded products, outmoded development methods and an unattractive place to work. They wanted to join companies like Glockenspiel, Merrion Gates and Generics, where the working culture was similar to their own. According to Generics founder Robert Cochran, Tony Kilduff's strategy was very explicit. He took a formula that mainframe companies had used and applied it on minicomputers. Kindle tried to lock its customers into products based on very mature technology. It was very good at customer support, but deeply suspicious of new software fads. "It was a good strategy but an old mindset," Cochran says.

The Kindle story began in 1978, when hardware vendors were still the market makers and software developers had to follow their lead. ICL Ireland needed a software partner for a new System Ten minicomputer installation at Waterford Savings Bank. It linked up with a Scottish consultant, Matthew Aird, who had experience on the ICL platform. His company, MA Systems, set up an office in Dublin.

MA Systems grew steadily, partly by acquiring other software service operations and partly by performing well on the projects that ICL steered its way. Triple A Systems, which developed the branch software for Ansbacher, was an offshoot of the firm. It released the Bankmaster package in 1981.

ICL spotted its potential. The computer maker, which was headquartered in London, sold many systems into countries that had once belonged to the British empire. These markets, it knew, seldom bought large mainframes, but would consider combinations of inexpensive hardware and packaged software. Bank branches in developing countries tended to operate on a standalone basis, offering a basic range of services on the premises. The software that Triple A developed for Ansbacher was distinctly old-fashioned. For example, it did not include a database. But it had the functionality that those branch offices required. ICL launched a minicomputer sales drive in retail banks across Africa and Asia. Its software partner in Dublin would supply the applications.

Standard Chartered Bank, which had branches in many former British colonies, bought Bankmaster. The deal gave the application developer a major boost. It opened offices in London and Hong Kong. In 1983 Tony Kilduff led a management buy-out of the business from Matthew Aird and introduced the Kindle name. In the following year, the company received an industry award for selling more than $1 million worth of the latest edition of Bankmaster in its first year of release. By then ICL had replaced the System Ten with the System 25 minicomputer and Kindle's software was adapted to suit this machine. The company phased out its activities in areas other than banking software. By 1986 Kindle had 65 employees and annual revenues of more than $4 million.

Mick Cunningham joined Kindle in 1988, having previously worked in IBM, Irish Life and System Dynamics. The banking software company was very different from his previous employers. Tony Kilduff, he recalls, had a hands-on style, but seemed curiously disinterested in the deficiencies of his company's output. At System Dynamics, in contrast, Tom McGovern always knew which pieces of code were good and bad. Cunningham was also struck by the way that Kindle was embedded into

ICL's business plan. The computer vendor, for example, paid all the travel expenses for its partner's staff.

By the late 1980s the software firm recognised that the days of writing applications for specific hardware types were coming to an end. It loosened the ties with ICL by porting Bankmaster onto PC networks and onto the NCR, ICL and IBM versions of the Unix operating system. There was even a project to deliver a mainframe edition of the product for large financial institutions.

Kindle was also keen to shake off its image as a producer of software for less developed countries. After a spell as project manager in Malta, Mick Cunningham moved into a sales role. His new task was to establish Kindle in eastern Europe. He started in Bulgaria, then explored East Germany, Czechoslovakia, Poland and Romania. Hungary, however, was the most receptive market for Bankmaster. The state-owned KFKI Technology Institute became a distributor for Kindle and in 1990 the company announced a $500,000 deal with this partner. Together they would supply three Hungarian banks with networked computer systems, complete with support features for cash dispensers and cheque clearance.

According to Cunningham, Kindle's software got overstretched on this project. "It was a third world banking system and there was nothing wrong with that," he says, "But when we sold it into eastern Europe the customers had first world ambitions." Single-branch organisations in India and Africa did not notice the absence of a database in Bankmaster. But this caused problems in Hungary. Kindle eventually released a retail banking package with a central relational database in 1992. It also added a branch banking system, Branchpower, that delivered applications on a central host system. The company, though, had trailed too far behind the technology for too long to succeed in the developed economies. "Kindle," Cunningham concludes, "was a third world company, but it pretended not to be."

Its achievements, though, should be acknowledged. At its peak, Bankmaster was installed by 120 banks in over 50 countries and Kindle employed more than 200 people. In 1991 International Computer Programs honoured Bankmaster with an award for confirmed cumulative sales in excess of $50 million. No contemporary Irish software product was in the same revenue league.

The company was sold in November 1991. The British-based ACT Group paid an initial $50 million for the business, mostly in shares, and later added another $10 million for hitting a profit target. The deal was preceded by a major win for Kindle at the State Bank of India, which selected Bankmaster and Branchpower for the country's largest ever banking automation programme. This project promised a steady cash-flow from the Kindle applications and enhanced the company's valuation. ACT kept open the Kindle office in Dublin. The operation also survived the takeover of ACT Group in 1995 by another British company, Misys. It scaled down slowly in the following years, but Misys retained the Kindle brand name until 2002.

Misys also bought up and scaled down Credo Group, another Dublin-based banking software producer. Credo had grown out of Cognotec, which was originally a videotex information provider. A cluster of videotex companies emerged in the 1980s, when Ireland attempted to emulate the Minitel online services that had become popular in France. Cognotec was the brainchild of Brian MacCaba, a hyper-energetic official at the Confederation of Irish Industry, which had participated in a public videotex trial in 1982. He championed online information services with a zeal that led him to leave the employers' body. MacCaba steered Cognotec through a succession of structures and business plans. At first it targeted two customer groups — insurance brokers and corporate treasurers. Its insurance service, Clientlink, connected life insurance offices to brokers and was endorsed by all the major insurance companies in Ireland. Cognotec supplied free terminals to the brokers, most of whom had never used computers before. Clientlink, however, was constrained by Minitel's technical limitations and was finally laid to rest in 1991. The information service for corporate treasurers generated twice as much revenue as Clientlink. Cognotec raised money to expand into the UK with an equivalent service, but sales were slow and development costs soon soaked up the finance.

In 1991 the troubled company split in two. Its name stayed with MacCaba, who went on to build a financial trading systems venture called Cognotec AutoDealing. The other group, led by Gerry English, set out to modernise the online banking application and took on the Credo name.

Gerry English understood how the financial services industry worked. He had been the corporate treasurer at An Post and, according to colleague Paul O'Dea, had personal credibility among the banks. Bank of Ireland selected the new outfit to develop and host a cash management service that would enable its corporate customers to monitor their account balances from PCs and to send instructions to the bank over the online connection. "We made the classic mistakes. We under-quoted and we delivered late," O'Dea admits. The bank, he says, was a good collaborator and helped the company to deliver the system, which went live in 1992. Other banks took notice and two years later Credo had supplied six bespoke online banking systems to customers in Dublin, London, the Isle of Man and Switzerland. All were built on a common engine that ran on Digital Equipment VAX computers.

The next version took the form of a product, called Fontis, that could be installed on Unix or Windows servers. It was designed to suit branches of international banks that wanted a shrinkwrapped product that they could implement quickly. Credo itself would provide all the system installations and technical support. Fontis went live in 1995 at the New York branch of the Union Bank of Finland, Mitsubishi Bank in London and Dialog Bank in Moscow, where the Dublin development group delivered a user interface with the Cyrillic alphabet. By then Gerry English was targeting prospective customers in London, New York, Singapore and Hong Kong and forecasting rapid growth for Credo.

Misys bought the business and achieved that sort of growth. But the organisation in Dublin, which once had more than 60 employees, shrivelled away after the acquisition. Credo would have liked a partnership arrangement with Misys, but the company was only interested in taking it over. The acquisition was announced in September 1996, when ten banks had live Fontis systems. The final price would be determined by future performance, but was expected to be around $8 million. Within three years Misys chalked up 45 Fontis installations and added internet features. The original development team, however, had broken up and, according to Paul O'Dea, Misys found it difficult to make the transition from PC-based to internet-based banking services. He stayed with the company until 2000, when Misys finally closed down the Credo office and moved its few remaining staff into the Kindle building.

Kindle's specialisation in third world banking, meanwhile, was inherited by CR2. Formed in Dublin in 1997 by two former Kindle employees, CR2 initially developed an internet banking application, BankWorld, that utilised Iona's Orbix middleware. This product scored early successes in the Middle East.

The company changed direction in 2000, when it acquired Interlink, a payment processing and card management software firm based in London. Interlink had sold its products into 70 countries. CR2 inherited a network of subsidiaries across Asia and Africa. It soaked up large sums of venture capital, signed implementation partnerships and embarked on an extended marketing drive across both continents. CR2's promotional roadshow travels constantly along an arc that starts in Cape Town, runs through the Gulf states and south Asia and leads all the way to Indonesia. The company is clearly the twenty-first century successor to Kindle.

Tony Kilduff left the board of Kindle in 1992, one year after the company was acquired. He bought a 29.9 per cent stake in Reflex Investments, a computer leasing and hardware maintenance group which was trying to establish an additional software products business. Kilduff became chairman of the firm and talked up the potential to turn Reflex into an international software supplier. A link of sorts already existed between Kindle and Reflex. The same venture capital company, DCC Corporate Finance, had bought shareholdings in both. Reflex offered a variety of minicomputer software applications for distributors, retailers and freight transporters. It was one of the last exponents of the generation two model. The products were gradually abandoned or sold to spin-offs.

By 2002, when Misys finally killed the Kindle name, Reflex was operating health centres in Britain and Tony Kilduff was chairing a preschool childcare company in Dublin.

Radical in the 1990s

Where Kindle was the flagship software development company in generation two, another banking applications supplier embodied all the highs and lows of generation four. In contrast to its predecessor, Dublin-based Eontec defined itself by running ahead of the technology curve. Eontec championed Sun's Java platform in its early years and challenged the banks to embrace a Java-based approach to applications software.

This was a brave stance to take in a market that had always shied away from unproven technologies. Many banks, indeed, spent the 1980s avoiding PCs because they appeared to threaten the centralised control that their mainframe systems afforded. These cautious institutions were similarly loath to adopt Microsoft's server software in the following decade. What Eontec proposed was much more radical.

According to company founder Jim Callan, financial institutions retained an attachment to bespoke and semi-custom software long after the rest of the world moved over to packages. This, he adds, was especially true in Europe, where banks continued to commission service companies to write once-off applications. Callan points out that there were plenty of packages around in the 1980s — monolithic mainframe suites with non-relational databases from vendors like Hogan System or products for minicomputers from developers like Kindle. But it was always difficult to persuade the banks to install packages and he finds that the old attitudes have persisted to the present day.

"If you can get a package going in banking, it is a good space to be in," Callan says. "The risks are huge, but the rewards are significant." Convincing the banks is only part of the challenge. Big name system integrators make many of the technology choices and have become key intermediaries in the sale of banking software.

Jim Callan admits that Eontec — or Eon Technologies as it was known in its early years — was established to keep its three founders in employment rather than to pursue a strategic plan. The three had previously worked for a British company, Third Wave, which opened an office in Dublin in 1990 to support a customer project at ACCBank. Third Wave assisted the bank to implement its Tamar retail banking system, which went live in 1991 on a Stratus computer. Three years later Third Wave disintegrated. ACCBank still needed technical support. Callan and his colleagues suggested to the bank that they would not only keep the Tamar applications running, but could also supply its next generation of software. They launched the firm in 1994 with ACCBank as a captive customer.

The Eon trio, like many other developers in those years, believed that the future of software lay in object technology. They set about creating object-based applications for ACCBank. A former colleague from Third Wave, who had moved to India, assisted with software modelling.

Eon's early efforts for ACCBank used the Smalltalk programming language. In 1996, however, Java became the main rallying point for the object-oriented software faction. Eon jumped onto this new bandwagon and started coding in Java. Developed by Sun as a programming language that enabled applications to run on variety of hardware platforms without modifications, Java quickly attracted a cult following. It promised to uncouple hardware products from systems software, and databases from applications, creating a level playing field for the developers in each category. Java represented openness and signified modernity, whereas vendors like IBM and Microsoft were perceived to lock in customers to their technologies.

In September 1996 Sun counted 441 Java-based applications on the market from independent developers. Two months later the corporation reckoned that the total had increased to more than 1,000. In spring 1997 Sun convened a developer conference, JavaOne, in San Francisco. Jim Callan trekked over to this event, expecting to find a bunch of banking applications and hoping to choose products that he could resell in Ireland. Nobody at JavaOne, however, was showing any software for banks.

"We had the world's first Java banking application, two years ahead of anyone else," Callan says. And no one was more surprised than the company team in Dublin. Sun was keen to support developers that could fill application gaps in the Java catalogue and offered to assist Eon. The Dublin firm was invited to participate in a Java Objects For Finance consortium and was offered display space at different Java conferences and promotions. Sun, however, lacked the resources to advise its software partners on business development, especially when those companies were small and inexperienced.

Eon delivered a web banking application called Java NetBank in 1997 and pledged that all its applications would be "pure Java" by the middle of the following year. In autumn 1988 the company launched BankFrame, a framework of Java software components for multi-channel banking applications. BankFrame was designed to be as comprehensive as possible. It could support internet applications, but the development firm insisted that the internet should be treated as just one of many channels. This stance was unusual in the late 1990s.

"We wanted to get into the chunky applications," Callan explains. Eontec wanted recognition as a provider of core banking software, not just the fringe applications. Most of the other Java-based software for financial institutions catered for trading rooms. When BankFrame was launched, technical director Colin Piper moved to Boston to drum up interest in North America. Eontec raised $10.4 million in venture capital in 2000 and used the money to build a US management team at a new office in North Carolina. By then BankFrame had expanded into a collection of more than 1,500 reusable components. Eontec obtained another $25 million in the following year, with American venture capital firm Warburg Pincus as the lead investor.

"We got early hits in Scandinavia, South Africa and Canada — pioneering territories," Jim Callan recalls. One of the company's reference sites was in Nova Scotia which he describes as "a great place to blood a package". It then won deals in quick succession at Bank of Ireland, ICCbank, EBS and Yorkshire Building Society. These were sizeable projects and the company's revenues passed the $10 million threshold when it had just six paying customers.

By the turn of the century the banking software development business was polarised into two groups. One supported Java and the open systems philosophy. The second was aligned to Microsoft, which had put forward its own component software framework. Dublin companies CR2 and JLS Software Solutions were among the banking application developers in the Microsoft camp.

The software suppliers on both sides of the fence also positioned themselves in relation to internet applications. One of Ireland's generation two veterans, Vision Consulting, was notably successful in this area, delivering banking systems to Dime Bank in the US and Halifax, the biggest mortgage lender in the UK. Vision, however, never tried to turn its projects into products. Orygen, which evolved out of the Irish subsidiary of Texas Instruments Software, made that effort. In 1998 it tried to build a product business out of bespoke software that it had originally supplied to Bank of Ireland. After the company was acquired by a US network operator, Level 3 Communications, it focused on marketing an internet banking system for corporate customers. Orygen always made it clear, however, that it was selling the template of a product, not something that was fully finished. This emphasis on componentry required a bigger commitment from customers than installing a software package. Another internet-centric developer, Information Mosaic, launched an electronic banking platform for branchless financial services and reported sales to Skandinaviska Enskilda Banken, Citigroup and Rabobank. Enba, a Dublin-based holding company, was also a client. Enba not only aspired to run its own internet banking system, but also to host operations on its systems for other financial service companies.

Eontec distanced itself from this bunch. It tried to avoid association with the internet banking bubble. Eontec, moreover, promoted itself as a supplier of tier-one products to tier one banks. "Why? Because we could build it," Callan says, "And because that was where the money was." Once you know the right names, he adds, you start to get calls from the big banks. Tier one was a tight-knit club. If Eontec could convince one member of its software's merits, the other institutions would soon know about the company as well. It found a tier-one champion in 2001. The Canadian Imperial Bank of Commerce was one of North America's top ten financial institutions. Linda Dentay, its chief information officer responsible for retail branch banking, chose the Dublin company's framework for a five-year programme to upgrade services for over six million customers. In 2003 Canadian Imperial implemented its software at 1,100 branch offices in less than seven months. Dentay also made public appearances with Eontec on the exhibition and conference circuit.

As Eontec's business expanded, its relationship with Sun was loosened. IBM became the customers' most frequent choice to install Bank-Frame. This followed the corporation's withdrawal from banking software development. In 1999 IBM announced that it would phase out all of its applications software. It would focus instead on selling middleware and infrastructure management software and would seek more alliances with independent software developers. Iona's Chris Horn had advised Jim Callan that Eontec would need to beat IBM in a competitive contest if it wanted a successful partnership with the systems and services giant. When IBM changed its business model, however, both companies saw advantages in working together.

There is more money in system integration than in software licence sales, but IBM needed access to retail applications to win that service business. IBM's salesforce swung behind Eontec's component suite. The companies agreed that IBM should make five dollars for every dollar that Eontec earned.

In the early years of the new century, however, financial institutions cut down their spending on information technology spend and avoided major new investments. Jim Callan suggests that the banks became more confident after 2000. During the web hype of the preceding years they had heard repeated assertions that their businesses were under threat from online start-ups. They felt obliged to increase their spending on internet banking systems and wanted to be seen to be doing so. When the web threat evaporated, the technology divisions of the banks reverted to more cautious timescales. New projects were cancelled. The working life of existing software was prolonged. The banks continued to buy or build new web-based applications, but they insisted that these must be integrated with their other systems and not rushed into service.

This change of attitude caused more pain for the product developers than the system integrators. The banking applications trade suffered three years of recession. Many vendors failed to survive. Enba's ambitions fizzled out in 2001. The group, which had seemed unable to decide if it wanted to be a bank or a technology vendor, wound up both operations. Orygen's parent company, Level 3, had little sympathy when its banking components failed to sell. It had inherited this line of business through an acquisition and only tolerated it as long as it was self-sufficient. It never put any resources into its Irish subsidiary. In 2003 Level 3 ordered Orygen to close. Information Mosaic, meanwhile, narrowed its offerings to cater for asset managers and private banks and survived in a scaled-down form.

Eontec survived the shakeout, but the number of employees in the company was halved to 150 in 2002. Its fortunes improved in 2003 when it won substantial contracts in Australia and Singapore. But Java was now a mature software technology, no longer the subject of a technical crusade.

Jim Callan was eased out of Eontec after the venture capitalists came on board and started to groom the company for a trade sale. His successor, Pat Brazel, was a former president of SunGard Capital Markets, which supplied systems to financial traders. Eontec found a buyer for the business in 2004. Siebel Systems agreed to pay an initial sum of $70 million in cash for the Dublin company, plus earn-out payments of up to $60 million during 2005. Callan, meanwhile, set up Erego as a new vehicle for enterprise software development. His future plans, he says, do not include any banking applications.

Dealing and Brokering and Coding

Customers felt comfortable when they walked into Quay Financial Software's office, because they found the atmosphere familiar. The company developed systems for financial dealing rooms and its employees were accustomed to the pressures of the trading room. Quay not only sold software products. It was also the in-house IT department of National and City Brokers (NCB), a financial services group with which it shared a building in central Dublin. When Niall O'Cleirigh joined in 1989, Quay was closely linked to NCB in another way. Investor Dermot Desmond was the majority shareholder in both firms through his Dedeir organisation.

According to O'Cleirigh, the day-to-day environment for the software builders was as frenetic as for the traders, but he describes the development team as stable and self-contained. Their well-heeled workplace was certainly different from the low-rent premises that other software firms inhabited. Visitors to Quay's office encountered a disciplined production unit, not a performance space for creative coders.

The software behind trading in currencies, stocks, bonds and other financial instruments has always come from specialist suppliers. The companies that developed the trading desk equipment also ran information services. Vendors like Reuters and Telerate sold not only workstations for dealers, but also the financial data feeds that appeared on the screens. Quay's founder, Gerry Giblin, worked for Telerate in New York in the early 1980s. He returned to Dublin in the middle of the decade and set up Dealformatics under the Dedeir umbrella. From the start this software venture wrote applications for low-cost PCs, rather than the proprietary trading workstations or Unix-based computers that other developers favoured.

Changes in dealing-room hardware were visible to all, but a more important technology transition was underway in the background. The content delivery side of the business was going digital. The information suppliers had traditionally distributed market data in the form of read-only video displays. Every dealer saw the same data on the screens. Digital feeds were introduced the late 1980s and offered a real alternative. For the first time the incoming numbers could be manipulated to meet the needs of individual trading rooms or customised to suit the job of a specific dealer. The industry started to sell trading data separately from the equipment. Software developers had a chance to loosen the big players' dominance of dealing-room technology by supplying add-on products that performed special calculations or extracted new insights from archived trading data.

Gerry Giblin hoped to capitalise on these opportunities when he formed Quay Financial Software in 1987. Quay was formally an operating subsidiary of Dealformatics, but it soon became the primary vehicle for Giblin's ideas. It won attention by pushing PC technology to the limits. Quay's InVision information delivery and presentation system integrated data from digital feeds, while its TeleCalc utilities provided dealers with customised calculations. Quay designed InVision to extract the essential figures, stripping out all other material, and thus presenting less data on the screen. Fast processing was vital. Quay used IBM's OS/2 Presentation Manager to strip clutter off the screen. InVision also included original windowing and local area networking software, while TeleCalc's data analysis features went far beyond the capabilities of ordinary spreadsheets.

"Most of the vendors picked Unix," Niall O'Cleirigh notes. "Ours was PC-based. That was the big differentiator. Essentially we rode the wave of PC adoption in financial services in the early 1990s." In 1993 he was promoted to technical director. Customers, he says, were attracted to the clever applications on the top of Quay's product stack. The company did not pitch InVision directly against the established platforms. Brokers and investment groups bought the underlying system because they wanted the tools that it supported.

"Digital feeds have shaken up the market to the benefit of the customer," Gerry Giblin declared in 1991. By then, four years after Quay was born, some 400 dealers in ten installations were using InVision. Most of the early adopters were in Ireland, but they also included Eurobrokers, which ran trading rooms in London and New York. Quay opened support offices in both cities and Eurobrokers became an important reference user.

The company also negotiated partnerships with major names like IBM and Unisys, which marketed its products on different hardware and in different territories. In 1992 it signed a three-year agreement with Connecticut-based trading room equipment vendor Micrognosis. A veteran of the video display era, its products were installed at 18,000 dealer positions. Quay granted exclusive worldwide distribution rights to Micrognosis for InVision and Telecalc on the understanding that it would use the software to move this customer base into the digital age.

Quay grew rapidly. Micrognosis was able to win large contracts for the software, such as a sale to Citibank that covered 500 dealer positions at 16 sites across Europe. Quay's revenues swelled from less than $2 million in 1991 to $9.3 million two years later. The company decided to invest more than $2 million in a diversification project and developed a real-time risk management system that could integrate with InVision. By 1994 the relationship with Micrognosis enabled Quay to claim 80 customers in 23 countries. By 1995 the partners had achieved their original three-year sales target of $19 million and 85 employees were working for the Dublin developer.

For Dermot Desmond, the main investor in Quay, the time had come to cash in his shares in the firm and move on to other projects. The company's three-year partnership with Micrognosis was nearing its end. Japanese conglomerate CSK, the parent company of Micrognosis, was willing to buy the business. A deal was struck in June 1995. "We were already engaged to CSK. So it was easier to get married to CSK than someone else," Gerry Giblin said at the time. Quay Financial Software became CSK Software. The new owner appointed Gerry Giblin, Niall O'Cleirigh and three executives from outside Quay to manage the business. Giblin also took on responsibilities for product strategy at Micrognosis.

CSK was a large computing services organisation with little experience in product development and a limited understanding of niche markets. It thought that the new subsidiary in Ireland should expand outside financial services and produce software in other fields as well. Slingshot was a step in this direction. Niall O'Cleirigh came up with the concept. Unlike InVision, which ran over local networks, Slingshot was designed for the internet. The product would integrate live trading data into standard web pages, combine it with other information and enable financial institutions to distribute updates to any user in any location. CSK Software tested the system with data feeds from Reuters and launched it in

1996 as a "financial server". It sold Slingshot in this form to more than a dozen installations, including Eurobrokers in New York.

The company then started to promote its web application beyond the banks and brokers. In 1997 O'Cleirigh and business development manager Colm Toolan set up an office in California and trawled around Silicon Valley, seeking allies that might adapt Slingshot for aviation or medicine or some other industry. They found interest in areas like online auctions and gambling. CSK Software also joined a European Commission research project to experiment with its technology in other settings.

From the outside, CSK Software now looked like thousands of other web application developers that were hustling for deals. On the inside, however, Niall O'Cleirigh was acutely aware that its parent corporation moved at a much slower pace than the internet community. He became increasingly frustrated with the Japanese firm's hierarchical management structure. In 1998 O'Cleirigh and five senior colleagues, including the principal developer of Slingshot, walked out of CSK. The defectors proceeded to launch Macalla Software and to produce middleware for mobile e-commerce applications in financial services. According to O'Cleirigh, they broke away so that they could be their own masters instead of taking someone else's orders.

Colm Toolan took charge of the Slingshot project and tried to keep it going with a smaller development team. The Japanese conglomerate finally axed its Dublin organisation in 2001. It then restructured CSK Software as a European services company with headquarters in Frankfurt.

Quay Financial Software was the most ambitious of Ireland's trading software developers. When CSK killed off the business, it left little trace. Other generation three companies had more staying power. The latterday Cognotec targeted large banks with AutoDeal, an automated system for foreign exchange and money market dealing. By 1998 Brian Mac-Caba's company claimed 150 employees, including 110 people at its software development centre in Dublin. Software Vineyard found a niche with MoneyMate, an investment analysis tool built on a database of information on managed funds in Europe. Focus Solutions, later known as

Broker Focus, introduced a deal settlement system and later added front-end applications for online trading.

International Financial Systems was another boom-and-bust story. Founded in 1992 and led by former Reuters executive Ken Coldrick, its flagship product, MarginMan, was a risk management system for foreign exchange traders. The company secured investment money from Deutsche Bank and Intel and, by the turn of the century, claimed annual sales of $6 million in 2000 and an employee count of more than 100. Crisis struck in the following year, following a failed attempt to acquire a British company that sold automated financial trading software. It scaled down to a skeleton team of eight people in Dublin. The end came in early 2002, when a US developer, Integral, scooped up its assets and intellectual property rights. Integral retained a sales group for MarginMan in Ireland, but transferred development and support responsibilities to India.

The financial trading applications business has also produced one of the great survivors of Irish software. Salmon Software was a 1985 start-up that believed that PCs could run treasury management applications. It wrote its Treasurer product to suit money managers in corporations and small banks instead of those in large financial institutions. According to founder John O'Brien, 30 software companies around the world offered competing products in the 1980s. By 2003, Salmon was one of just five developers still in the field. Treasurer, which supports foreign exchange, money market, treasury and banking transactions, evolved through successive operating systems and eventually embraced the web. O'Brien attributes Salmon's longevity to how the company paid its way by selling its product and never sought external investments.

Only a handful of generation two software companies made it intact to the twenty-first century. Salmon Software not only succeeded, but has also guided a single product through changes in financial services and software technology. Quay's innovations in the dealing rooms brought transient fame, but Salmon's careful build-up and consolidation was a more lasting achievement.

Hard Ways to Get Paid

The smart card was invented in Europe and the potential for the technology seemed vast in the mid-1980s. Many and various tasks could be entrusted to a programmable chip mounted on a sliver of plastic. It could store personal identification data. It could hold medical records. It could be used to switch on or unlock different items of equipment. First and foremost, though, the smart card could replace the magnetic stripe cards issued by credit card companies, while supporting a far wider and richer range of payment processes. Was this the key to a cashless society, where auditing software would combat fraud and only criminals would want to pay with printed notes?

The European Commission was especially keen on the smart card as the enabling device for new products and services. Its research programmes aimed to give European companies a global lead in these applications. Large corporations like Bull and Philips got involved, but most of the advances, including the creation of software tools, were made by smaller firms. The complexities of establishing new infrastructures soon became apparent. Industry politics and inertia got in the way of the grand visions. The credit card companies always called the shots and they moved very slowly. The smart card manufacturers found an alternative market in mobile communications, supplying the user identity cards for GSM handsets. The software developers and system integrators that specialised in smart card payment systems struggled to remain in business.

Payment processing has never been a hospitable environment for application software developers. But a number of Irish firms moved into this area in generation three. Card Services International offered a multi-function card payment system called CardBase and later renamed itself after this product. Peregrine Systems came from a background in rules-based systems and produced software for resolving disputes over credit card payments. Flexicom sold end-to-end card payment processing systems with multi-currency capabilities until it was absorbed into CR2. The best known of the bunch was Trintech, whose software transferred electronic payments information.

Brian Caulfield joined Peregrine in 1989 and became its managing director three years later. He was 27 years old and his salary was halved when he was promoted. "I became captain of the sinking ship," he recalls. Peregrine had previously been taken over by Landis & Gyr, an engineering conglomerate based in Switzerland. The Dublin company had originally developed expert systems to customer specifications. Landis & Gyr treated its 20 employees as an internal software group. The parent organisation ran into difficulties in 1991 and informed its Irish staff that they would be laid off at Christmas. One of Peregrine's external customers, a financial institution in Ireland, reacted angrily to this decision and threatened legal action. The Swiss firm responded by retaining five Peregrine employees. Caulfield describes the situation as rather surreal. "The lawyers," he says, "had to figure out whether they could withdraw a redundancy notice."

This muddle was resolved when Landis & Gyr formally sold off the assets of Peregrine for one Swiss franc. In April 1992 Caulfield and three colleagues took charge of the business which, he says, "bumped along at the bottom for the best part of four years." The new incarnation of Peregrine picked up some service projects in Ireland and started work on its application for the credit card industry. The concept came from technical director Bill O'Connor, who wanted to apply rules-based methodologies to "chargebacks" or disputed card transactions. He believed that banks could achieve real cost savings with such software and would avoid losses through invalid processing. The company, however, was in a fragile condition and progress with the package was slow. Two of the four founders departed because they found it hard to take the insecurity. Peregrine finally produced a saleable product after four years of penny-pinching and hard graft.

In 1997 Visa International agreed to market and distribute the chargeback processing software under its own brand name. Peregrine had high expectations for this agreement. In retrospect, however, Caulfield says that it had little practical value. Selling software was not Visa's business. Two years after the deal, just ten organisations had adopted the chargeback application. Peregrine had twice as many users of Credit Enquiry Manager, a country-specific credit reference product that was designed for sale in Ireland.

The company now had about 50 employees and had opened its first international office in Birmingham, England, close to premises of a flagship customer, Barclaycard. It had made its first sales into the US and tried unsuccessfully to identify an executive who could grow its business in North America. In 2000 it recruited a new chief executive officer instead. Terry McWade joined from the Boston Consulting Group. Bill O'Connor bowed out and Brian Caulfield took over the role of chief technology officer. The company changed its name to Exceptis Technologies shortly afterwards.

All this activity attracted industry attention. Following a merger proposal from an American company the new chief executive entered into discussions with other prospective partners. These included Dublin-based Trintech, which bought Exceptis in November 2000 for approximately $26 million in shares, of which $10 million was dependent on its future sales performance.

Trintech had also encountered the hazards of partnering with major corporations. Founded in 1986 by brothers Cyril and John McGuire, the company launched its own range of point-of-sale transaction terminals two years later, differentiating its products with a capability to receive lists of stolen card numbers through radio broadcasts. It initially grew its terminal business inside Ireland, followed by Germany in the early 1990s. The company's revenues rose more gradually than the brothers forecast, but exceeded $5 million in 1994. The software applications that supported Trintech's products came to be worth more than its hardware.

In 1996 the company announced a strategic partnership with Visa International. This was followed closely by an endorsement from Microsoft. Trintech integrated its software with Microsoft's Merchant Server, adding authorisation, transaction management and order fulfilment features. Both relationships centred on the adaptation of Trintech's payment processing software for the internet. The company opened a subsidiary in California, headed by John McGuire, to seek new business on the back of its alliances. The financial institutions that issued credit cards showed little enthusiasm for the internet applications, but they were bought by online merchants and internet service companies. Sales to fixed and mobile telecommunications operators also increased.

In 1999 the company achieved sales of $30 million, half of which came from its internet products. In the following year it went on an acquisition spree, buying its Texas-based rival Globeset, a UK electronic payment firm and a Latin American card management applications specialist, as well as Exceptis. Trintech promoted its expanded portfolio as the only integrated software suite for physical transactions and e-payments, contrasting this approach with rivals who could only offer pieces of an online payment processing system. The four acquisitions required a combined investment of $112 million. Speaking in 2001, Cyril McGuire justified the series by arguing that they had brought a broader spread of customers to Trintech and reduced its dependence on technology expenditure by banks.

The acquisitions did not deliver the sort of growth that Trintech hoped for. It recorded net losses for four years in a row, while sales slipped to $43.0 million in 2003. The big alliances did not deliver big contracts. Instead the company buoyed up its sales by adding new customer categories like restaurant chains, cinemas and sports clubs.

Trintech kept adapting and survived. By 2002, however, John McGuire had had enough and resigned. The company had been created to expand on his research as an electronics engineering student. When Trintech reached its eighteenth anniversary, Cyril McGuire was still at the helm as CEO.

The Irish software firm that showed the greatest faith in smart card technology was Card Services International — or CardBase Technologies as it was renamed in January 2000.

Aonghus Geraghty set up the business in 1993 after working for Trintech and for Wordnet Banking Automation. Wordnet's software added an "electronic purse" option to cash, credit card and debit cards. Geraghty's Dun Laoghaire-based venture took the same approach to pre-loaded spending power on plastic cards. It contracted out the development of its first electronic money system to the ICL software centre in Leopardstown.

It also collaborated with the French card technology vendor Gemplus and card reader supplier VeriFone, incorporating their products into its applications. Later in the decade the company added a marketing relationship with IBM and launched CardBase2000, its second generation suite of control and monitoring software for multi-function cards.

CardBase was willing to take on electronic payment projects that the established vendors viewed as too specialised or too risky. Early in its career the company sold a system in Russia to manage dual-purpose cards that identified the holder and contained his or her salary. Bandit attacks on workers who had been paid in cash were a problem in the former Soviet Union. Employers were willing to consider alternative payment methods. The money system was piloted in a Russian town where most of the inhabitants worked for the same organisation. Abu Dhabi's national oil company, meanwhile, implemented the purse-on-a-card system at 300 filling stations. The technology was also selected for schemes in Malaysia and Costa Rica. And Aonghus Geraghty trekked all over Africa, including parts that travellers were advised to avoid, promoting the merits of cashless transactions.

By the turn of the century the CardBase product set covered card management, transaction processing and settlement. In 2000 the company added internet transaction tools, digital signatures and support for electronic purse specifications drawn up by Visa International. In the same year CardBase Technologies announced a $7.7 million investment package. This gave Gemplus a 20 per cent stake in the company and added a Japanese venture capital firm to the shareholders.

Since its inception, the company had contributed to many trials and pilot implementations. But all this effort delivered just two major customers. British Airways chose CardBase to set up a travel allowance scheme for its flight crews. It then commissioned a system to manage payments to passengers who volunteered to give up seats on overbooked flights. In both cases the airline asked for smart cards that could be configured as electronic purses and used to obtain cash. ValuCard Nigeria, a banking consortium that built a national electronic purse scheme, also picked CardBase. It designed a system to manage offline transactions as easily as online payments. ValuCard extended the system across 38 banks and more than 3,000 merchant locations.

CardBase always struggled to make money from mainstream payment processing. It was difficult to win business from banks in the developed world. Rival software vendors fared no better. By 2001 the number of technology suppliers was shrinking. Aonghus Geraghty resigned from CardBase at the start of the year. In the summer the company applied to the High Court for an examinership — the Irish equivalent of the American Chapter 11 procedure for restructuring companies with financial difficulties. The process enabled CardBase to negotiate another investment package — €5.4 million from a combination of previous and new shareholders. The owners appointed Vincent Nolan as chief executive officer.

A former director of private banking at Bank of Ireland, Nolan had also held sales positions in computing and networking companies. He reckoned that CardBase had been distracted by implementation projects that did not fit into its core business and refocused on product marketing. Nolan undertook to stop "chasing rainbows". The correct niche for CardBase, he declared, was in the second-tier retail banks that issued credit cards. These would soon be obliged to replace all magnetic stripe cards with smart cards. CardBase pointed out that its multi-application card management systems would enable them to launch additional customer services during or after this changeover.

The new CEO's criticisms of the old regime annoyed Aonghus Geraghty and other CardBase veterans. They argued that there was nothing new in Nolan's business plan, except that he was walking away from revenue-generating projects. In the end, the new chief increased the company's sales to €2.1 million in 2003 and reduced its losses to €1.7 million — about a quarter of the previous level. Along the way, however, he shrank the CardBase development team from 60 people to 34. "If asked to do it again," he admitted at the end of the year, "I do not think I would take on such an underfunded company." A new owner agreed to take it on in 2004. ID Data, a British smart card systems company, acquired CardBase Technologies for €3.42 million.

The payment processing business has never lived up to software developers' expectations. But this section of the industry never went away. The newer payment software developers have stayed away from smart card applications. Many channelled their energies instead into mobile payment applications. Other generation four start-ups were more interested in security for online payments. Orbiscom, for example, patented a controlled payment technology in almost 100 countries before its initial product launch in 2000. With a technical team drawn largely from former Credo employees, Orbiscom invented a process for generating a unique, controlled authorisation number for individual internet payments. This allowed buyers to keep their real credit card numbers confidential and thus safeguard themselves against fraud. Orbiscom rapidly achieved one of the highest capitalisations ever attributed to an Irish software firm.

Sideways into Insurance

In the mainframe era, when there was little computing education in the universities, Irish Life was one of the few places that trained large groups of programmers and treated software development as an element of its business strategy. Mick Cunningham was a systems and programming manager at the insurance firm. He admits that the work was "sweatshop stuff". But he says that there was genuine job satisfaction for the youthful workforce. Most of the programmers joined the company at 18, passed an aptitude test and were given far greater responsibilities than their peers in policy management or claims processing. Many of the software industry's leading figures in generation two learned their craft at Irish Life.

These roots in the insurance business did not, however, lead to widespread software product development for insurance firms. Other subsets of the financial services industry have always attracted more interest. Insurance is one of the few areas of applications development where a single supplier holds a dominant share of the international market. Computer Sciences Corporation (CSC) achieved this through acquisitions that covered all the subsets of insurance company management and gave it a near-monopoly in packages for policy administration. Anyone who wanted to break into the business faced two hurdles. First they had to overcome the continuing preference of many insurance firms for bespoke software. Then they had to compete against the muscle of CSC.

There are, however, side paths that lead into the information technology divisions of insurance firms. The industry is known for its dependence on workflow processes, document management and customer relationship management. In the 1990s it became apparent that developers could gain a foothold in the insurance industry by meeting these peripheral needs.

FM Systems was an early example. It released its Financial Advisors Modelling and Information System (Famis) for the life assurance industry in 1990. This supported salespeople with the data gathering, needs analysis and counselling routines that precede the creation of each new insurance policy. The Leopardstown-based developer claimed that the marketing support and cross-selling functions of Famis set it apart from the applications offered by bigger software vendors. FM Systems also tried to sell products for central policy management and branch office administration. But sales support became its speciality and enabled it to win business in Britain and the US. By 1995 Famis could also be integrated into call centres and one user organisation was using telephone calls to process all of its customer transactions. Support for e-mail and the web followed in due course. In 1998 FM Systems launched its Allfinanz Original Software framework for automating the insurance sales channel. The company subsequently changed its name to Allfinanz, but kept its focus on new business processing and underwriting.

Zarion and Phoenix Technology Group both gained admission to insurance firms with other companies' document management software, then went on to become product developers. Zarion, originally known as Aspect Software International, was established in 1995 by a team of document imaging specialists who had worked together at Wang. At first they implemented Wang's imaging and workflow applications. In time the company created its own business process management products for customer service groups, including a special edition for the life and pensions subset of the insurance industry. Phoenix started life in 1997 as an implementer of FileNet's Panagon document management software. After a couple of years of project experience the Dublin company designed web-based applications for insurance work processing and content management. While it kept up its relationship with FileNet and continued to draw most of its revenues from service projects, the company established reference sites for its own applications in both Britain and Germany.

The best example of an applications developer that started on the margins, but aimed for the heart of insurance computing is Fineos. Other companies cite this generation three venture as the best in the business at structuring and positioning product families.

Fineos was founded in 1993 by Michael Kelly, who had previously worked in the Benelux and Scandinavian regions for Paxus, one of the insurance software vendors that got swallowed up by CSC. Originally named Managed Solutions Corporation, the company started quietly. It took on consulting projects. It mastered Iona's Orbix middleware and it explored the positioning of object technology in insurance applications. One of its few public appearances in the early years was in an educational television series in Britain. A BBC Open University course in computer science featured its demonstration of object technology in a commercial environment and alerted potential customers to the company's approach.

By 1997 it could offer two products based on an object technology — a life assurance administration system and a customer care application for insurers. In some instances Kelly's firm found that it was competing directly against CSC. Over the following years it concentrated on the customer contact end of the insurance industry. It gradually added more internet options to the product set and introduced web portals for various participants in the business process.

The strategy that Fineos adopted was to sell front-end applications that would integrate with the existing systems in an insurance company and then outline to customers how it could also replace their ageing applications at the back end. It also eased its way into banking with products for loans administration and mortgage applications processing. By mid-2001, when the company's revenues climbed over the €20 million mark for the first time, it had installed its software at seven insurance firms and five banks, mostly in Britain and the Netherlands. In the same year Fineos made its debut in the US with the launch of a workflow system for disability claims management. This was a US-only product, designed for a particularly complex subset of the insurance industry. The company opened a sales and consulting office in Maine and announced the first sales of the disability claims system in early 2002.

In summary, Fineos started as a specialist in the front office and systematically fleshed out its product range until it had a comprehensive portfolio. After ten years in operation it reshuffled its offerings into six distinct packages, each based on the same set of software components. This meant that the company could not only present itself as a sector specialist in US-style disability claims, but also in life assurance, pensions administration, general insurance, banking and loans processing. The front- or back-office modules of each package could be installed together or on their own. And if necessary they could co-exist with CSC's systems.

The emphasis on vertical markets was a throwback to earlier years. But the way that Fineos stalked its way into the heartland of insurance applications was something new. Fineos set a precedent for how to develop a software business in generation five, then benefited from the revival in industry-specific packages.

Chapter 9

THE NETWORKING STORY

Cannes Do

The Palais des Festivals on the seafront in Cannes is best known as the home of the film festival that takes place at the start of every summer. The climate in the Mediterranean city is cooler and wetter in February, but the conference complex can get pretty hectic when the mobile networking industry comes to town.

The building was full to capacity in February 2000 and the organisers of the GSM World Congress were turning away unregistered visitors. Network operators, equipment providers, software developers and a plethora of information service providers were trying to extend the World Wide Web into the mobile world. The industry wanted to drum up interest in the Wireless Application Protocol, but there were signs of trouble with this strategy. All these interest groups and their hangers-on converged on Cannes and the crowd inside the Palais swelled. Some of the more well-heeled participants had anticipated this crush and were conducting their business on yachts in the adjoining marina. The whole town was talking wireless.

At many IT industry conventions the real action takes place in the auditoria or the seminar rooms, while the exhibition area only gets busy during coffee breaks. The GSM congress was different. The promotional stands buzzed all day long. It was easy to forget that the venue was in the south of France. Judging by the accents, it could be Dublin. Irish companies had turned out in force.

By the turn of the century, indeed, this annual show had become a favourite showcase for Ireland's software developers. As a rule, this community performed much more effectively on technical committees than in exhibition halls. The GSM event in Cannes was a striking exception.

The attendees in 2000 included a number of new companies created by old hands. Network365 was the latest brainchild of Isocor veterans Andy DeMari, Raomal Perera and Denis Hennessy. Networking consultant Robert Baker had recently launched Xiam with Hugh O'Donoghue, Warren Buckley and a bucketload of venture capital. Another start-up, Anam Wireless Internet Solutions, was headed by Mike Brady, who had worked for Siemens' SSE subsidiary. Directory enquiries company Conduit had branched into software and introduced a WAP edition of its directory enquiry application at Cannes. Jinny Software, led by a former paging company chief from the Lebanon and a product engineer from Irish GSM operator Eircell, made its first public appearance at the exhibition.

Microcellular Systems, a Tralee company formed in 1999 through a management buyout from ADC Telecommunications, was running demonstrations on the concourse in front of the Palais. It showed a compact mobile networking and switching infrastructure that it had scaled down to fit inside a van. Norkom Technologies unveiled an industry-specific version of its Alchemist analytical software that assisted mobile network operators to study customer behaviour patterns and to utilise the findings when they introduced new services. The GSM Association, an industry body with headquarters in Dublin, ran presentations in the conference theatres. Add in the Irish representatives of international companies like Logica, Tellabs, Lucent, Motorola, Tecnomen and CMG Telecommunications, various consultants and entrepreneurs researching new business ideas and the Irish presence at the congress was palpable.

In terms of the number of companies, the mobile communications brigade made up the largest subgroup in the software industry in 2000. This shift of emphasis made sense in an international context. The buyers of corporate applications had put their fingers on the pause button. Web applications development had been tarnished by the failures of many online service companies. The one place where technology was advancing rapidly and people seemed willing to spend real money was in mobile communications. The handsets were changing all the time and the operators were willing to experiment with new services — as long as they were not expected to take much of a financial risk.

What was surprising, though, was the speed at which the software products industry had reorganised itself around wireless applications and descended in such force on Cannes. Some of the companies in the new wave were headed by telecommunications industry veterans. Most, however, came from other parts of the software spectrum, from backgrounds in payment processing, customer relationship management or financial trading systems.

The agility shown by these software companies and developers was not unprecedented. In earlier years one of the strongest clusters in Irish software had also been forced to evolve or die. These were the developers who had honed their skills in networking standards that the internet swept away.

X.men and X.women

Systems Network Architecture (SNA) belonged to IBM. Introduced in 1974 to provide data transfers between host computers and terminals, SNA expanded over the next decade to support communications among the various computer families in its portfolio. Other manufacturers also released communications protocols for their own systems. By the mid-1980s, however, customers were pressing the industry for vendor-independent standards, so that mixed collections of computer brands and architectures could communicate. The International Organisation for Standardisation took up the challenge in a project known as Open System Interconnection (OSI).

The seven-layer OSI model not only defined all the elements of computer connectivity and information exchange, its application layer also set out the procedures for handling specific tasks like data transfer on the factory floor or document formatting in an office. By the end of the 1980s OSI was a framework for dozens of interrelated standards, such as X.25

for packet switching, X.400 for electronic mail, X.435 for trading documents, FTAM for file transfers and MAP for manufacturing automation.

The European Commission was particularly enthusiastic about OSI and its research programmes included projects that fleshed out pieces of the model. The Commission also supported multi-vendor networking demonstrations. The 1990 CeBIT show in Hannover, for example, spotlighted intercontinental messaging, showing how X.400 services in Germany, Japan and the US could route messages across different computer systems, public networks and time zones. This exercise was co-ordinated by the 50-company EurOSInet consortium and the demonstrators at CeBIT included members of two research groups from Ireland — the Nixdorf R&D centre in Dublin and Retix Ireland in Dun Laoghaire. The Nixdorf group had worldwide marketing responsibilities for OSI applications, while the Retix operation built products based on different elements of the OSI model. In another section of CeBIT that year Baltimore Technologies was showing two X.400 products — its Sitric message management centre and its Dictum test tool. Both had grown out of a long-running relationship between the Dublin company and Jutland Telephone in Denmark.

OSI development in the late 1980s provides a rare example of Irish companies and Irish-based branches of international corporations working in the same fields and interacting with each other at a technical level. ICL's information technology centre in Leopardstown took on X.400 software projects and contributed to interoperability standards for text and multimedia documents. Digital Equipment's subsidiaries were involved in the company's OSI projects in Europe. Ericsson and the state-owned network operator, Telecom Éireann, created Broadcom Éireann Research as a joint venture. Ericsson Systems Expertise built a portfolio of OSI-related technology-based training packages. CBT Systems brought out a similar suite called Openlink. And when the Nixdorf centre in Dublin came under the control of Siemens, its OSI activities expanded into e-mail directories, data communications systems for factories and electronic data interchange among trading partners.

The ranks of the OSI protocol specialists swelled steadily. The X.men and X.women who built products and applications on the network standard became a distinct cluster inside Irish software.

Retix was the epicentre of OSI networking. Anyone with a passing interest in the communications standard soon encountered the company's posters — densely populated maps of the seven-layer OSI universe with colour-coded ellipses to represent the X-prefixed specifications and connecting lines to explain how they related to each other. No graphic artists were employed to produce these charts. They were designed by Andy DeMari, who had founded Retix in 1985 in southern California. The company developed a selection of software products that implemented OSI standards on computer terminals. It subsequently introduced OSI migration products that enabled users to run OSI applications on non-OSI networks. It sold these engines to computer manufacturers and other equipment vendors. According to Raomal Perera, who joined Retix in 1987, it embraced emerging network standards in the same way that Iona latched onto Corba middleware in the following decade.

The company set up its European software development and support centre in 1987 with an initial team of 14, including ten graduates straight out of college. This operation in Dun Laoghaire was headed by Fergus O'Connell, who had led the software team at CPT in Ovens and subsequently worked for ICL.

It started well, developing a product based on the OSI common management information protocol. This generated a steady revenue stream for the company, which then transferred an X.400 development project to the Irish group. According to Perera, this initiative had previously run into problems in the US and the young team in Dun Laoghaire lacked the experience to turn it around. The gaps in its management ability and technical knowledge were exposed. "We totally underestimated the size and complexity of the task," he admits.

Nonetheless, when the Irish software industry was at its lowest ebb in the late 1980s, Retix was an uncommonly vibrant place. Its staff worked on advanced technologies and contributed to industry consortia. Some were organised into a professional services unit which developed products for larger vendors. The company interacted much more closely with the Irish universities than other US firms, awarding scholarships for final-year student projects and hiring a fresh batch of graduates each summer. Like CPT some years earlier, Retix became a springboard for future industry leaders, such as Raomal Perera, Openet Telecom cofounder Declan Conway and Triona Mullane, who became chief technology officer for Anam.

By the end of 1990 the headcount in Dun Laoghaire had risen to more than 60, but it dropped thereafter. Andy DeMari established Isocor in February 1991, planning to sell software packages to users instead of to computer makers and to focus on messaging applications rather than the complete OSI spectrum. Raomal Perera headed the new development team, which soon included 20 former Retix employees. Shortly afterwards Fergus O'Connell and two of the other senior managers from Retix launched an OSI consulting and training company, Synaptics, which lasted until 1995. Another batch of Retix staff migrated to Euristix.

Their former employer underwent a sharp decline in the 1990s. Retix missed opportunities to grow its e-mail software business, opting instead to develop network equipment and finding itself ill-equipped to compete against Cisco. The company split in the middle of the decade. The OSI part of the business was renamed Telegenics, renamed a second time as Vertel, and changed its focus to middleware for telecommunications operators. The Dun Laoghaire office took on responsibility for standards-based air-to-ground communications for the aviation industry. The depleted operation was sold to a start-up firm, Airtel ATN, in 1998. Xelas Software bought the remnants of the Vertel business in the US six years later.

Isocor, whose name was an acronym for International Standards Open Communications Resources, succeeded Retix as the leading centre of OSI expertise in Ireland. "We were like religious zealots when we set up Isocor," Raomal Perera says. "The early 1990s was a great time to set up a company. Iona was the only other company doing greenfield development. We were able to attract high-quality engineers. It was ingrained in people that if they could work with the leading technology, it would set them up for their future careers".

Although Isocor was registered in California, the company in its early years carried out all development and support, packaging and order processing in Ireland. Potential investors objected to DeMari's choice of location. Financiers who had supported his previous ventures refused to back a company whose intellectual property resided outside America. Isocor nonetheless raised $7 million in its first two years, finding as much of this money in Europe as in the US. Most of the software developer's executives were based in California and in 1995 the *Los Angeles Business Journal* ranked it as the fastest-growing private company in LA County. But Isocor's sales were always skewed towards Europe.

There were other ways in which DeMari's latest vehicle behaved more like an Irish business than an American one. Its developers in Dublin made technical decisions instead of waiting for instructions from California. Isocor used Irish customer installations as trial sites for new products. And at a time when other firms were granting equity to Forbairt in exchange for financial support, Isocor requested the same facility from IDA Ireland, the agency that dealt with international companies. The IDA duly agreed to buy a stake in the e-mail application specialist.

Although its original mission was to bring X.400 e-mail to the masses, Isocor evolved into a supplier of high-end messaging engines. It pushed its products up the performance scale and concentrated on the needs of larger enterprises and service providers. Then the spread of the TCP/IP stack and other internet standards disrupted its strategy.

Much of the communications software industry had long regarded TCP/IP as a temporary phenomenon that would wither away as the OSI model matured. Most of the Irish universities, therefore, ran networking courses based on OSI, even though their internal computing services were installing internet connections. One of the world's pioneers of internet communications, indeed, came out of Irish academia. In 1985 Dennis Jennings took a sabbatical from University College Dublin to work on a project at the National Science Foundation in the US. This early implementation of the internet protocol enabled researchers to access supercomputers over an inter-institutional network. Academic and industrial researchers embraced TCP/IP in the following years. The standard was closely associated with the Unix operating system, but proved particularly good at linking different computing environments. Internet e-mail also had distinct advantages over X.400, including a far better address structure. Up to the early 1990s, though, commercial traffic on the internet was discouraged and service providers required new customers to sign an undertaking that they would respect its research-oriented ethos. Business users were therefore the last group to accept the internet. But they migrated en masse in the 1990s, especially when the World Wide Web was added to the applications on offer.

When Isocor saw the impact of internet e-mail, Andy DeMari set up a separate development group in the US to produce internet versions of its applications. The first of these appeared in 1996. Isocor underwent an initial public offering that year and listed its stock on Nasdaq. The company's revenues climbed above $26 million in 1996, but never returned to this peak. The Dublin office eventually got to work on the internet products. It also became more deeply involved in directory software, collaborating with a group in ICL and introducing products that bridged the OSI and internet worlds. As the years passed, though, Isocor looked increasingly isolated at the top end of the mail server trade.

In the second half of the 1990s the balance of power in the communications industry shifted from product companies to service providers. Isocor tried to grow a service capability, but also sent out signals that it was interested in being acquired by a bigger player. Names like Microsoft, Netscape and Novell cropped up in discussions, but the company was eventually bought in 1999 by Critical Path. Based in central San Francisco, this two-year-old venture supplied managed e-mail services to internet service providers and enterprises. Like other service firms in the dotcom era, Critical Path had achieved an inflated stock market valuation and gone on an acquisition spree. It agreed to pay $287 million for Isocor in an all-stock transaction. By the time the deal closed, the price of Critical Path shares had risen and Isocor was valued at $450 million. Andy DeMari marked the end of the venture by having a star named after Isocor.

Isocor's X.400 applications continued to generate revenue right up to the end of its existence. But the OSI model faded rapidly as the world took to the internet. Ireland never produced a pool of internet tool companies in the same way as it had a discernible OSI cluster. The software products industry adjusted to the internet in a different way. Development companies availed of the core technologies, most of which had originated in the universities, using these to web-enable just about every application on the market.

The 1990s opened with a show of strength by the OSI products brigade. But the decade closed with clusters of communications software development in two very different areas — mobile applications and telecommunications network management. In each of these fields the foundations had been laid by a single company that, like Isocor, aimed high and sold out at a premium price.

The Parallel Ascents of Euristix and Aldiscon

Michael Purser's company, Chaco Computer Consultants, was part-owner of Baltimore Technologies when the communications software firm was launched in 1984. Three years later Chaco assumed full control of Baltimore. Purser became chairman of the company and combined the two organisations under the Baltimore name. He was one of the few computing academics who involved themselves in commercial ventures during generation two. But his philosophy was that software companies should be self-financing and always live within their means. He liked consulting projects and research contracts because the revenue streams were stable and predictable. He also understood the way that the European Commission ran its research programmes.

Jim Mountjoy, as managing director of the restructured Baltimore, held a very different view of the company's potential. By the late 1980s its annual revenues had grown to about $1.5 million. At any time, however, most of its business came from one big project. When each of these contracts was completed, Baltimore walked away and got stuck into the next one. Mountjoy believed that it could build something more sustainable.

The company had recruited graduates whose competence and self- confidence impressed him. He wanted to capitalise on their abilities. He wanted Baltimore to take more risks. He wanted to break away from the fiscal conservatism that Michael Purser imposed.

The chairman and the chief executive disagreed on one issue after another. By 1989 they were even having rows about the heating system in the Baltimore office. Jim Mountjoy decided to quit after Purser blocked the hiring of two experienced software engineers, because he was unwilling to pay fees to a recruitment agency. Around the same time, however, network operator Telecom Éireann approached Baltimore and signalled its interest in acquiring or investing in the firm. Mountjoy held back from submitting his resignation in the hope that Telecom might buy it out.

In December 1989 the Baltimore board of directors formally rejected Telecom's proposals. Jim Mountjoy resigned. He spent the early months of the new year raising money and obtained more than $160,000 to set up a new venture that would follow the route that he had wanted Baltimore to take. Tom McGovern and Dennis Jennings chipped in at the inception of Euristix. System Dynamics, as a company, also invested in the start-up, but University College Dublin turned down an invitation to join the backers. The new firm was officially launched in April 1990. Its name was both a pun on "heuristics" and a signifier that it aimed to be the best of its breed in Europe.

Aldiscon Information, which was two years older than Euristix, was another newcomer with an interesting pedigree. It started as an offshoot of Murray Telecommunications Group, a company built on cable-laying contracts for public networks. Group founder Jay Murray invited two former associates to officiate at a reception to launch Aldiscon in February 1988. One was Albert Reynolds, the future Taoiseach, who had accelerated state spending in telecommunications as a government minister a decade earlier. The second was Tom Byrnes, a former chief executive of Telecom Éireann who had moved to Litel Communications, a long-distance carrier in the US. This was a reunion with a meaning. The business and political establishment that had fixed the phones in Ireland was making a statement. Now that the trenches had been dug and the fibre optic lines were laid, the time was right to begin cutting code for communications software.

Euristix, under Jim Mountjoy's leadership, and Aldiscon, which was headed by Gilbert Little, grew up side by side. Both started as service businesses and transformed themselves into product developers. The product strategies in both companies were shaped by their technical directors. Joe Cunningham in Aldiscon and Bryan Alton at Euristix channelled employees' skills into emerging technologies. The first focused on wireless messaging, while the second specialised in telecommunications network management. Both were uncharted territories for Irish software at the start of the 1990s, but Aldiscon's Telepath short messaging software and Euristix's Raceman network management package opened doors for dozens of other firms in associated areas. Both companies set the template for software development in generation three — Aldiscon was arguably more influential because of its higher public profile. Finally, both were acquired by international corporations when they were nine years old. And these transactions made the founders and shareholders wealthy.

Early on, indeed, Euristix and Aldiscon considered a merger. Gilbert Little contacted Jim Mountjoy soon after the formation of Euristix and suggested that they combine their talents. Mountjoy turned down this approach, but the companies maintained regular contact and a mutually supportive relationship evolved. In 1994, for example, they formed a joint venture called Contrenet to arrange temporary staff placements inside other companies, mainly in the US. This sort of contracting was the core business for both companies in their early years. Assignments from established manufacturers and operators ensured that they did not need to borrow money, while giving them time to research and select opportunities for product development.

What really set this pair of companies apart from their contemporaries, however, was the way that they understood the telecommunications services industry. Telco software was always different from networking software. Telecommunications had its own rules and conventions, its own relationships and dependencies, its own technical leaders and market influencers. Until the 1980s voice telephony was largely a government function and most of the technology came from vendors with good political connections. Large countries had enterprises, often described as national champions, that supplied the network infrastructure to the operators. In Ireland the big contracts had gone to corporations, most notably Ericsson and Alcatel, that had been willing to set up branch plants in provincial locations.

The telecommunications technology business had opened up by the time that Aldiscon and Euristix got going. The operators had expanded far beyond basic voice services into data services and mobile networks. And it had become much easier for the equipment makers to sell internationally. It was still extremely difficult, though, for software companies to get access to operators outside their own countries. According to Jim Mountjoy, Bryan Alton had a special talent for conceiving products that the big technology vendors would buy and implement, while Joe Cunningham at Aldiscon had a similar knack for product designs that would appeal directly to operators.

Aldiscon's technical leader had worked as a telecommunications engineer at Nortel and STC Telecommunications. Cunningham had learned how the industry worked by observing their sales strategies. He had also tracked the deliberations behind the 1987 memorandum of understanding that established Groupe Speciale Mobile (GSM) as the underlying technology for digital mobile communications in Europe. The GSM standard was designed to support data services as well as voice communications. Joe Cunningham was aware that no other company had produced a robust message management system based on the specification. Aldiscon set out to build one.

The Dublin company showed its hand for the first time at the International Telecommunication Union's Telecom convention in Geneva in 1991. Aldiscon unveiled a pilot version of a Short Message Service Centre (SMSC) with which operators could offer a basic data transfer service to their customers. Telecom 91 was supposed to be a launchpad for GSM. Aldiscon was one of the first firms to demonstrate the messaging functions that later became known as "texting". The company went on to launch its Telepath SMSC in late 1992. The system stored short messages, routed them to the correct recipient and confirmed the deliveries. It proved that GSM networks would do more than carry speech. When Aldiscon released Telepath there was still no GSM service in Ireland — just an ageing and rather expensive analogue network. No one was talking yet about mobile communications as a mass medium or about the potential impact of texting on youth culture. If short messaging was ever discussed, it was usually as a perk for corporate chiefs or a method for millionaires to keep a watch on the changing values of their stocks.

When the service providers became more aware of short messaging, Telepath was ready for implementation. It soon became the most widely used SMSC. Aldiscon learned that it could sell the system to rival operators in the same market by selling add-on products or custom modifications that would differentiate one company's text messaging service from another. It found a way of introducing its technology into the US, which had not adopted the European network standard, by developing a messaging system for the clearing houses that managed the interconnections among mobile networks.

Former Enterprise Ireland official Tom Weymes attributes Aldiscon's success to Joe Cunningham's early grasp of the significance of short messaging and to the clarity of his vision. "They never put a foot wrong until they sold the company," he says. Weymes supported Aldiscon in 1994, when the company wanted to raise money for an expansion plan. It applied to the board of Forbairt for an investment of about $3 million — an exceptionally large sum for the state agency to give to any native software firm. The board approved the investment and acquired a ten per cent shareholding in Aldiscon. By 1997 more than 100 wireless operators had bought Aldiscon messaging centres, often installing them at more than one site, and the company's annual sales had risen to $45 million.

The company was sold for $85 million in July 1997 to Logica, a British software and consulting firm. The new owner retained the SMSC organisation in Dublin for more than five years, changing its name to Logica Mobile Networks. It was finally wound down after Logica

merged with CMG in late 2002 to create an Anglo-Dutch services conglomerate. Logica Mobile Networks had been a direct competitor to a
CMG unit that was based in the Netherlands but also ran a satellite development team in Cork. The companies had created very similar product sets, but CMG was deemed to have produced better multimedia
software. The former Aldiscon operation lost out. It probably suited the
new entity, LogicaCMG, that it could rationalise its mobile messaging
activities by laying off staff in Ireland instead of in its home countries.
The decision, however, sent shockwaves through the communications
software cluster in Dublin. Hundreds of developers had passed through
Aldiscon and Logica over the years. To them, the pull-out seemed like a
death in the family.

The plotline of the Euristix story was broadly similar to Aldiscon's.
In 1990 Jim Mountjoy and Bryan Alton drew up a business plan to develop a product in an area where the company had appropriate experience — they just did not know what the area would be! In the meantime
Euristix supplied consultants to the Irish government, the European
Commission and commercial clients. It also worked on fixed price development projects, producing communications protocol stacks for other
companies' products. Soon, the majority of this development work was
coming from the US. The company also promoted its services in Europe
and Israel and later placed one of its managers in Japan, but it got the
best response to its proposition in America. By 1995, when Euristix was
a 50-person organisation, its client list in the US included telecommunication equipment vendors, internetworking systems developers, communications software firms and computer makers. The company opened an
office in California that year, locating some its engineers there as well as
account managers.

Euristix also introduced its first product prototype in 1995. The company's contracting work had deepened its knowledge of large-scale telecommunications switching and of shortcomings in the available tools for
managing the network infrastructure. Its first attempts to develop network management software addressed the high end of the market. According to Jim Mountjoy, this attracted the interest of engineers in the

big equipment companies, but it also ran up against the realities of telecommunications industry politics. Euristix was floating ideas that
breached the proprietary preserves of vendors like Ericsson, Alcatel and
Lucent. Potential customers declined to talk to the company. Euristix
examined the obstacles and decided to design products that would suit
the equipment makers that were willing to deal with it — the challengers
rather than the incumbents. It targeted companies with niche technologies that wanted to expand their range, not the big names with the comprehensive portfolios. It kept the services business going as well and restructured its workforce into two business units.

The name of the Euristix product suite, Raceman, denoted its suit-
ability for rapid deployment. It enabled developers to build element
management systems for the transport and access equipment in telecommunications networks. Raceman spanned a variety of fixed line and
wireless technologies. Equipment vendors could configure the Euristix
toolkits to meet specific management requirements for their systems and
devices. Unlike most network management software, moreover, Raceman could be implemented on commodity computer hardware. It ran on
Microsoft operating systems.

Raceman was behind-the-scenes technology — something that was
fitted into someone else's system that was sold to support some other
company's service. Unlike Aldiscon, whose software could be seen in
action as text messaging spread, Euristix's products were delivered to
development labs and deals were struck without fanfare or publicity. The
recruitment of more engineers at the company's operations in Dun
Laoghaire and San Jose indicated, though, that the company was doing
well. By 1997 its headcount had risen to 130 and it claimed a client list
of more than 60 telecoms equipment vendors.

Fore Systems was the sort of customer that Euristix had in mind
when it chose how to position Raceman. Founded in 1990, Fore specialised in asynchronous transfer mode technology, developing switches,
adapters and software for high bandwidth computer networks and constantly broadening its capabilities by taking over smaller companies. By
the late 1990s the company's annual revenues had grown to more than

$500 million and it was targeting telecommunications and internet service providers as well as corporate networks. It had adapted its acquisition strategy to focus on what it called "the new public network".

In February 1999 Fore announced that it had bought Euristix for approximately $81 million worth of shares and stock options. Raceman would add significant management functions to its internet backbone switches. It also suited Fore that Euristix would no longer hire out engineers to help its rivals to design their products. It soon transpired, however, that the Pennsylvania company was itself a takeover target. Just two months after the Euristix deal, London-based General Electric Company announced an agreement to acquire Fore in a cash transaction. General Electric Company, which changed its name to Marconi in late 1999, paid a premium price for Fore, driving up the value of the shares that had been issued to buy Euristix to approximately $175 million. The former owners of the Dun Laoghaire firm could, moreover, convert their shares into cash much sooner than they had envisaged in February.

Euristix, it should be recalled, had paid its way into the product business by selling service contracts. It had never offloaded equity chunks to venture capitalists. Jim Mountjoy and Bryan Alton reaped the biggest rewards, followed by the initial backers of the company and by other individual investors who had contributed in the early years. As Euristix rolled out its Raceman products, moreover, the company had offered shares to its managers and employees to compensate them for the increased risks. Dozens of Euristix staff thus received financial windfalls from the acquisition of Fore.

Spending on telecommunications infrastructure declined after the turn of the century. The services industry suffered from too much capacity and too few customers. Network operators scaled down, merged or disappeared. The telecommunications equipment vendors battened down the hatches and told their acquisition departments to take it easy for a few years. Marconi, the new owner of the Euristix organisation, suffered more than most. A restructuring process in 2002 transferred most of the shares in the company to its major creditors. None of the other communications software developers in Ireland could now hope to achieve the sort of valuation that had been placed on Aldiscon and Euristix. But the success of these companies encouraged others to enter the sector. The number of firms kept expanding. Most tackled some aspect of mobile communications. Others opted to address the challenges and complexities of pricing and billing for network services.

The Billing Brigade

Around the end of the 1980s much of the talk at telecommunications industry events concerned the "intelligent network". With more and more digital technology in their infrastructure, the operators had realised that they could start offering a greater variety of services, targeting these at different groups of customers and pricing them at different levels. At this time the carriers were also coming under pressure to make their charges more transparent. In many cases their fee structures dated back to the years when networks were run by government departments and pricing was the prerogative of politicians. Increased competition, the spread of data services, the growth of mobile communications and the emergence of specialist information and transaction service providers transformed this old regime.

The service management tools that had served operators in the past were no longer adequate. The telcos installed more bandwidth, upgraded their switches and started to meter functions that had never been measured in the old days. They also needed better financial systems. Most carriers had previously written and maintained their own back office software or bought customer management applications from other network operators. When they went out to tender for more sophisticated billing and administration applications, another segment of the communications software business opened up.

By the second half of the 1990s independent software vendors were touting a bewildering array of applications and tools for fixed and mobile network operators. These were all designed to co-ordinate aspects of network planning and management with aspects of service pricing and customer billing. Different suppliers had different priorities. Some focused on mediation — the collection of traffic information for each customer from the various points around a network. Others specialised in the setting and administration of rating plans, contact centre services, revenue sharing among service providers or revenue assurance applications that trawled through billing records in search of errors or inconsistencies.

The participation of Irish developers in these areas became evident during generation four — the turn-of-the-century period when the majority of software start-ups were funded by external investors. The first visible projects, though, were in a small group of foreign-owned operations.

A group at EDS Ireland won a local contract to implement billing applications from a joint venture between Ericsson and Hewlett-Packard, then went on to become an international centre of expertise in this product set. Accuris, a Dublin-based software services venture part-owned by Telecom Éireann, also claimed special skills in the billing and mediation processes. The former Retix organisation in Dun Laoghaire, meanwhile, turned its attention to network interoperability and management information protocols. Saville Systems, a customer care and billing software supplier that had originated in Canada, opened a development centre in Galway in 1994 to work on its convergent billing platform. The senior management of the company was based in Boston, but when it listed its stock on Nasdaq in the following year, it designated Galway as an official headquarters. ADC Telecommunications bought Saville in 1999 and retained this operation.

Several Irish-owned ventures also surfaced around the turn of the century. Interconnect Billing Systems developed an inter-carrier settlement application for smaller operators — a system that produced bills for the traffic that came into their networks from other carriers and checked the accuracy of bills received from those partners. Sepro Telecom started up in 1997 in Dublin and Am-Beo was formed three years later in Galway by a development team drawn largely from Saville/ADC. Both firms focused on the rating part of the telecommunications billing process. Their rating engines offered operators more flexibility in the pricing of their services, enabling them to introduce more tailored discounts, incentive packages and special promotions. Cape Technologies developed RevenueOffice, which automated the checks and controls in carriers' administration systems and tracked down revenue leakages or billing mistakes. Another late 1990s start-up, Interactive Enterprise, tackled another aspect of customer service. Its founder, Tom Higgins, had previously worked for a cable TV service provider in Ireland and the company concentrated on provisioning and service activation software for cable network operators.

Barry Murphy moved into the telco applications business in 1999, when he became chief executive officer of a company that exemplified the capabilities and the flaws of generation four. After five years as National Software Director and three as the European representative of investor John Cullinane, he wanted to return to active management in the software development industry. He did so by taking charge of Openet Telecom.

This was a successor company to Openet International, which two Retix alumni, Declan Conway and Darragh Stokes, had established in the mid-1990s. The earlier firm distributed and supported other vendors' communications software, including a mediation application developed by ISR Global Telecom. In 1999 Openet raised $2.7 million from the Dublin-based Cross Atlantic Technology Fund, bought the rights to ISR's mediation technology and hired some of the most experienced software developers in town to expand its product offerings.

Barry Murphy was soon enthusing about the opportunities that mediation in general was creating for software vendors and that internet-related mediation in particular represented for Openet. This technology, he argued, held the key to transforming internet services from a business of flat fees and undifferentiated quality to one where tariffs could be based on bandwidth requirements, usage levels, performance guarantees or content delivery. Openet joined an industry consortium that planned to establish IP detail record standards and declared its intention to capture a significant share of the emerging market.

In retrospect, Murphy says that he was applying theories that he had come to believe in during his spells with the National Software Director-ate and with Cullinane. Openet, for example, kept its R&D group separate from its customer services department. It set out to target key influencers of industry opinion, such as the research departments of investment banks, in the hope that they would make the company better known. This strategy, he says, proved much more productive than participating in exhibitions. He concedes, though, that it was sometimes useful to book a room in a hotel next door to a major trade show and to hold discussions there.

He describes the first buyers of Openet's IP mediation software companies as "tier three companies". The mediation specialist broke into the top tier late in 2000 when a major US operator chose its Fusion-Works platform. AT&T Wireless selected this product to support the introduction of more data services and value-added services on its infrastructure. Openet was one of the four final contenders for this contract. According to Barry Murphy, the Dublin company won because it was able to respond within two weeks to 30 different scenarios put forward by the operator. "That's the thing I love about American companies," he says. "Even an AT&T Wireless will take a risk if they think that a company has the best technology. European companies, especially of a particular vintage, tend to be very conservative about your pedigree."

Openet's success at AT&T Wireless led other large operators to evaluate FusionWorks and the average value of the company's sales rose steadily. Big billing application suppliers and systems integration players approached it to discuss partnerships. By spring 2001 Openet had ten customers, annual revenues of approximately $10 million, more than 100 employees and a burning desire to raise a second round of external investment. It found a new backer later that year.

This time around the money came from the US — or, to be more accurate, from a fund established by Silicon Valley venture capital firm Benchmark Capital to invest in European companies. Benchmark Capital committed $20 million to Openet so that the company could accelerate its international expansion. As soon as the deal was announced, however, the new investor set about ousting the chief executive. In early 2002 the Openet board named John Rainger, who had been chief operating officer of Lucent Technologies software products group in the US, as the company's new CEO. Barry Murphy did not leave without a fight. A five-month stand-off followed, during which he brought his case to the Employment Appeals Tribunal. By the time he obtained a compensation package, the treatment that he had received from Benchmark was the talk of the industry.

Other chief executives of billing software companies lost their jobs after institutional investors put money into their companies. The senior management casualties reflected the tough environment for all companies that sold technology to telcos, but the circumstances varied from one case to another.

Sepro's co-founder Declan Ganter stepped down in 2001 when the company was having difficulty landing new business. After his US-born successor, Desmond Pieri, slimmed down the company's workforce, Sepro slowly expanded the customer base for its rating engine. The company's valuation, however, kept declining until 2003, when Openet acquired it and rebranded the rating product. At Am-Beo, where the investors included Intel Capital, CEO John Brady held on until early 2004. Here again the directors chose a new chief executive with industry experience in America.

Accuris underwent a change of ownership in 2002, when it was bought by a group of individuals previously associated with Aldiscon. It was also given a change in its mission. The company resurfaced as a specialist in lawful interception tools for internet service providers. It subsequently moved into mobile roaming applications.

Interconnect Billing went into liquidation in 2001. The company's assets were bought by Dennis Jennings, who had now become a frequent investor in technology firms, and Pa Nolan from online financial services group Fexco. They hired key members of the software vendor's team to form a new entity, IconX Solutions, which sold the billing applications as a managed service rather than a packaged product.

Barry Murphy remained in the communications software business after his departure from Openet. In 2003 he took charge at Netsure Telecom, another Dublin company with a software application for network operators. Netsure's Capman system assists telcos to map their forecasts of customer demand against data extracted from their network inventory and operations management systems. Murphy welcomes the calmer mood in the industry today compared with the frantic environment he experienced at Openet. "I like being in a start-up at this time," he says. "The pressure to grow in nanoseconds is gone."

The Mobile Gold Rush

The GSM mobile network standard was a spectacular success. In the aftermath of Telecom 91, and the pilot demonstrations in which Aldiscon participated, the standard's cross-border roaming capabilities made it popular in Europe. The first million users signed up by 1994. Five years later there were more than 200 million customers on GSM services and the specification had been adopted around the world. The user count rose over the one billion mark in early 2004.

This was a triumph of collaboration and committee work over the winner-takes-all dogfights that American corporations regard as normal. The global standard for digital mobile networks had come from Europe. So did most of the service providers' administration tools and the applications that their customers looked for when they realised that GSM was designed to carry data as well as speech. By the turn of the century the biggest cluster of development firms in the Irish software industry was writing applications for mobile networks. Some developed products for the network operators. Some extended enterprise information systems into the wireless world. Others focused on computing engines for the providers of mobile information and transaction services. In short, the late 1990s was a hectic time for communications software start-ups and more entered the fray in the early years of the new century.

These companies carried all the hallmarks of generation four. They sold software products and were wary of becoming dependent on service revenues. The mobile applications start-ups looked for external funding and some found that the lenders were willing to give them more money than they expected. In most cases the technical leaders had previously worked for more mature companies and wanted to get back into a smaller firm. The firms in the mobile cluster differed from their contemporaries, though, in their geographic priorities. Like the GSM standard itself, they targeted Europe first. Some entered the Asia-Pacific region as well. But North America seldom featured in their plans.

The mobile technology industry took its lead from the Nordic countries — the home of Nokia, Ericsson and the earliest adopters of every new consumer device and business application that worked without wires. Service providers and software developers tracked what was happening in Sweden and Finland on the assumption that new trends in these territories would be replicated across the rest of Europe in the following years.

Peter Bennett took charge of the Enterprise Ireland office in Stockholm in the late 1990s. It had been four years since he had had any contact with the software industry. He had become familiar with its abilities and shortcomings when he had compiled the Connect Ireland directories of information technology companies. When he moved into his new post, he was surprised to discover how much had changed, especially in communications software. In contrast with their predecessors, young firms with mobile applications had learned how to establish themselves in Scandinavia. In 1999 Bennett counted 30 Irish-owned developers that were active in the region. It seemed, he says, that there had been a seismic shift in the way software companies operated. The new contenders appeared to think of themselves as invincible.

Two of the companies in this wave were led by veterans of the Workmate project at CPT. Mike Brady founded Anam in 1999. This was one of many developers whose products delivered corporate information to employees over SMS services, but tried to set itself apart by adding systems for mobile operators. Within a few years it could claim technical leadership in WAP gateways and MMS gateways. Network365 was another 1999 start-up. Raomal Perera, under the tutelage of Andy DeMari, launched the company to develop mobile commerce applications. Its interests soon broadened to support different categories of networks and devices and gradually led the company deeper into transaction processing systems.

In 1999, according to Mike Brady, getting started was relatively easy if you had contacts. "There was money on the streets. And if you were well networked, there was evidence that you could be a player on the world stage," he says. The biggest problem for software entrepreneurs was staff recruitment. Companies, he says, had to accept that there were few top-flight graduates available for hire. They settled for personnel with lower qualifications and struggled to meet their productivity and quality targets. Raomal Perera encountered similar problems. "The disappointment for me at Network365 was our inability to attract good people for the right reasons," he says, "It was difficult to get people who wanted to do more than make a quick buck and leave. Everyone was in for the quick kill."

One of the regular set-pieces at the annual mobile congress in Cannes is an international awards ceremony run by the GSM Association. Network365 was named the best mobile application developer in 2002. By then the company was winning highly visible contracts in competition against much larger vendors. It made two major sales in 2002. One was a deal to supply Hutchison 3G with an "electronic wallet" system for payment processing. Hutchison planned to introduce this on its third-generation mobile networks in eight countries. The other involved a secure mobile payment service for NTT DoCoMo in Japan. In the following year Network365 acquired an American payments technology company and changed its name to Valista. The GSM Association gave its application developer prize to Valista in 2004. In addition, two of the three commendations in this category went to Dublin-based software firms. Macalla Software and Xiam also made the shortlist.

Macalla was the company set up in 1998 by former members of the Slingshot product group at Quay Financial Software. According to CEO Niall O'Cleirigh, the company saw Iona as its role model. Macalla's first applications were designed for banking and financial trading, because these were the areas where the founders had contacts. Dresdner Kleinwort Benson in Britain and Staalbankiers in the Netherlands soon became reference customers. Subsequently, though, the company diversified into payment systems and content delivery applications for network operators and enterprises outside the finance industry.

Xiam, like Anam, developed SMS gateways that used text alerts to extend companies' messaging systems beyond their computer networks. It tried to recruit network operators as resellers. Founder Robert Baker accepts that the company was one of many SMS gateway suppliers, but says that its Xiam Information Router stood out because it could be implemented without programmers. It was designed to enable users without technical knowledge to produce their own applications.

Aldiscon, meanwhile, had spawned a diaspora all of its own. Not only were there staff who left the company to set up new ventures; Gilbert Little also encouraged the formation of new business units inside Aldiscon. In one of these sideline initiatives the company acquired intellectual property rights to a network information system developed by Dublin-based operator Eircom. Aldiscon set up a unit to handle this product. The network information system business broke away after Logica bought the company and was restructured as Altion. Apion, meanwhile, started life as Aldiscon's satellite development unit in Belfast. It went independent in 1997 and developed gateway technology based on the Wireless Application Protocol. Apion was acquired in 1999 and subsequently became part of Openwave Systems. Following that transaction, however, Gilbert Little and his colleagues retained Apion's services division, renamed it Aepona and proceeded to grow another business with a "network operating system" gateway based on specifications from the Parlay Group. By 2004 Aepona had 140 employees and, with more than 20 live customers, claimed more gateway implementations based on this standard than any other vendor. The emergence of Apion and Aepona in Belfast from under the wing of a Dublin company was one of the few instances of cross-border synergy in the history of Irish software.

Many of the other mobile software vendors tried to apply the Aldiscon business formula — identifying new ways of using mobile networks and bringing products to market in time to win over the early adopters. At different times, the Irish communications applications bunch included subclusters of companies that connected private e-mail systems to public short messaging services, built security toolkits for mobile data or opened up the payment systems for online services to accommodate mobile customers with pre-paid phones. Whenever there was talk of a new type of service, hitherto unknown firms announced their intention to supply the enabling software. Several developers, for example, emerged simultaneously with alternative strategies for using mobile phones to pay parking fees.

The opportunities to be original were diminishing. Some observers detected signs of a throwback to the me-too products of the 1980s. Robert Baker, for example, argues that Irish communications software companies have generally been undistinguished in technical terms. They proved good, however, at making the most of their international sales opportunities. He credits the successes in the cluster to Enterprise Ireland and to the support structures that its international offices provided to software exporters.

Few of the mobile application development firms showed real staying power. Consider what happened to the attendees at the GSM World Congress in 2000. Within a year Jinny had been bought by Italy's Acotel Group and Microcellular Systems was absorbed into California-based InterWave Communications International. Tellabs and CMG subsequently axed their development groups in Ireland. Another batch of contenders was waiting to step into the spotlight. Companies like Agile, Alatto Technologies, Am-Beo, Cape Technologies, ChangingWorlds, Cibenix, ItsMobile and Selatra began to report international deals. By the middle of the decade, however, the flow of mobile software start-ups had flowed to a trickle.

There were only two first-timers at the Cannes show in 2004. One of these, Saadian, was a four-year-old outfit whose e-mail-to-SMS gateway product was already widely used in Ireland. The second, OpenMind Networks, owed its existence to the dismantling of the former Aldiscon organisation by LogicaCMG. Some of the employees that the SMS specialist had made redundant regrouped at OpenMind, where they devised new ways for operators to expand the range and improve the performance of existing messaging services. This was a start-up with an emphasis on continuity.

It was evident that the mobile gold rush was over. There had been surprisingly few start-ups led by developers who worked for Logica in Dublin before its owner pulled the plug. Mobile communications had become a mature technology. Operators were giving preference to established vendors and taking a more cautious approach to software purchases. It was harder for product developers to find new niches. The available opportunities involved plugging minor gaps instead of creating new markets. By 2004 some industry analysts were forecasting a decline in SMS traffic — the area where many of the Irish software developers had positioned themselves.

Institutional investors, meanwhile, were focusing on other software categories and on other industries. The large venture capital firms were no longer touting for mobile software projects and generation four companies that had benefited from their largesse in the past discovered that fundraising had become much more difficult.

Some software vendors disappeared. Others underwent major overhauls. Anam was restructured in 2003 and a new management team of former Logica executives was drafted in. Agile, which offered payment processing services for mobile network operators, was acquired by MoreMagic Holdings, a developer whose technologies had been incorporated into Agile's applications. Cork company Comnitel Technologies was merged into WatchMark from Bellevue, Washington. Comnitel had raised €30 million from institutional investors between 1998 and 2002 to develop fault management and service assurance systems for mobile networks. Over those four years, however, it identified only one customer in Ireland and none outside the country. It also abandoned the fault management product because operators kept postponing purchase decisions. The investors kept supporting its work on quality of service issues and eventually steered the Cork operation into WatchMark. This gave it access to a customer base of more than 100 wireless service providers.

According to Niall O'Cleirigh at Macalla, there are still too many small companies in Ireland developing mobile applications and only the larger ones are likely to survive. This sounds like the way that the financial applications business consolidated, so that a small group of established companies now supplies the core technologies. The opportunities for new entrants are limited to specialist applications on the fringes of the market.

The mobile cluster is already consolidating. The pace of change is also slowing down. And some of the developers are seeking new business that does not depend on GSM networks. After Network365 evolved into Valista it took to describing itself as a payments software company rather than a producer of mobile commerce systems.

Just as mobile communications superseded middleware as the central interest of the Irish industry, the mobile software companies of generation four are now showing the signs of middle age.

Chapter 10

DISCOVERING AMERICA

Knocking on Doors

John Carolan was more successful at selling Glockenspiel's products than anyone that he employed in a sales job. His way of obtaining orders was as unorthodox as everything else he did.

Declan McCarthy, one of the original investors in the company, accompanied Carolan on one of his scouting expeditions around the business parks off Route 128 in Massachusetts. "John was the Jesus freak. I was the suit," he recalls. McCarthy watched in awe as his charismatic, precise-speaking colleague found customers for Glockenspiel's software.

Marketing types might describe the process as cold calling. John Carolan would walk into an office building and ask which companies in the neighbourhood were developing software. He narrowed down the list of names to those with an interest in C++. Then he strolled up to the reception desk at each target firm and asked if he could speak to someone technical. As soon as he began to talk to junior staff, they passed him over to their superiors. Carolan usually ended up in conversation with a senior technologist with whom he could debate the finer details of object-oriented development. He came away from these unscheduled meetings of minds with product orders.

This was a classic demonstration of personal networking. The economic relationship between Ireland and the US has always been based on personal networking. But this display did not involve tax concessions or appeals to ethnicity — even in Massachusetts where Irish influences are strong. John Carolan exploited his knowledge of software engineers and their subcultures. He understood their fascination with new design and development concepts, their preferences and prejudices, their sense of a professional hierarchy and the one-upmanship that comes from mastering the latest tools.

Other companies back in Ireland heard how Glockenspiel was operating in America and learned from its approach. Iona achieved its early success by modifying the Carolan method so that it could take advantage of the internet. CBT Systems and Euristix applied their own variations in California. These firms and others broke down the barriers to trading in the US that had scared off their predecessors.

Generation two companies saw the US as distant, expensive and difficult to penetrate. Technologies took time to cross the Atlantic. IBM, for example, launched its original PC in the US in 1981, but waited until early 1983 before introducing it to Europe. The technology traffic flow accelerated in the following decade and Irish software developers became more confident about selling into the US.

At the start of 1996 about 20 software firms had set up sales and customer support offices in America. The number doubled in the next two years. By 1998 companies like Iona, Mentec and Trintech were running multiple offices in North America. In 2000 Enterprise Ireland reported that 70 software companies were active in the US and that half of all the exports by Irish-owned software developers were going there. The value of this business was reported as €460 million in 2000 and over €550 million in the following year. It should be noted, though, that a high proportion of the transatlantic exports always came from a small group of companies.

When Barry Murphy became National Software Director in the early 1990s, more than half of the software exports were going to Britain. He encouraged the companies to sell into the US which, unlike the UK, acts as a springboard to the rest of the world. Older companies like Dillon Technology, GC McKeown and Systems Software put so much of their energies into the British market that they ended up with localised products that could not be sold anywhere else. Developers that proved themselves in America, in contrast, found it much easier to increase their sales in Europe. According to Murphy, American companies are more open than others to buy software from small vendors. But they have to establish their credentials in the US. Previous achievements in other parts of the world count for nothing.

The software export surge in the 1990s owed nothing to the philanthropy of Irish-Americans. Nor did it have much to do with emigration. Irish computing graduates never swarmed into Silicon Valley by the planeload and there have been few cases of returned expatriates setting up development companies. Graduate migration to the US — including illegal emigration — did, indeed, run at a high level in the 1980s. But these movements contributed very little to the subsequent improvement in software export capability. The people who made the sales take off had previously learned hard lessons inside generation two software companies.

Tony McGuire, for example, recalls that Insight Software found it tough to establish its credibility when it set up sales offices in New York, Chicago and Los Angeles in the early 1980s. Prospective customers looked blank when they heard that the company had developed its product in Dublin. This was an era when it never occurred to them that someone might try to sell them a non-American product. In contrast, McGuire says, being Irish was a distinct advantage in the late 1990s when the US press was full of positive stories about the Irish economy.

CBT Systems was another early entrant to the US. Pat McDonagh says that the company decided to target America after landing a once-off order from NCR for its Protocol 90 telecommunications courseware. Quay Financial Software also scored early transatlantic successes. As a trading room software vendor, however, it never concerned itself with the continent beyond Manhattan. From Quay's perspective, North America meant Wall Street.

Irish software suppliers that have sold products into North America often say that the process was made easier by their familiarity with the way that US corporations operated inside Ireland. Some also suggest that the absence of a language barrier gave them an advantage over development firms from other countries. It may be more accurate to say that Irish companies were more willing than other European software firms to take on an American persona, especially if they accepted funding from US investors or hired US executives. In some instances the businesses were eventually driven from the US and Ireland became a back-office location where the coders lived. The larger e-learning firms, for example, straddled the Atlantic in this way. Firms from other European countries also went through this transition, but Irish companies seemed to have fewer reservations about the changes in their identity. Israeli technology developers, incidentally, had even fewer qualms and routinely wrapped themselves in the stars and stripes.

Some vendors suggest that US industrialists accepted Irish software because they did not see it as a threat to its own interests. The individual developers were too small to challenge the status quo. That made it easier to sell their products. On the other hand, the software buyers knew that small firms might not be able to provide the technical support that they would require.

Brian Caulfield promoted Peregrine Systems' credit card chargeback processing software in North America and won four customers without setting up an office there. The company, he recalls, had a workforce of 50 people and $1 million on its balance sheet. By the standards of the Irish software industry this profile represented solidity. In the US, Caulfield discovered, it made the users wonder whether the company was going to be viable.

Paddy Holahan was one of the first Irish software developers to set up a sales operation in America. He did it on the cheap. East Coast Software was a young Dublin firm that developed PC utilities. Holahan and Alan Kilduff set up the business in 1986 while they were still in the third year of a computer science degree course. They modelled their company on Intelligence Ireland and on Borland, which had sold its Sidekick package for just $79 but still managed to make a fortune. According to Holahan they wanted to play at the cool end of the software industry and thought that they had nothing in common with the "stuffy old men" who sold applications for minicomputers. East Coast produced a fast PC file transfer utility called 5:30. Holahan was convinced that this would sell in huge quantities if the price was kept low. America was where bulk sales could be made. In 1990 Holahan decided to try rustling up new business in the States. He was still young enough to qualify for a youth fare on the westbound flight.

Atlanta became Holahan's base. Once the company had an American address, nobody needed to know that the coast mentioned in the company's name was the one with Dublin Bay in the middle. Holahan started to place advertisements for 5:30 in US magazines. He pushed the software into retail chain stores that had never previously put a European product on their shelves. He went to meetings of the Southeast Software Association where he could speak with the chief executives of large software firms. "You can never be seen as foreign," he observes. "You have got to be local. There was never a problem that we were developing software in Ireland as long as I was living there." East Coast sold more than three million licences for 5:30, although the company never knew how many copies were actually in use.

Paddy Holahan never planned on staying in Atlanta for long. After five years he wanted to return home. He claims, indeed, that he became the first person to buy a house in Ireland over the internet when he made arrangements to come back in 1995. East Coast was wound up after he returned, mainly because the founders disagreed on what should happen next. They decided to split the assets and go separate ways.

In 1996, when he was based in Dublin again, Paddy Holahan attended a seminar on selling software into the US. The keynote speaker, consultant Mary Cryan, had written a guidebook on the subject called *New Pioneers* and told the audience that companies should plan to raise $1 million if they wanted to enter the market. Holahan dissented from this view. "I did it for $5,000!" he informed the meeting.

Observation Posts in the Valley

Euristix landed its first substantial development contracts from the US in 1993. They came from Stratacom and from the American wing of Ascom Timeplex. These projects provided the company with the type of work that chief executive Jim Mountjoy wanted to win. He knew that most of the innovations in network technology were happening in the US and he felt that the best strategy for Euristix was to assist the smaller players there to bring new products to market. There was, however, a catch in the first contracts. Stratacom and Ascom Timeplex were direct competitors and the tasks that they allocated to the Dun Laoghaire firm were uncomfortably similar. Mountjoy had heard many scare stories about projects that went wrong and the scale of the damages that contractors could incur. If either client believed that Euristix had transferred technology to the other, the litigation could become a nightmare.

Jim Mountjoy put protective measures into place. He ensured that the two project teams worked in different physical locations. Euristix drew up undertakings that the contracts would be kept totally separate and lodged letters to that effect with a legal practice. In the months that followed, Stratacom and Ascom both heard that Euristix was also working for the other firm. Mountjoy received phone calls from both customers' lawyers. In each case he said that any development that Euristix was doing for the other company was under a non-disclosure agreement, but he explained the steps that he had taken to avoid conflicts of interest. This satisfied the legal advisers.

"The lesson was that we were doing the right thing and could articulate that we were doing the right thing," Mountjoy says. Euristix had not only proved to its clients that it understood how American corporations operated. It had also proved the point to itself.

The skills that Euristix could provide to network equipment companies were in short supply and the company's American business snowballed. In 1995 it set up an office in California and moved a dozen of its employees there. "I wanted us to do as much of the work as possible from Ireland and resisted setting up an office in the US until we had scale," Mountjoy says. The new operation would liaise with the company's American clients and seek new projects. It would also enable Euristix to track the day-to-day politics of Silicon Valley at first hand. The company also thought that California might provide it with a stepping stone into Asia.

IT Design also opened an observation post in the valley. It settled on the west coast one year earlier than Euristix. The company had been launched in 1990 by John Hearne and Ronan Rooney. They had developed an internal reporting system for Apple Computer Sales in Dublin and believed that they could improve the information analyses in other organisations as well. IT Design offered consultancy and development services and won a series of projects that involved graphical user interfaces and object-oriented programming.

The company's first product, Viper, followed in early 1993. Designed to run on the Apple Macintosh, this client-server toolset offered fast access to items of information in different areas of a large computer network. According to John Hearne, more than 50 of Apple's biggest international customers bought Viper. This success prompted IT Design to set up a US office near Apple's headquarters in Silicon Valley. The company recruited local staff to handle its relationship with the hardware maker and to promote Viper in corporate America. It implemented the software on more computer platforms and launched a single-purpose version, Directory Xpress, that co-ordinated the internal phone lists in large organisations.

Viper, Hearne admits, led the company into a cul de sac. IT Design could not build a sales channel. Viper was designed for the large corporations that software resellers avoided because their purchasing cycles were too long. "We realised that this was a horizontal product," Hearne says, "That meant that it was 20 per cent about development and 80 per cent about marketing. We did not have the visibility or the confidence to put money into marketing. This was an eye-opener for us on what it took to bring a product to market."

IT Design spent three years trying to drum up interest in its information retrieval software, then decided that it should focus on a vertical market instead. The company redirected its resources into an applications framework for social welfare authorities. The California office was given a different mission. It picked up service contracts to build systems and products. The American subsidiary always paid its way, but never contributed to the development of Curam, the social welfare product that the company released in 1998. Five years later IT Design changed its name to Curam Software. By then it had a sales office in Washington, DC that targeted potential customers in state administrations and the Silicon Valley office was a historical anomaly. Having a presence in California, however, had enabled the Dublin company to keep an eye on the US technology scene during its years of transformation.

By the late 1990s there was a network of Irish software companies with California offices, including CBT Systems, Iona, Trintech and WBT Systems. If one firm needed advice on, for example, how to find a good lawyer or accountant, it might contact one of the others. But the companies never discussed their shared concerns in a systematic way. Enterprise Ireland marketing adviser Marina Donohoe convinced her superiors at the agency that it should do more to support the migration into the valley. In 1998 she moved to Campbell, California and opened the agency's first technology marketing centre in the region.

The office suite in Campbell included five rooms that individual companies could rent. Over the next two years 18 companies, including electronics hardware designers as well as software developers, chose it as their first address in the US. The facilities at the centre were absolutely basic — a room that was just big enough for a desk and a parking space outside. But the address looked good on business cards. It allowed the companies to negotiate with others as neighbours instead of as visitors to the region. A few of the tenant companies established a permanent presence in California. AEP Systems and Cape Clear Software were notable examples. Others were acquired by American firms after making themselves known through the Enterprise Ireland address.

The real significance of the Campbell centre was the message that it sent back to the Irish software industry. It had become the norm for product development companies to try to break into the American market. Enterprise Ireland had institutionalised this process. Irish expatriates never built ethnic business networks and support structures in Silicon Valley in the way that entrepreneurs and engineers from several Asian countries did. European influence in the area, indeed, has never been substantial or visible. But the Irish companies had learned how to raise their profile when they needed it.

In later years Enterprise Ireland moved its office from Campbell to Palo Alto and shifted its focus in Silicon Valley from software to other industries. This made sense because generation five software companies are less inclined than their predecessors to sell products to other technology firms. It is more appropriate for them to establish US offices in the regions where their customers and prospects are clustered.

By 2004, moreover, Irish software companies were making strategic investments in the US instead of simply opening sales offices or observation posts. The value of the dollar has declined against the euro and it has become more economic to hire American staff for development work or customer support. Companies that derive a significant portion of their revenues from implementation projects or customer services are finding that this option is increasingly attractive. Fineos and Performix Technologies, for example, have increased their headcounts in the US to reduce their exposure to currency fluctuations. American salaries no longer appear excessive beside the average rates in Ireland and most of the costs in the software business are people-related.

It is ironic that, at a time when the biggest talking point in the American software industry is the outsourcing of jobs to economies like India and China, Irish exporters say that they are saving money by creating additional employment at their offices in the US.

Chapter 11

WHO'S PUTTING UP THE MONEY?

Software Engineering Meets Financial Engineering

Malachy Smith went prospecting in California in 1984. He toured around the offices of several venture capital firms in Silicon Valley to ask if they would provide finance for his company, Intelligence Ireland. Wherever he went, the response was the same. They thought that Intelligence was interesting, but they would never invest in Ireland. Iona's Chris Horn heard these arguments nine years later, when he held discussions with investors on the west coast of America. He met two firms. Both said that they would back Iona if it moved to the US, but they did not think that they would be able to monitor a company in Dublin.

Business textbooks recommended that technology-based companies should team up with technology-oriented investors. Entrepreneurs were supposed to raise seed capital to get their companies started, then follow up with successive rounds of venture capital and development capital as they brought products to market, found buyers and managed their customer relationships. Good investors, the textbooks said, did more than put up the money. They also became proactive advisers and found additional business partners when their clients needed them. The developers and the financiers would thus work together to maximise the returns on their efforts.

These options were seldom available to Irish software firms until generation four. They had to survive without the financing structures that their American counterparts took for granted. And they had to operate on budgets that were many times smaller.

Generation two companies complained constantly about the banks. The big problem was that banks did not want to lend money to businesses that lacked physical assets and almost all software developers fell into that category. "In the 1980s bank branches made decisions and the local branch managers were like gods," Barry Murphy says. When he worked at Insight Software in that era, the company traded profitably every year. But the directors had to give personal guarantees when Insight sought an increase in its overdraft facility. An embryonic venture capital industry also existed in the 1980s, but the banks controlled most of this as well. Venture capital, moreover, was generally reserved for companies with established products and trading records. None of the institutions offered seed capital for new companies.

Some firms found ways to skirt around the bankers' policies. Mentec, for example, purchased a building with IDA grants, then raised money from a bank on the basis that it owned property. Other developers opened accounts in international banks and reported that these treated them better than the Irish institutions.

Even if Silicon Valley-style venture capitalists had been active in Dublin, few generation two software entrepreneurs would have dealt with them. They instinctively recoiled from giving equity away. Most preferred to get by on debt finance and state agency grants than to swap any shares for cash.

The contrast between this environment and generation four is stark. By the turn of the century, institutional investment had ceased to be just another business input like electricity or internet access. Commentaries on Irish software invariably treated venture capital as the main event. Financing agreements received vastly more attention than strategic positioning or quality issues or distribution channels. Product launches and major contracts passed by virtually unnoticed. Investment deals had become the standard measure of a company's health, while the total volume of venture capital coming into the industry was regarded as an index of its overall condition.

The constant speculation about initial public offerings was unhelpful. The value of shares has some significance in commodity-based businesses, where a company's prices and unit shipments can be measured objectively against those of its competitors. Such comparisons have little meaning in the software product trade. One middleware toolset vendor may choose to live off licence revenues, while another bases its business model on service contracts. And both may face an erosion of their market by free code from an open source project. Software company share prices can arguably be read as fashion statements. Often, however, stock market listings damage software firms. The treadmill of quarterly reporting, analyst briefings and public speculation about the personal wealth of their executives distracts them from long term strategies and planning.

The role of financial engineering in the software story has often been exaggerated. The changing character of the investors nonetheless deserves attention, because it helps to explain how the industry evolved.

When the banks failed to support the software developers of the mid-1980s, they turned to the public service for support. The National Enterprise Agency (NEA) was the first state-run organisation to offer seed funding to Irish companies. It commenced operations in 1984 and allocated $7.6 million to 29 projects across a range of industries by March 1986. The NEA was then subsumed into a new agency, Nadcorp, which had a much bigger revolving investment fund. Soon, however, Nadcorp lost interest in early-stage financing and focused instead on more established companies. It closed in 1991. The IDA inherited its portfolio and it, in turn, became the primary supplier of venture capital to Irish-owned firms. At the end of 1991 the authority held shares in 37 software firms. Most of these had exchanged redeemable preference shares for payments under the agency's support schemes.

The priority for the NEA and Nadcorp was always to develop knowledge-based industries in Ireland rather than to find the best return on their money. Software was a small element in their investments. Both agencies preferred to finance electronics hardware development. The NEA's main software investment was in Omnicorp Technology, a short-lived Limerick company that sold materials management applications to manufacturers. Nadcorp looked for bigger projects. It put money into

Peregrine Expert Systems and East Coast Software, which both had staying power. Its flagship software investment, however, was a $590,000 package for Software Laboratories in 1987. The size of this deal was regarded as an advance from previous fundraising exercises in the Irish industry, but Software Laboratories ceased trading two years later.

In 1992, shortly after Nadcorp's own demise, National Software Director Barry Murphy produced a discussion document on venture capital. This argued that Ireland needed a pool of competing venture capital firms — and not just investment groups controlled by banks. Murphy had also noticed that generation three software firms were more willing than their predecessors to allow external investors to take part of their equity. In the years that followed, a locally based venture capital industry emerged in the way that he advocated.

Delta Partners was the first firm to specialise in financing young technology companies. It was founded in 1994 by Frank Kenny, who had recently returned from working in the US and wanted to import the American venture capital model to Ireland. Delta built up its software portfolio steadily to include companies like Credo Group and Qumas, WBT Systems and Xiam. Trinity Venture Capital, which was established in 1997, backed developers such as Aepona, ChangingWorlds, Mapflow, Norkom Technologies and Valista. IACT Venture Capital grew out of AIB Bank and supplied finance to Am-Beo, Cape Clear Software, CR2, Soft-ex and others. The number of funds has steadily risen to the point that some complain there is now too much competition instead of too little.

By the turn of the century, several international funds were also actively seeking investments — or, at least, they asked their London offices to keep an eye on the Irish software industry. Some investors came from unexpected sources. In 1996 Barry Murphy joined one of the new operations, Cullinane Group — a vehicle established by Massachusetts-based software veteran John Cullinane to acquire shareholdings in new development ventures. He admits that there was no preconceived plan as to what he should do. He evaluated many Irish software firms, but invested in only two — Expert Edge, which was sold to Wall Data for $3 million in 1997, and Piercom, which had good technology but struggled to achieve sales. Soon most of his work for Cullinane was in Northern Ireland and in Israel. The investment firm shut its Dublin office in 1999.

Dave Miller was another software veteran who joined the venture capitalists. He left Iona, attended an executive education course at Stanford and moved into consulting in 1999. He wanted to get a foothold in the venture capital business, but knew that many others had the same ambition. In America he encountered MBA graduates who were willing to work for free in venture capital firms so that they could gain frontline experience. When Agincourt Ventures came along, Miller saw it as his golden opportunity. An Irish-based fund whose primary sources of finance would be American, Agincourt announced its arrival in 1999, declaring that it would invest at least $30 million in early-stage technology companies over the next twelve months. Miller joined this operation and read all the software business plans in town. "At that time," he says, "Everyone had the attitude that 'If I get venture capital, then I have credibility'." Agincourt, however, never completed an investment. It announced a $4.3 million deal with Sepro Telecom, but the promised funding from America did not materialise in Dublin. Sepro raised money from Trinity Venture Capital instead. Miller joined the billing software firm in 2000 as chief operating officer.

Brian Caulfield also crossed the line from software management to venture capital. After he sold Peregrine Systems, he launched Similarity Systems, which developed data quality management software. Trinity Venture Capital appointed him as an investment director in 2002. Caulfield is positive about the quality of the business proposals that he has seen since joining the company and comments that there have been few wacky plans in circulation since the internet hype died down. But he says that development firms have been slow to adapt to present-day realities. Software companies, he points out, should no longer expect to raise significant sums before they can demonstrate a product prototype. Many, he adds, do not understand the dynamics of competition. "Anything that is an alternative for your customer to buy is competition," he explains.

The venture capital business has become more fragmented in generation five. Different sets of investors have declared an interest in companies of different sizes and stages of development. Multi-stage investment has become the norm and the financiers have refined their offerings for each stage. The most significant change, perhaps, has been the involvement of software industry veterans in new funds that focus on the very early phase of company formation. Organisations like Mentor Capital and 4th Level Ventures are seeking brand new start-ups and university projects with commercial potential.

Mike Peirce chairs Mentor Capital. He stepped down from the CEO role at Mentec in 2001 so that he could give more time to selecting and supporting young ventures. Mentor, he says, has received high quality referrals, especially from the universities. But most of these projects have come from areas like optical networking and semiconductor testing. Iontas and OpenMind Networks are Mentor's main clients in the software industry.

Generation five companies are not creating instant millionaires. Peirce points out, indeed, that it is now acceptable to follow gradual timescales and for companies to go through three or four loss-making years before their sales start to build up. "It's going to be a grafting model again," he says, "but it's a different world from ten or fifteen years ago. Companies can raise equity that is disproportionate to their cashflow." What they need, he explains, is sustained expenditure on development and financial stamina so that they can withstand unexpected events. He is concerned, however, that the software industry may not have enough business brains to take full advantage of its development capabilities and suggests that this factor could determine how well it performs in the coming years.

4th Level Ventures was founded in 2002. The official launch of its €20 million venture capital fund followed two years later. This money, which includes €8.6 million from Enterprise Ireland, is reserved for companies whose intellectual property originates in research projects at educational institutions. Although it is structured as a subsidiary of a financial services company, Dolmen Securities, 4th Level Ventures is managed by internet pioneer Dennis Jennings and Ray Naughton, a former chief executive of Siemens Nixdorf in Ireland.

For Jennings, indeed, 4th Level was a way of formalising a role that he moved into after cashing in his shares in Euristix. As a private investor he backed several companies, including WBT Systems, online reservations system developer TourIT and IconX Solutions. Like Mentor Capital, however, 4th Level finds that the strongest projects in the universities are in areas other than software. He suggests that new software start-ups on the campuses may come from engineering projects or from multi-disciplinary research units, not out of the computer science departments.

With more investment funds with more targeted strategies than ever before, software start-ups have a clear financial trail to follow. The terms of the deals will be more stringent than in generation four, but there is no sign of any return to the funding famines of earlier times. Since 2001, however, more companies have tried to finance product development without institutional investors. Some take on service contracts or other cash-generating projects. Others are paying their way through partnerships with pilot customers. These companies have heard too many tales of developers that had bad experiences with venture capital and have reverted to old modes of fundraising until they can negotiate with investors from a position of strength.

Perhaps the venture capitalists are much less essential to the process than they are willing to admit. Tom Weymes, the former Enterprise Ireland official, poses an interesting question. "How many guys made it with venture capital money who would not have made it without?" he asks. "My guess is that there are very few."

Payback Time

The closing years of the twentieth century were defined by internet-fuelled illusions that the economic order was undergoing a fundamental change. The rapid diffusion of the World Wide Web prompted assertions that outfits with "dotcom" in their names were poised to depose the Fortune 500. The First Tuesday movement organised monthly gatherings for believers. These meetings spread into Ireland in 1999.

In the early days the First Tuesday clubbers met in pubs. Attendees were discouraged from wearing ties, but they donned badges that showed whether they wanted to invest money or to receive investments. Thus labelled, they were free to mimic the courtship routines of venture capitalists in Silicon Valley — or, at least, to act out their perceptions of those rituals. First Tuesday began as a bizarre attempt to import an American business promotion formula. Some meetings, for example, included "elevator pitches" where entrepreneurs delivered the briefest of presentations and hoped that venture capitalists would look at their websites to find out more. Over time, however, the club introduced more conventional seminars and discussions. The venues changed from bars to hotel rooms with platforms and rows of chairs. The organisers even allowed the ties to creep back in.

Most dotcom projects involved some form of business service or the sale of consumer goods. There were also plenty of consultants and website designers offering to transform mundane commerce into e-commerce. The software industry was not swept up by this hype to the same extent as others. Nonetheless, developers moved fast to ensure that their applications could be fronted by web pages. And a number of software product firms were among the recipients of large venture capital sums in the midst of the frenzy. Some of these produced lookalike applications that presented a web store's merchandise or made it easier for employees to access company documents. But there were others with established businesses that were less naive and took more calculated risks. They reckoned that the rush to the web and collaboration with the financial engineers could raise the scale and the value of their operations.

Two of the most prominent examples were Baltimore Technologies, which was reborn in the late 1990s as an e-business security software company, and airline communications protocol specialist Datalex, which reinvented itself as a supplier of web-based booking systems. Both proceeded to undertake expensive acquisitions, ballooned to an unprecedented size and had their energies sapped by bruising experiences on stock exchanges.

After Jim Mountjoy quit Baltimore in 1990, an Ericsson technologist, Pat Cremin, took charge of the organisation. It continued to bid for consultancy work and for contracts to develop communications software, but online security and cryptography came to account for an increasing proportion of its work. Michael Purser agreed to sell the business in 1996. Dermot Desmond, whose previous investments had included CBT Systems and Quay Financial Software, was the new chairman, while Fran Rooney, a financial engineer who had previously worked at Quay, became managing director. Paddy Holahan signed on as sales and marketing director. When the new regime took over, he says, the Baltimore team had shrunk to just seven people, including five mathematicians. Over the next two years the company built a product family on their expertise in cryptography, hired dozens of additional developers, joined all the relevant standards bodies and opened offices in Boston, San Mateo, London, Amsterdam and Tokyo. Further restructuring followed at the start of 1999 when it merged with a London-based network security firm Zergo Holdings.

According to Paddy Holahan, the revamped Baltimore never compared itself with any other software firm in Ireland. The new regime chose Oracle as its role model. When Oracle started, he explains, no one believed that a database supplier could grow into one of the biggest players in the industry. But Oracle pushed for growth and pushed more aggressively than anyone else in its field. Online security still looked like a niche business in the mid-1990s, but Baltimore was confident that the size of the market would soar. Encryption was also an area where European firms could gain competitive advantage, because they were not encumbered by the technology export restrictions that existed in the US. "Encryption was big enough and technically complex enough for us to be at the top table," Holahan says.

Baltimore promoted its public key infrastructure and digital certificate software with as much determination as Oracle had applied to databases. The demand for dedicated security products was punctured, however, when the incumbent players at the top table, including IBM, Microsoft, Oracle and Cisco, embedded encryption-ready features into existing

products. Their customers could obtain additional security without dealing with specialist vendors. The financial engineers behind the new Baltimore had designed their company to command a much bigger business
than the one available to it. In the end they had to sell off the product
lines one by one. BeTrusted, Clearswift, HP and AEP Systems picked up
pieces of the portfolio.

At Datalex the decision to change was initiated by founder and chief
executive officer Neil Wilson. The company developed slowly and organically from 1985 to 1998, starting as a local supplier of computer networks, then fixing its sights on the travel trade. It developed communications software that enabled PCs to access airline reservations systems,
installed it throughout Ireland and began to win international deals in the
early 1990s. By 1997, Datalex had annual revenues of $6.7 million, three
offices in the US and about 40 employees. Wilson decided that he wanted
promotion into a higher league. He sold 25 per cent of the company to a
venture capital consortium and hit the acquisition trail. It purchased
around a dozen companies, reducing the range of competition in its sector. One of these deals made Datalex the owner of a Java-based internet
booking engine called BookIt! and this became its flagship product.

By 2000 Wilson estimated that half of all online travel transactions
employed Datalex software but, as happened at Baltimore, the company's revenues lagged behind its aspirations. Annual sales peaked at
$33 million in 2000, when it reported a loss of $66 million. In the following year the losses climbed to $98 million. The company's market
capitalisation was slashed during an unhappy 18-month listing on the
Nasdaq exchange. Datalex scaled down and survived, but had little to
show for the tens of millions that it had spent on acquisitions.

The merger and acquisition process works two ways and several of
Ireland's more prominent software firms were sold during generation
four. At first these deals looked benign. The people who had founded
and built up Aldiscon, Expert Edge, Euristix and Software Architects
International were major beneficiaries of takeover transactions. After the
turn of the century, however, more of the acquisitions were forced
through by institutional investors. In these instances financial engineers

had taken control of the businesses, got rid of the founders and packaged the companies for sale. They received a payback, but left wounded organisations and individuals in their wake.

Irish investors and foreign funds were equally keen to get their money back and to pocket a bonus. For the most part, though, the locals entered into financing deals in the expectation that they would work with the existing managers. The international venture capitalists usually wanted to place their own nominees in charge. If they did not change the chief executive at the time of the investment, they made their move when a performance target was missed or some other setback arose. This resulted in a cull of chief executives that had a demoralising effect on whole sections of the software industry.

The ritual reports of investment deals as "success stories" never mention the less pleasant side of the venture capital ideology — the attitude that people can be treated as commodities. The rougher edges of this American philosophy are often smoothed over in Europe. By the turn of the century, however, much of the money that was being pumped into the Irish software industry originated in US-based funds. Soon venture capitalists were pushing the companies for faster growth at a time when corporate information officers were cancelling or deferring software purchases. Logic suggested that sales directors should shoulder the blame, but the American model plays down collective responsibility and always spotlights the figure at the top of a company. The chief executives became the fall guys.

Among the casualties in Ireland were the chief executives of Eontec, where Warburg Pincus had led a $25 million equity investment, and International Financial Systems, where the shareholders included Deutsche Bank and Intel. The story was the same at Openet Telecom after Benchmark Capital invested $20 million and XML forms specialist Vordel, where an international consortium had pumped in $10 million. The pattern was repeated in other companies where the investments had been smaller.

It would be wrong to conclude that the development companies were always blameless for their problems. The same mistakes appeared over and over again. According to Pearse Coyle at consulting firm Cloynes

Technologies, the recipients of venture capital paid too little attention to trial customers and user testing, because they found it easier and more pleasant to work on the technical aspects of their projects. When these companies were ready to sell products, moreover, they splashed out money on sales staff whose pay was not tied to performance. "When people with a technical vision could raise money with a limited amount of commercial sales," Coyle says, "they came up with a seriously rose-tinted view."

Not every venture capitalist was a slash-up and cash-in merchant. Curam Software's experience showed how software companies could make smart use of external investment. The company, which was originally known as IT Design, delayed dealing with venture capitalists for as long as it could. It had been trading for 12 years in 2002, when Fidelity Ventures put $10 million into the firm.

IT Design had its first encounter with social security computer systems in 1991, when its ability to display data from multiple systems on a desktop computer screen caught the attention of the Department of Social Welfare in Dublin. The company became a subcontractor to Praesidium, a joint venture between this government department and Digital Equipment, which wanted to sell software to social security agencies in other countries. IT Design gradually inserted itself into the niche that Praesidium had picked, working on an implementation project for the National Social Security Authority in Zimbabwe and deepening its knowledge of the data integration needs of welfare services. "It became clear that, if we were to develop a product, it would have to be a framework that would be customised for every customer," chief executive John Hearne says. In 1998 the company launched Curam, its sector-specific development framework, and signed a non-exclusive reseller agreement with IBM. Guernsey was the first customer to select Curam and was followed by a number of US states.

"IBM had defined a strategy to partner with the best of breed. We were the beneficiaries of that," Hearne says. IBM, which held only eight per cent of the market for social welfare administration systems, was keen to identify a product that would enable it to win more systems integration contracts. Curam was the only developer in its field that had taken a framework approach. In 2000 IBM upgraded the relationship to a strategic alliance that included provision for the Dublin firm to obtain financial support. The following year, however, proved difficult and the company failed to close expected sales. It decided to accept venture capital so that it could place more management and professional services personnel around the world. Fidelity came on board and its investment sustained the company until the orders picked up. In 2003 Curam made its landmark sale to the UK Department for Work and Pensions. By the end of the year, ten welfare authorities had paid the company for a software licence or for a proof of concept demonstration.

According to John Hearne, Curam chose Fidelity because it wanted a backer with an international profile. There was also a meeting of minds on ethical issues. Curam wanted to protect its reputation as a software employer that did not engage in redundancies, while Fidelity had a policy of retaining the existing management at companies that it invested in. Hearne says that Fidelity's studies of European software firms show that all of the larger ones have maintained continuity of leadership.

This analysis is dramatically at odds with the more commonly heard anecdotes of ousted managers and disillusioned development groups. Who said that venture capitalists were all the same?

Chapter 12

CODING CULTURE AND
INDUSTRY POLITICS

A Geek Inside the Gin and Tonic Brigade

Donal Daly joined the Irish Computer Services Association (ICSA) in
the late 1980s. The software industry was in trouble and the industry
group had commissioned Coopers & Lybrand to study its condition.
Daly already understood the day-to-day realities of running a software
development company. Inside the ICSA, however, he encountered an
unfamiliar world. He belonged to a different generation than his new
colleagues. But the gulf was wider than that. Donal Daly entered the
industry association with a passion for software development. He had
lived inside a geek culture, where technology was seen as an end in itself. If the other ICSA members were passionate about anything, he says,
it was about running businesses.

When Daly had entered University College Cork some years earlier,
his qualifications were not good enough for a place in civil engineering.
So he studied electrical engineering instead. After graduating in 1982 he
worked for Softech and Zentec Microsystems, selling personal computers in and around Cork. Then he chanced upon an emerging software
category. Artificial intelligence had been a theoretical discipline for decades. In the mid-1980s many believed that the time had come to put it
into practice. The processing and storage capabilities of PCs had advanced to the stage where a single desktop machine could hold a
"knowledge base" — all the rules and conventions behind a specific task
or process. Users could consult this computer to find the correct course

of action in any set of circumstances. According to their promoters, expert systems enabled employers to capture and preserve the knowledge of their key staff. The humans might leave the organisation, but their skills would remain on the premises.

Donal Daly launched Expert Edge Computer Systems in 1986. He promoted expert systems with the same enthusiasm and persistence that had made him a successful seller of PCs. In its early days the company acted as the Irish distributor for Crystal, an expert system builder from a British company, Intelligent Environments. Within a few years, however, Expert Edge was developing its own applications. Daly travelled regularly to Dublin to seek new customers and opened an office in the capital in 1987. In the following year he set up a London office to sell a graphics software product that Expert Edge had designed for expert systems developers. In the same year Daly co-authored an introductory book on expert systems with Price Waterhouse consultant Frank Bannister and Jurek Kirakowski, who led a human factors research group at University College Cork. The book was sold with a trial version of Crystal inside the cover. In later years Expert Edge sold financial counselling applications with built-in knowledge bases. Then Daly decided that this work was no longer technically challenging and redirected his company into computer connectivity products.

In 1988 the fast mover from Cork was rapidly gathering experience and thought that joining the ICSA would enable him to gain some more. He was aware that few of his contemporaries had any dealings with the association. He also knew that it was run by generation one veterans like Tom McGovern from System Dynamics, Insight Software founder Matt Crotty, Kindle's Tony Kilduff and Tom Winters from Future Technology Services — people who had introduced the first computers to many Irish workplaces. He describes this group as a "gin and tonic brigade". When he joined their association, he felt like the only person at the meetings who understood how the software industry had evolved. "I got in there because I knew nothing about what I was doing," Daly says, "I thought that I could learn from them." He soon discovered how little the old guard knew about the world that Expert Edge inhabited.

Companies like Insight and Kindle were the accepted leaders of the software industry in the late 1980s. But they belonged to a world of large systems for large organisations with large business applications. And they did not employ geeks. Daly's experience was in a technical milieu, where the best ideas came out of the colleges and geeks could be heroes. If they had commercial strategies, they usually targeted personal users or work-groups as Expert Edge had gone. According to Daly, the rift between the old guard and the Young Turks was widest when it came to their visions of the future for Irish software. The low ambitions of the ICSA establishment in the international industry took him by surprise. "It was an accepted fact that we could never get a company that was a leader," he says. "The gin and tonic brigade did not know what was going on."

For years the old guard had been preoccupied with the local trade. More specifically, they objected to the tendency of government departments and agencies to import software products and services. In other countries the governments championed local developers and often provided them with reference sites. In Ireland there were frequent allegations of discrimination against the locals, whenever consultancy projects or development contracts were up for grabs. Almost all of the computer hardware used by the public sector came from US manufacturers with assembly plants in Ireland. The software companies suspected that their proposals were brushed aside in favour of foreign developers that might also invest in Ireland. These concerns came to a head in the early 1980s when the Department of Health nominated an American product as a national healthcare standard. The ICSA protested that its members had lost out to a US vendor, McAuto, even when serious shortcomings were uncovered in the functionality and price competitiveness of its hospital administration software. The McAuto affair still provokes rancour today.

By the end of the 1980s, however, the high failure rate among generation two software product companies had become the most pressing issue for the ICSA. The leaders of the association had less direct experience in this area. Robert Cochran, who was running Generics Software at the time, points out that they had come from a tradition of bespoke software development in which long-term customer relationships were regarded as all-important and software quality was a minor concern. "People who had worked in bespoke software tended to apply the same ways of working to products," Cochran says, "For them, delivery was only one stage in a much longer process." He attributes the spate of company collapses at the end of generation two to the high incidence of bugs in their products.

Donal Daly was the first software entrepreneur from the PC package trade to play an active role in the ICSA. The organisation was keen to attract younger members and welcomed his contributions. Daly was elected vice chair of the association less than a year after he had joined it. Paddy Moore, who headed IBM's development operation in Dublin, was the new chairman. His predecessor, Pat Talbot, had been a management consultant. Moore and Daly set out to give the ICSA a sharper focus on software development. This started a transition process at the industry association. In the years that followed it tried to recruit more product developers and to articulate their interests. By 1995, when the ICSA changed its name to Irish Software Association (ISA), the transfer of control from the gin and tonic brigade appeared to be complete.

The ISA, however, was never overrun by geeks. It changed its agenda to reflect the interests of product exporters, addressing issues like the availability of investment funds, software quality standards and certifications, the US software trade and the scarcity of international sales and marketing personnel. But the association still found it hard to persuade software company executives to join its policy committees and strategy groups. Its executive council has been chaired by marketing consultants, magazine publishers and investment intermediaries. Its conferences have attracted a disconcerting number of venture capitalists and legal advisers. Sometimes, indeed, the ISA looked curiously like an Irish Software Wellwishers Association.

Another problem was that the ISA's parent organisation, the Irish Business and Employers Confederation, was primarily a mouthpiece for large enterprises. The Irish branches of international companies supplied much of its funding and were active contributors to policy formulation. This meant, for example, that members of Microsoft's officer corps could end up making public pronouncements about the needs of cash-strapped software start-ups.

Paul O'Dea now runs a consulting firm, International Ventures, with Donal Daly. O'Dea chaired the ISA for one year in the mid-1990s and was elected to the position again in 2002. He acknowledges that collaboration among Irish software companies has always been bad and that it has been difficult to attract a broad range of companies into the association's initiatives. "We went through a period where people did not need to network," he notes. "There were muddled perceptions as to who was a competitor." O'Dea adds, however, that the level of interaction improved during the lean years at the start of the twenty-first century. This happened in much the same way as the gin and tonic brigade rolled up their sleeves and worked together to respond to the crisis of the late 1980s.

During O'Dea's second term in the chair, the Irish Software Association launched a sales and marketing education programme for senior managers. A new self-help group, the CEO Forum, started at about the same time. Membership is limited to chief executives of companies that have passed the start-up phase. About 20 people are actively involved and members allowed to raise any topic at its discussions, which take place four times a year. These initiatives suggest that high-level information exchanges among software firms may be improving.

It seems strange, though, that inter-company communications have been so poor in an industry that sends a disproportionate number of delegates to international standards groups and has networked so assiduously in places such as Silicon Valley. Paul O'Dea points out that the international networking has usually been done by technical people. Perhaps the chief executives are belatedly catching up.

Goat Tracks and Border Russians

The Atlantic Technology Corridor (ATC) had been taking shape for a couple of years before the group held a conference in May 2003 to announce its agenda. It introduced itself as a representative body for companies from the information technology, communications and medical technology industries. The ATC declared its intention to become the catalyst for establishing a knowledge-based economy on the 100-kilometre axis from Limerick through Shannon and Ennis to Galway. The organisation would also co-ordinate, and in some cases take over, the projects and services of two existing software associations in the region — Limerick-based ShannonSoft and the Information Technology Association of Galway.

This was the latest and largest in a series of initiatives to challenge the dominance of Dublin in software development and other technology-centred industries. The ATC aimed to grow an alternative development hub in the west of Ireland. The alliance would be led by industry, while state agencies, local authorities and universities would play supporting roles.

Taoiseach Bertie Ahern attended the Atlantic Technology Corridor conference in Bunratty, declared his support for the initiative and offered some encouraging comments on the provision of broadband access, which had been a contentious subject in the Shannon area. It was striking, however, that most of the ATC activists who greeted and escorted the Taoiseach were employees of American corporations. Only one of the 12 industry representatives on the ATC board came from an Irish-based enterprise. And when speakers at the event highlighted the capabilities of the technology cluster on the corridor, they presented lists of foreign-owned companies instead of homegrown successes like Narragansett Technologies in Limerick or Am-Beo and BrightWork in Galway.

The ATC concept was born when the subsidiaries of US firms started to share ideas on how they could persuade their parent organisations to give them tasks with higher value. Even in 2003, there was still an implicit assumption in the Corridor counties that inward investment would provide them with a knowledge-based economy. The further one goes from the eastern seaboard, indeed, the higher the profile of US corporations in commercial life — not only in the role of employers, but also as the customers of local technology companies. In the west the software industry still talks more often about importing jobs than about exporting products.

This may explain why the Information Technology Association of Galway campaigned for road construction during the general election of

2002. An American software executive had recently complained that the route from Shannon to Galway was like a goat track. The locals cringed. They also studied the project schedule at the National Roads Authority and saw that all the big schemes were on the eastern side of the country. At a time when industry associations all over the world were campaigning for investment in high-speed communications, the Galway group lobbied election candidates to improve the roadways first. Its members were preoccupied with the image that their city presented to foreign investors.

Software development in Ireland has always been concentrated in and around the capital. Analysts have speculated for years about the distribution of employment to telecottages and other rural retreats, but the industry thrives on critical mass. Developers like to work in conurbations where they can transfer easily from job to job. They want the supports of an urban environment with taxis and courier services, maintenance technicians on standby, coffee shops, convenience stores and pizzerias that deliver in the early hours of the morning. The workforce, indeed, has shown a strong preference for inner-city locations, especially when their employers have tried to move into suburban business parks with much lower office rents.

A study by McIver Consulting in 1998 found that 83 per cent of the software industry's employment was in Dublin and its hinterland. The Limerick-Shannon area had the second-largest concentration with six per cent. Cork, where a cluster of companies wrote applications for civil engineers, pharmaceutical facilities or agribusiness groups, and Galway, where Compaq and Nortel accounted for large blocks of employment, had about four per cent each. Just three per cent of the software jobs were scattered among all the other towns and cities. The McIver survey, incidentally, prompted industry groups in both Cork and Galway to launch schemes to push up their percentages. Cork focused on improving the facilities for start-ups and created the NSC campus.

Patricia Byrne, the director of knowledge enterprise at Shannon Development, points out that the clusters outside Dublin started later and that they started from a lower base. Until the 1980s, she explains, there was little employment in the Shannon region other than in manufacturing

plants and the skill set was correspondingly weak. When Byrne joined
Shannon Development in 1980 she was given a portfolio of 40 existing
companies to work with. When she met the chief executives of these
firms, she discovered that only one of them was a graduate. Patricia
Byrne regards the educational standards in local companies as a measure
of the economic status of an area. Limerick, she says, started to absorb
more graduates when software firms and electronics design companies
began to emerge in the 1980s. By the end of the decade more than 40
ventures had been formed through Shannon Development's entrepreneurship and high technology programme. Since the mid-1990s, she
adds, skill sets in the region's smaller towns have also started to climb
up the educational ladder.

National and regional authorities have made numerous attempts over
the years to encourage software development outside the four main centres. In particular, these programmes targeted towns with third-level colleges that produced computing graduates. They offered low-cost accommodation for start-ups. They identified academics with entrepreneurial flair. They trawled through the manufacturing facilities in search of
executives with business ideas. Until the second half of the 1990s, however, the companies that they assisted were short-lived and the developers usually drifted back to the big cities.

In the final years of the century, in contrast, software firms began to
surface in these locations in a more natural way. A general shortage of
development skills, coupled with escalating costs in the cities, spurred
investment in the college towns. Software employment rose in places
like Dundalk, Letterkenny, Sligo, Tralee and Waterford, partly through
the formation of local companies and partly through the opening of satellite offices by Dublin-based firms. In some cases the decentralisation
movement spread to more remote locations. Integration middleware vendor Propylon, whose commercial offices are based in Dublin, runs a
software engineering team in Enniscrone, a tourist resort on the Sligo
coastline best known for the type of surfing that requires a wetsuit. Iontas, which produces management software for contact centre systems,
started life in 2000 at a vacant holiday apartment complex in Moville on

the Inishowen peninsula, but moved to a business park in Letterkenny four years later. When the company needed to expand its development team, it reckoned that it would be easier to attract new recruits to a more accessible location.

Datacare Software Group is the outstanding example of a software company that grew up and remained in an unlikely location. Its founder and chief executive, John Kelly, came from the border town of Monaghan and was determined to build his business there. The company started off in 1983 as a computer systems reseller. When demand for its Unix platforms was slow, Kelly thought that he could attract more customers by hiring developers to write accounting applications. In 1986 Datacare added a corporate records management product for company secretaries and their filing agents.

The company had discovered a niche. It soon learned that it was better to be the leader in a narrow area than a bit player in a larger market. Its first corporate reporting applications were based on Irish regulations. Datacare worked on electronic filing processes in collaboration with the Companies Registration Office in Dublin. In 1994 it launched the first Windows-based corporate records management software in the UK. It added a version for Canada in 1998 and one for the US in 1999. In 2000 the company raised $5.4 million in venture capital to support its transatlantic expansion. As it expanded outwards, it also moved higher up the enterprise pecking order. Its latest records management software is designed for the world's 2,000 largest corporations, but John Kelly says that his priority is to cater for the top 500. These users keep the company informed of their requirements and Datacare does its best to meet their expectations.

Datacare today runs sales offices in London, New York and Toronto, but all of its software development has stayed with a 30-person group in Monaghan. This team has an unusual profile for an Irish software company. Its members are predominantly female and include several Muscovites.

John Kelly admits that the company has found it hard to attract software developers to the border region. Over the years, however, it learned that female employees who had settled in, and identified with, the area

were easy to retain. Datacare has benefited from the loyalty of these employees. Its salaries do not match the peaks in central Dublin, but its staff
are better paid than other office workers in Monaghan. The Russian connection was established in 1999, when the company hired three programmers on one-year contracts from IT-Combi, a recruitment agency
affiliated to a computer science research centre in Moscow. Their work
was good and Datacare has continued to employ Russians ever since.

The company puts a great deal of effort into its customer relationships, but seldom interacts with the mainstream software industry. "You
can get by without any dialogue with other software developers," Kelly
says. Thus, despite its location, Datacare has never sought synergies with
software companies on the other side of the border. The industry in
Northern Ireland has specialised in applications for local authorities and
other government organisations. It has always had a large service element and its software product companies make most of their sales in
Britain. Some industry analysts have tried to draw parallels between its
evolution and the regional clusters in places like Cork and Galway. It
would, however, be inappropriate and unfair to depict the Northern Ireland software story as another initiative to lessen Dublin's dominance.

Strong opinions can be found in the software industry for and against
encouraging the distribution of development around the country. Many
argue that companies must congregate in the same area to keep the innovation process going. In theory, the cluster could be moved from east
coast to some other region as long as the skill base is not allowed to
wither. Others suggest, though, that Ireland is small enough for the entire
software community to be considered as a single cluster. Datacare's international achievements, moreover, prove that isolated development
groups can succeed, if local champions have the determination to make
things happen in their home towns.

Grunt Life

Tom Murphy completed a degree in mathematics in 1991. Over the next
three years he learned how to write software by working in a series of
companies. Quinnsworth was the first. According to Murphy, he told the

supermarket operator that he knew the Cobol programming language, was offered a post shortly before Christmas and spent the holiday break reading Cobol manuals. When he reported for work, Quinnsworth placed him in a technical architecture team and never asked him to write a line of Cobol.

In subsequent jobs he learned about financial services applications, about software product lifecycles and about the importance of quality control. By 1994 Murphy had become one of the industry's buccaneers — a software contractor with, he says, "the ultimate gun-for-hire mentality". He sold his skills through an agent for three months at a time. He would only accept contracts with customers in Dublin city centre, because he insisted on being able to walk to work. He made more money than he could spend and sometimes took long breaks between assignments.

According to Murphy, a revolution took place in the ranks in the mid-1990s. At the start of the decade coders in Dublin were willing to accept sweatshop conditions and a pay regime below the European average. People routinely worked six days a week for 14 hours a day and received little credit from their employers. "You were treated like dirt," he says, "and measured by deadlines that were unrealistic because they were set by non-technical people." After the revolution, he argues, the techies called the shots. They asked for, and received, much better pay and conditions. "The programmers realised that, far from being the 'grunts', they were the actual stars of the industry," he asserts.

In later years Tom Murphy set up a content management software company, Spin Solutions, and got to look at grunt life from an employer's perspective. Younger programmers, he says, had more business savvy than his contemporaries. When they came out of college they already understood their place in the industry machine and were familiar with American business models. They entered the labour market with a more mercenary attitude than their predecessors. They also saw themselves as part of a technical hierarchy with its own concepts of fraternity and celebrity. Programmers are loyal to each other, Murphy explains. The best developers assist others, even if they work in rival companies, in return for peer recognition. Proficiency in a specific technology is the source of their status.

The development community is divided according to members' affiliations to either Microsoft or Java, by the use of different coding tools and environments and by the lines of business that applications are written for. That means that it is a constellation with many tight-knit star systems. Programmers interact with others in the same orbit and have little contact with the other groups. Developers in, for example, e-learning companies know the real experts in courseware authoring tools and methodologies, but have no idea of who's who in wireless data applications.

Employers are very much aware of this star system and seek out the techie celebrities. Some argue that one exceptional performer is vastly more productive, and therefore worth much more to a software company, than a dozen average developers. The rankings are not always reflected in job titles and there are obvious reasons why companies never broadcast the names of their backroom geniuses. Often, however, chief executives quietly acknowledge the contributions of some brilliant individual.

Back in the 1960s those star systems were labelled IBM, ICL and Honeywell. The Irish Computer Society (ICS) was formed in 1967 as an initiative to bring these groups together for the first time. The association has always focused on computing as a profession rather than on commercial issues. It continues to formulate policies on education, qualifications and career paths. For example, it has put considerable effort into enabling software developers to participate in the Institution of Engineers of Ireland's professional hierarchy.

In the early years of the ICS, most systems ran financial management applications and programmers were expected to understand how accountancy functioned as well as how to construct pieces of code. Computer staff still learned their craft on the job more often than in academic institutions. According to Trinity College Dublin lecturer Dudley Dolan, who has been active in the ICS since its inception, software work became more stratified in the 1970s. Promotion options for programmers appeared. Systems analysts emerged as a separate group who talked to customers and assessed their requirements. The analysts had their own skill sets and seniority structures. Dolan points out, however, that the managers at the top of the computing job ladder were still reporting to accountants. The situation changed in the following decade, when hundreds of software companies sprung up and much less of the work on offer was inside user organisations. In the 1980s, Dudley Dolan says, the programmers came under fierce pressure to deliver value for money and found themselves working harder and working longer hours.

As the number of software writers increased, a new breed of employees that had studied software at university began to define itself through an affinity with technology. They gravitated to the companies that undertook research projects or developed software engineering tools. Today's geek culture evolved as this group's attitudes and expectations permeated the wider software workforce in generations three and four. Paul O'Dea at International Ventures says that the developers of the 1990s showed a better understanding of the processes needed to build good software. But they also put less passion into their work. At the start of the decade staff wanted to "own" pieces of code and had a strong belief in their integrity. By the end of the decade software development was less like a vocation and more of a job. "Twenty years ago," O'Dea says, "people wrote code because that was what they wanted to do. Later on people came in with more of a financial motivation." Productivity and quality, he adds, declined as a result.

Towards the end of the century, the arrogant element of the mindset was more evident than ever. One anecdote told of a 21-year-old developer who quit his job after taking offence at being asked to test some code. He proceeded to sell his services as a contractor for €400 a day.

The subjects of such tales were invariably male. Women were always a minority in the workforce and the imbalance seems to have increased since the grunt revolution that Tom Murphy describes. There have, of course, been outstanding women in the Irish software story, such as database pioneer Jane Grimson at Trinity College Dublin, National Software Director Jennifer Condon and company founders like Cadco's Anne O'Leary and SoftCo's Susan Spence. The majority of female executives in software firms, however, work in areas like marketing, customer services or personnel management.

There is a striking predominance of females, indeed, at the meetings of a human resources circle run by the Irish Software Association. When this group came together in 1998, the industry was struggling to fill vacant jobs and searching for staff retention strategies. Its agenda changed after 2001 when some of the largest employers slashed their headcounts, graduate recruitment dried up and debates about incentive schemes made way for discussions about redundancy packages. The industry avoided a meltdown on the scale of the late 1980s, but human resources specialists estimate that the total workforce in software development declined by ten per cent or more after 2001.

Some of the displaced staff pocketed their redundancy money, declared that they were leaving the software business or went travelling in Australia. Others returned to college. There has been a marked increase in the number of postgraduate students since 2001. People who had moved into software development from other lines of work, such as financial services, drifted back to those areas. User organisations, especially in the public sector, rebuilt information services groups that had been depleted in the 1990s. In short, geek culture had to sober up.

The reactions and attitudes differed according to age group. Younger members of the coding teams became disillusioned. Some who had entered the industry with unrealistic expectations about share options and initial public offerings spoke of changing their careers. But the thirty-something developers, who understood the cyclical nature of the software industry, were better prepared for the tightening up at the end of generation four. They could recognise it as business as usual.

Chapter 13

FRONTIER TALES 2

Hatched from an Incubator

Waterford Technologies held a reception to introduce itself and its technology in August 2001. The event followed all the standard practices for a twenty-first century software launch. The company had plenty of precedents to follow and groundrules to observe when it brought the MailMeter product to market. It had been born into a business environment that guided new ventures along well-worn paths.

In terms of function and positioning, however, MailMeter was curiously reminiscent of one of the earliest Irish software products. It bore striking similarities to Insight, the minicomputer package that AMS wrote more than 20 years earlier. Both products were designed to make more effective use of data that was already sitting inside enterprise applications. Insight extracted financial information and reworked it in a way that enabled managers to understand the operation of their businesses. MailMeter sieved through e-mail traffic records. It showed companies how their employees actually used messaging systems to communicate internally and with the outside world. It also assisted administrators to set and implement policies on acceptable mail usage.

The echoes of Insight extended to the export strategy for MailMeter. Like AMS before it, Waterford Technologies consciously chose to write a software package for international users, then decided to target Britain and the US before it entered other markets. The company opened offices in both countries.

Where Waterford Technologies differed dramatically from its predecessor was in the process through which the company was formed. AMS, like most of its contemporaries, began life as a supplier of bespoke software to local customers and switched to software packages later. Waterford Technologies was hatched in an incubator.

The South East Enterprise Platform Programme was one of a series of regional company formation initiatives. Waterford Institute of Technology co-ordinated this 12-month training and support scheme for local entrepreneurs. One of the participants, Lorcan Kennedy, had plans to develop document compression software that would integrate with Microsoft Exchange e-mail servers. Brendan Nolan was interested in setting up a company to commercialise the development skills in a telecommunications software systems group at the Institute of Technology. Fiona Mulvaney joined the scheme to set up an information technology training business. As the programme progressed, these three participants decided to band together in a single company. Brendan Nolan, who had previously worked as a software contractor in Ireland, Britain, Netherlands and the US, took on the role of chief executive.

At first, according to Nolan, the trio backed Kennedy's compression software project. They demonstrated a beta version to a group of IT managers from the finance industry in Dublin, but found little interest. Some of the managers commented, however, that their companies needed reliable data on e-mail usage. Waterford Technologies took up this challenge and started work on MailMeter.

The company developed separate versions of the product to work with two e-mail server applications — Microsoft's Exchange and IBM's Lotus Domino. But is did not seek strategic relationships with Microsoft or IBM. "Our product just sits on top of their platforms," Nolan says. In the past the potential market for software applications was defined by computer hardware. Today, however, software products complement one another and the type of hardware underneath is almost incidental.

Brendan Nolan claims that MailMeter is still unique and has evolved to cater for larger organisations and their mail servers. Other vendors offer plenty of applications that inspect and filter the content of electronic messages. But he does not know of any other firm that has focused on the behaviour of employees as mail users.

Since it emerged from the business incubation programme, Waterford Technologies has availed of other support mechanisms for generation five start-ups in Ireland. It raised money through the Business Expansion Scheme (BES), which offers tax concessions to private investors in emerging companies. When it hit the maximum sum allowed under the BES rules, two of the contributors agreed to provide additional finance outside the scheme. Enterprise Ireland supplied funds through its research technology and innovation initiative, enabling the company to accelerate its development work. Waterford Technologies raised €2 million through these routes. If it wished, it could have sought institutional investors as well.

Waterford Technologies was born into a world of business parks that offer special terms and facilities for start-ups. Generation five companies can avail of Enterprise Ireland's shared offices in major cities abroad. They can access a plethora of translation and localisation services, often based inside Ireland. They can market and deliver products via websites. They can make themselves known through internet search engines that steer users to new products.

The existence of this support infrastructure shows how much has changed since the first software exporters ventured outside Ireland. A product like MailMeter, on the other hand, shows how some things stay the same.

Hijacked by Venture Capitalists

Long before dozens of mobile software companies sprouted up across the city, Dublin had Silicon and Software Systems. S3, as it was commonly known, opened in 1986 as a contract designer of integrated circuits. When the European telecommunications industry agreed on the GSM standard for digital mobile networks, S3 took on GSM software projects. Philips, which was the majority shareholder in the Dublin firm, commissioned it to develop the operation and maintenance system for a

GSM base station. S3 also designed digital signal processors that made their way into other vendors' products for the new mobile infrastructure.

Robert Baker joined S3 in 1988. It hired him to install and look after its communications infrastructure, not as a GSM software developer. He spent two years there, then moved on to a new job at a system and network implementation firm. Almost a decade later he was running his own company, Baker Consultants, which installed private intranets and advised its clients on network security matters. Then he chanced upon an opportunity to return to the GSM software business. Baker joined forces with Hugh O'Donoghue and Warren Buckley and set up Xiam in 1999.

Warren Buckley was a software developer in Bank of Ireland Group Treasury. "He was a purist — an academic who went into business because he found it more interesting than university," Baker says. Buckley had written an application that enabled the bank to send currency rate updates to selected customers in text messages. Robert Baker suggested that this software could be commercialised and sold more widely as an SMS gateway. Such a product, he reckoned, could make big money quickly in a way that his consulting firm could not. He kept the service business running in the background, but took on the chief executive's position at Xiam at its inception and held it until December 2001.

Generation four was still in full swing and software start-ups assumed that venture capital was easy to find. Xiam started by targeting one of the big names. Robert Baker had previously had close connections with TGV Software, a California company that Cisco acquired in 1996. He approached the venture capital department at Cisco and asked if it would back the SMS gateway. The networking technology giant replied that the product was outside its areas of interest, but it referred Baker to Vertex Venture Capital in Singapore. Vertex offered to finance Xiam if the start-up brought in a local investor as well. Dublin-based Delta Partners came on board and Xiam, which was still in its infancy, secured a total package worth more than €2.5 million in 1999. "We got more venture capital than the company was worth because the area we were in was perceived as sexy," Baker says.

Two years later Xiam pulled in a further €6.75 million from the original investors plus ADD Partners in London. It also received an alternative offer of €20 million from Paribas, but turned this down because Paribas wanted total control of its business.

Xiam's situation in 2001 showed the central paradox of generation four. The company had plenty of cash at its disposal from institutional investors and could have chosen to accumulate much more. But it was struggling to make money from sales of its Xiam Information Router. Other developers had come up with the same SMS gateway concept. Xiam found it hard to sign up distribution partners and even harder to sign up customers. "We had lots of competition, but we had the only product that could do it all without requiring any programmers," Baker claims. "Our biggest problem was that in every single country there was some local GSM applications company with an SMS solution."

Xiam's first partner was an Irish network operator. Eircell undertook to promote the gateway among its commercial customers and to share the resulting revenues with the software firm. Robert Baker believes that this was the first time that a mobile service had agreed to this type of revenue split in relation to an SMS product. Xiam tried to negotiate similar deals with other network operators, but none were interested. It supplied its package to the GSM Association, the industry organisation that promoted the GSM standard. This move attracted plenty of enquiries but few orders. It released a Japanese version of the SMS gateway and became the first software firm outside Japan to obtain product approval from both J-Phone and NTT DoCoMo. But the sales were sluggish. The company scored a success in 2001, when it landed an implementation project with Vodafone Fiji. This sounded impressive, but Robert Baker points out that the SMS market in Fiji was about the same size as the SMS market in Limerick.

In retrospect, he says that the SMS Gateway was never going to sell in large volumes because Xiam was a late entrant to the market. Mobile operators preferred to source text messaging technologies from established names like CMG, Logica and Nokia. Other organisations that wanted SMS applications turned to local suppliers. Xiam probably performed as well as it could. It signed and supported hundreds of customers, but never broke through to the masses. The company catered for a steady stream of enterprises and information providers with special messaging needs. It expanded its list of reference sites and developed new content management features for the gateway. But it was merely a niche player and SMS was moving into the latter stages of its natural life cycle.

Warren Buckley, meanwhile, had given Xiam a second product. XML had emerged as a document integration technology. He noticed at an early stage that the XML format could also record the properties of an internet protocol packet and thus combine content handling and networking functions in a new way. Hugh O'Donoghue took charge of technical strategy for the SMS gateway, so that Buckley could concentrate on creating an XML router.

This product was launched in autumn 2001 by a new Xiam division called PolarLake. Buckley's initial concept had expanded into a large-scale framework for developing XML applications and integrating them with existing enterprise applications and middleware. According to Baker, PolarLake's technology was much more flexible than other, better-known vendors could supply and represented the start of a new breed of software for information distribution. Once again, much of the early interest came from the mobile communications industry in Japan and PolarLake set up an office in Tokyo.

In early 2002 PolarLake broke away from Xiam and became a separate company. Ronan Bradley, a former vice president of product management and business development at Iona, was appointed chief executive officer. Delta Partners and ADD Partners invested another €1 million in the project and became the majority shareholders.

Over the next two years the XML framework expanded. Sun and Hitachi endorsed PolarLake and became resellers of its platform. Other partners steered PolarLake towards the financial services industry, where its technology appeared to meet changing requirements for data integration in trading rooms. The company appears to have made steady progress, not only in Japan but also in Europe and North America.

Robert Baker, however, objected to the PolarLake spin-off. In his view Xiam's greatest asset had been hijacked by the external investors. He suspected that the venture capitalists would take a profit by selling off blocks of shares and that the PolarLake technology would not achieve its full potential if its ownership was diluted in this way. He feared that the company would be dismantled before it could reap the rewards. Time will tell. But Robert Baker will not be involved. He resigned from Xiam in protest at the start of 2003.

The Standard that Stagnated

March 2002 was an eventful month for Sean O'Sullivan. His company, Rococo Software, shipped its first product, ran demonstrations at the JavaOne developers' convention in San Francisco and presented a pitch to an investors' conference in Dublin. Established just over two years earlier, Rococo had 18 employees, a $3.7 million stash of venture capital and a handpicked set of beta customers spread across Asia, North America and Europe. Best of all, it was following a proven business model. The company had participated in the setting of a new middleware standard and had released a product based on that standard earlier than anyone else.

Rococo's founders knew that this formula worked. Sean O'Sullivan, Ross O'Crowley and Karl McCabe had worked together at Iona and studied the company's success from the inside.

Perhaps the industry had changed. Perhaps the ex-Iona trio chose the wrong standard. Perhaps the world's enterprise software buyers were suffering from technology fatigue and avoiding new concepts. By the end of 2002 Rococo had ceased all development work on its product and was looking for a new line of business.

According to O'Sullivan, the Dublin-based company had been convinced that a volume market existed for a development toolkit that enabled Java applications to run on mobile phones and other consumer devices. Rococo understood middleware, distributed systems and networking. In its first year it had carried out technical architecture projects for

Vision Consulting and AIB Group while it explored development opportunities. The new firm found that it could made good money from services and could take its time to draw up a product strategy.

Bluetooth, however, looked rather interesting. This wireless standard
promised easy connectivity among portable devices. Hardware designers
would be able to integrate low-cost communications components into
new products. Users would have fewer cables to worry about. The Rococo team studied the recently agreed Bluetooth specification and was
struck by the absence of a common application programming interface.
Software developers had to cater for different Bluetooth protocol stacks
when they wrote applications for different devices. Someone should design an integration product.

Rococo Software joined the Bluetooth Special Interest Group, the industry consortium that steered the wireless standard. It also linked up
with IBM, Motorola, Nokia and Extended Systems and formed a Java
expert group that would produce a specification for Bluetooth interfaces.
Rococo had a clear product strategy. It planned to release tools for developers, to sell a core reference stack and to expand its Java/Bluetooth
portfolio as the standard gained acceptance.

The company launched its Impronto suite in 2002 in conjunction
with the release of the Java working group's JSR-82 specification. It
suggested that developers could start by buying a low-cost simulator for
wireless applications. Then they could progress to the Impronto development toolkit and create those applications. The company also introduced a technology licensing kit so that the developers could embed its
software into their products.

Industry veterans praised Rococo's pilot trial, describing the exercise
as a role model for the rest of the software community. The company
chose developers from different industries and different geographies to
evaluate the pre-release version of its software. These testers worked for
software companies, network operators, automotive corporations, universities and system integration firms. The mix was exemplary.

Unfortunately, though, few software developers wanted to work with
a Java/Bluetooth combination. There was little demand for Impronto.

Sean O'Sullivan does not think that the toolkit would have fared any better if it had come from a large and established vendor. Bluetooth was problematic. The Bluetooth Special Interest Group was putting too much effort into expanding its standard and too little into getting implementations of the basic specification. Few devices were reaching the market. The first commercial hardware with a built-in JSR-82 interface did not appear until June 2003, fifteen months after the release of the standard.

By the start of 2003 Rococo had reduced its headcount and returned to the software services business. It targeted Irish organisations that wanted to link mobile devices into their enterprise systems and won a series of bespoke development contracts. Later in the year it branded this part of its work as MobileFrontier Enterprise.

It also found a new path into the product trade through a partnership with Belfast-based Aepona, the developer of the Causeway platform for fixed and mobile telecommunications service providers. Causeway uses Open Service Access (OSA) programming interfaces from the Parlay Group to integrate new applications into the operators' network infrastructures. Rococo designed a family of applications that run on top of Causeway and other OSA/Parlay gateways. It launched this suite in 2004 under the MobileFrontier Operator name and identified potential users among its partner's contacts.

The Java/Bluetooth business trundled on in the background. In fact, the Impronto technology generated half of Rococo's revenues in 2003, even though all of its 12 staff were assigned to MobileFrontier projects. Ericsson Technology Licensing bundled the Java middleware with its Bluetooth protocols in response to customer requirements. Then Aplix, a Japanese company that had recently entered into a partnership with Motorola, integrated Rococo's technology into its Java environment for mobile handsets. Sean O'Sullivan foresees a continuing royalty stream from the 2002 vintage middleware. "The product is in good shape," he says. "If someone calls and asks for something, we can deliver."

In mid-2004 the Bluetooth Special Interest Group announced that its radio communications technology had been built into 150 million devices and another two million units were shipping every week. Much of this momentum, though, involved the motor industry and consumer electronics rather than mobile phones and handheld computers. The JSR-82 specification will probably live on as an occasional requirement for developers, but will never be the hot technology that Rococo envisaged back in 2001. The company expects that MobileFrontier Operator will soon become its core business.

According to O'Sullivan, Rococo's financial backers welcomed its move away from Java/Bluetooth middleware, where the company has a whole market to itself. Its OSA/Parlay applications will face direct competition from other products. Vertical market software is now a safer bet than development tools. And driving the introduction of a new industry standard is much less attractive than it used to be.

Sailing with Microsoft

Chris Byrne was starting a software development operation in Limerick for the third time around when he launched Narragansett Technologies in 2001. The company's chief technology officer Richard Coady and senior architect Ned Keniry had also been around the block before. These three colleagues had previously worked together at Software 2000 and in Software Architects International (SAI).

Software 2000 was an American outfit that sold financial management applications for IBM's mid-range computer families. Its salesforce had a strong reputation, but it had to compete in one of the more crowded sections of the applications trade. In 1988, when the company wanted to expand into Europe, it opened a development centre in Limerick. Chris Byrne, who had previously worked at Software 2000's headquarters in Massachusetts, was appointed to lead this new operation. Three years later he left the firm and set up SAI with assistance, in the form of employment grants and accommodation, from Shannon Development. Software 2000 withdrew from Ireland soon afterwards.

Like the US developer, SAI initially positioned itself in the IBM camp. Its Cashbook product integrated cash management functions into standard ledgers, supplementing the features in bigger vendors' accounting packages. The company landed OEM agreements with SSA and Hoskyns. By the late 1990s it had added electronic banking and treasury applications to its portfolio and in 2000 a new SAI subsidiary, Redeo Technologies, offered multi-currency settlement software for transborder electronic procurement transactions. By this time SAI had developed a preference for Microsoft platforms and, more specifically, it had latched onto Microsoft's server technologies for electronic commerce services.

The Limerick company was one of the big winners in the acquisitions frenzy at the turn of the millennium. In 2000 Atlanta-based Clarus Corporation, which was also strongly committed to Microsoft technologies, offered a whopping $175 million in shares for SAI and Redeo. The SAI team, who had never involved any venture capitalists in the company, negotiated an alternative deal. They agreed to sell the business for $30 million in cash plus $30 million in shares. After the Limerick operation was absorbed into Clarus, the American company's fortunes nosedived. In 2002 Clarus sold all of its core products and operations for just $1 million in cash. By then, several members of the former SAI team had regrouped at Narragansett.

The company took its name from a piece of coastline in Rhode Island, where Chris Byrne liked to go sailing. This nautical theme was extended to Narragansett's first product, an e-mail marketing campaign application called SpinnakerPro, which emerged in the second half of 2002.

"Web services seem to have mushroomed and have become a whole sector in its own right," Byrne commented when he launched the new firm. It based its technology roadmap on this approach to data integration and on its expectation that Microsoft would not make any disruptive changes to its operating system. Narragansett Technologies introduced itself to the world in October 2001 at a Microsoft developers conference in Los Angeles. It was not yet saying much about its product intentions. But the start-up wanted to be seen as a supporter of the Microsoft .Net platform and to identify potential allies among the other supporters. In 2002 it forged a partnership with enterprise applications developer Epicor Software, which agreed to make SpinnakerPro available through its distributors and resellers as part of its own Clientele product set. Epicor bought most of the remaining assets of Clarus at about the same time.

Chris Byrne draws a parallel between the positioning of IBM's mid-range computers in the early days of SAI and the space that is occupied today by Microsoft .Net. Customers, he explains, put considerable effort into their own relationships with these platforms and have shown themselves willing to pay for new applications. He adds, however, that he has found IBM better than Microsoft at partnering with independent software developers.

According to Byrne, Narragansett is a more focused business than SAI, which kept spotting new areas where applications could be developed and dived into them opportunistically. Narragansett remained a single-product company until 2004, when it extracted a web survey management module from the SpinnakerPro system and rebranded this as SensorPro.

The software industry as a whole, Byrne adds, has become more focused, making it harder to start new ventures. In the 1990s, he explains, companies were deemed to be delivering the goods if they could demonstrate a product prototype and give an availability date. Today they are not taken seriously until they have working applications and paying customers. This requires substantial sums of money upfront. This, he says, is why the availability of venture capital is so important.

Narragansett ensured that it would have cash at its disposal in 2001, when it announced a €2.25 million private placement backed by ABN Amro. This money was never actually drawn down. Chris Byrne and Richard Coady paid for the development of SpinnakerPro. The company built its own office block beside the former SAI premises on the technology park. Its sales began to rise in 2003 and by the middle of the following year it had chalked up 30 client installations. Most of these were in Europe, but the Epicor partnership had produced a scattering of users in North America and the company outlined an expansion plan for Asia.

The Narragansett software is available as a licensed product or as a hosted solution. The majority of customers to date have preferred the second option and access the campaign management software online for the duration of their marketing promotions. Chris Byrne says that it takes less time to get the applications up and running if they are installed on the development company's own computers. These systems, of course, are powered by Microsoft .Net. The Limerick firm continues to assert its loyalty to its chosen platform.

Friend of the Top 400

Robert Winters and Kevin Glavin worked together in the mid-1990s at the Euristix office in California. They forged contacts with American network technology vendors, watched what the key companies were doing and identified prospective customers and partners. Winters subsequently moved to Japan and China to cultivate more industry relationships. These travels convinced him that the networking business is actually rather small. He encountered plenty of developers and plenty of companies but, he reckons, there are only about 400 people who really matter. The best way to understand the industry, he concluded, is to find out who these individuals are and then follow their careers.

In 2000 Winters and Glavin joined up with another former Euristix executive, Alan Robinson, and launched Shenick. Ten years earlier Euristix had chosen a business plan that treated consulting and contract development as stepping stones to a telecommunications product. Dun Laoghaire-based Shenick took the same approach. In its first six months the new venture hired two dozen network software engineers. It opened a branch in Silicon Valley and placed the data communications skills of its team at the disposal of its friends in the top 400.

From the outside Shenick looked like a twenty-first-century clone of its predecessor. Robert Winters points out that there were some differences. Shenick, he says, started life with a more complete service offering. Euristix generally took on pieces of a project that was already underway. When an equipment vendor discovered that its next product required an additional protocol stack, the software contractor was available to deliver it. According to Winters, Shenick preferred to get involved with product development at the planning stage and to work through the entire design and testing process. The company claimed that its engineers could shorten the end-to-end cycle.

Shenick also switched from services to products more rapidly than Euristix. It relaunched itself as a product vendor in 2003 and quit the contract development business completely.

The background of the company's founders had suggested that it might move into network management software. Robert Winters says that they considered this option, heard industry analysts forecasting tough market conditions and looked elsewhere instead. Mobile data technology seemed attractive, but Shenick was discouraged from entering this area by the large number of firms that had already targeted it. A project for a communications equipment vendor presented the company with an opportunity in a less crowded field.

The Dun Laoghaire firm assisted one of its clients to develop a multi-service internet switch. Through this project it encountered multi-protocol label switching — a technology that defines how traffic moves through a broadband network — in its embryonic state. Multi-protocol label switching would enable network operators to expand their ranges of communications services, to allocate different bandwidths to different customers and to charge a premium rate for guaranteed performance.

"We saw a couple of holes in the test process," Winters says. Operators would not only need to ensure that their pipelines ran smoothly; the new technology allowed them to split up those pipes and to sell different fractions for difference purposes. That would require testing the individual fractions as well. Shenick plugged these holes by developing DiversifEye.

Network testing is a low-profile line of business, but billions of dollars are spent on systems and devices that test point-to-point connections. Network operators are accustomed to buying test technologies from independent specialists, not from the suppliers of their switches or their cable infrastructure. The Shenick team reckoned that point-to-point testing was insufficient for multi-service switches that run a variety of applications. DiversifEye tests both the network equipment and the network management systems. It has integrated emulation processes and performance tests into a single platform. DiversifEye can be used in test laboratories or to analyse the quality of service on live networks. "We wanted a product that could be sold off the shelf and did not require one million dollars worth of customisation," Robert Winters adds.

Shenick floated the idea with some of its first division friends in 2002. Its California office showed an early version of the system to selected contacts. It also signed up Mitsui in Japan as a reseller. The first DiversifEye sale followed in April 2003. Six months later the company reported that it had found a pilot customer in each of the main regional markets — Europe, North America and Asia-Pacific. Additional orders followed from Japan, Korea and Australia.

Four years after its inception, Shenick is one of generation five's brightest hopes. It is positioned to benefit from the changing nature of the internet and the need for service providers to support diverse applications. It also hopes to take advantage of an expected recovery in capital investment in telecommunications after several years of depressed spending by the operators.

Shenick has also shown how to get a new firm off the ground before looking for venture capital. It waited until DiversifEye was ready to sell before seeking an external investor and opted for an Irish institution, Trinity Venture Capital, instead of one of the international funds. It has shown how to select and implement a clear business model. It has proved that companies can still sell software services upfront while building a product in the background. This traditional approach remains valid if the skill levels are high and the services are aimed at a specialist clientele.

Most of all, perhaps, the rise of Shenick highlights the re-emergence of the vertical market. The successful turn-of-the-millennium start-ups understood the dynamics of their customers' industries. Shenick tracked the telecommunications equipment vendors and service providers. AmBeo, Havok and Valista have been equally focused on specific markets. Promoters of communications technology have always argued that their innovations transform business relationships. But personal networking is as important in the twenty-first century as it has ever been. There is no substitute for knowing who's who among the top players.

Chapter 14

GENERATION FIVE AND BEYOND

Ireland's Place in the Software World Order

Marketing consultant Pearse Coyle was acting as an adviser to middleware developer Propylon, when the company bid for a contract in Belgium in 2002. The prospective customer was looking for a company with experience in XML information formats. Coyle attended a meeting with this organisation and asked whether it was realistically going to choose an Irish supplier in preference to a local software firm. He was told that the customer had never expected to find an appropriate product close to home. When it went out to tender it assumed that the strongest proposals would come from somewhere like Ireland or from one of the Nordic countries. Propylon, Coyle discovered, had got onto the shortlist because of its nationality.

Try looking at the world through the eyes of a buyer of business software. If you need an applications suite for a large enterprise, you look at vendors like SAP or PeopleSoft or Oracle — big corporations from big, wealthy economies like the US and Germany. Much of the world's security software comes from Israel. Australia has produced a wide range of accounting and insurance applications. Singapore is strong in embedded software. If you want customised coding or other labour-intensive services, the candidate companies are probably in populous, low-wage countries like India, Egypt or South Africa.

If, on the other hand, you require something specialised or technically tricky, you consider development firms in smaller countries like

Norway or Finland or Israel. Or Ireland. Small and flexible countries produce small and flexible software ventures.

This characterisation of the geography of software development may be wildly simplistic. But there is a ring of truth about it. It may also tell us something about Ireland's place in the world order in a much wider sense.

Over the past quarter century the country has shown how software development can thrive as a cottage industry. Hundreds of small companies have launched and exported specialised products. Individual businesses open and close all the time. Role models emerge and fade away. It is still a rare event for a software company to survive for a full decade under the same name and the same leadership. Collectively, however, the Irish industry keeps expanding, capitalising on its accumulation of development skills and its store of international contacts.

Sadly, the nature of this success has often been obscured by misconceptions. Some have originated inside the country. The tired old cliché that Ireland is the world's biggest software exporter has not gone away. This makes it easy for critics to suggest the country's main contribution to the industry has been to assist American companies to reduce their tax liabilities. Within Ireland, meanwhile, the public perception of what goes on in software companies has been coloured by a preoccupation with stock market listings and venture capital investments. Other misconceptions crop up in commentaries, especially from the US, that divide the software world into American and non-American camps. These complain that software services in India have taken work away from American programmers and list other countries, from Canada to China, as secondary offenders in this conspiracy. Ireland gets lumped in with the outsourcing centres as part of a giant anti-American conspiracy.

It is true that the country has been less affected than others in the west by the transfer of software assignments to India and other low-wage economies. That is because so many software developers in Ireland are employed by product vendors, not by software services firms or in corporate computing departments. The global trend has, however, touched some corners of the Irish software community. A couple of large financial institutions have awarded high-profile outsourcing contracts, while product companies like Curam Software and Propylon have off-loaded blocks of work to Indian developers.

According to Shemas Eivers, whose company Client Solutions is in the services area of the business, the offshore phenomenon may also have harmed the Irish industry in a less direct way. Many software product companies, he explains, started off by securing a big contract from a local customer and using this work to create the template for a future product. "When you got past being a two-man office, you had to get one of those contracts," he says. Those opportunities, he adds, are no longer being presented to start-ups in Ireland, disrupting the company formation process.

Valista CEO Raomal Perera — who was born in Sri Lanka, but has spent most of his working life in Ireland — believes that the Asian countries will gradually build an experience base for software development in the same way as Irish industry has done. Companies in Ireland, he suggests, should therefore focus on a higher tier of the product business. It will be difficult, he adds, to attract skilled programmers from the Indian subcontinent to work in Ireland. The best will always try to move into the US. He thinks that Irish firms should aim to recruit talent from eastern Europe instead.

Dublin-based consultant Pat Divilly has assisted Irish software exporters with their sales strategies and has advised companies from the developing world that want to attract service contracts. He says that the Irish industry should expect competition from places that it did not previously come from. The Baltic states, he notes, are technically very sophisticated and are partnering with software firms in Sweden and Finland in order to sell abroad. Vietnam is encouraging software development by giving tax breaks to individual programmers instead of to companies. Egyptian companies are buying market share by pitching their prices at a fixed discount on the international average. Divilly also expects that Indian companies will move into product development as their US-based executives become more familiar with the applications market.

Jim Mountjoy, the former head of Baltimore Technologies and Euristix, says that the newer software companies ought to become "more cerebral", developing applications that meet the higher order needs of their customer organisations. He also says that the standard of management in Irish firms will have to improve as more sources of competition appear.

Chris Horn at Iona points out that the movements of people determine the locations of software development. The industry follows streams of talent, not the availability of financial incentives. "Am I going to get top computer engineers in Lithuania or Estonia when I can go to China or Taiwan and get engineers with Silicon Valley experience?" he asks. Horn describes India and China as hotbeds of innovation — much more than outsourcing economies. The time has come, he argues, for Irish software companies to seek early adopters in these markets, especially in China which he describes as particularly receptive to new technologies.

In summary, the software industry in Ireland cannot hope to stand out in terms of human resources. Other countries will produce much larger numbers of software engineers and award more PhDs in computer science and mathematics. Companies will need to seek advantage through other means — their ability to network abroad, their knowledge of the international customer base and their understanding of how the software business works. More and more, they will also need an in-depth knowledge of the industries where their target customers operate, so that they can identify niche markets based on line-of-business trends as well as on technical considerations.

One factor that is unlikely to change is the pivotal position of the American market. The United States is still the primary target for software product developers. If their work is accepted there, they gain credibility in the rest of the world. Despite the best efforts of the European Commission to represent the EU as one big home market, it is still easier for a European developer to sell software into other member states after it has done deals across the Atlantic. This is as true for a French or a Swedish company as for an Irish one.

The contact networks between America and Europe, however, are now much looser and weaker than those that link the US and Asia. The software industry advances through the informal flow of information and ideas across these networks. In the minicomputer era there were healthy links between the east coast of the US, where most of the manufacturers were based, and western Europe. These assisted European developers to influence the evolution of software technology in the minicomputer era. Today the connections from California and Washington State to mainland China, Taiwan and India are growing stronger and firmer, while few European firms have made much impact in Silicon Valley. The transatlantic grapevine looks distinctly undernourished.

Micro-Multinationals

There is a neatly furnished office in a west Dublin business park where most of the tenants are clothing wholesalers. This room does not have a desktop computer or a fixed telephone line. But it provides a glimpse into the future of Irish software. Jim Callan, the founder of Erego, uses this office as his base. No one else works there. There is not even a brass plate outside the building. The rest of the Erego organisation is in India.

Jim Callan met Rakesh Jain in the early 1990s when they both worked for Third Wave. Their partnership continued in banking software company Eontec, which was one of the first development firms in Ireland to farm out blocks of work to India. Jain built up an operation in Delhi for Eontec and eventually became a director of the firm.

Erego is the two colleagues' latest project. It is building an enterprise software product but is saying little about its intentions. Unlike Eontec, though, it does not plan to sell banking applications. Callan says that offshore development in India often be difficult and can actually be very expensive if the management structures are poor. Investors, however, like software companies to have a presence in India. And he is confident that Jain can deliver the goods. "If you go to India you have to know the guys or else you have nothing to fall back on," he says.

If this business model works, Erego could pave the way for a new breed of "micro-multinational" software companies whose nationality will be hard to define. They may be registered in Ireland and their beneficial owners may be based in the country. The core competence of knowing how to build a product business will thus be Irish. A growing band of industry veterans has been through the process more than once before and some can fund the development of new products from their personal resources. Every other activity of the micro-multinational, however, will be located somewhere else.

The development team will typically go to a country where the wages are low and English is the business language. It could be India. Or Egypt or South Africa or the Philippines. If Jim Callan is correct, the quality of the local management may be more important than the quality of the programming.

Once the product has been built, someone has to promote it. The sales and marketing office ought to be close to the prospective customers. And, in most cases, the micro-multinational software company will want to target the US. America has the sales skills. So the company's commercial headquarters will probably go there. Sales and marketing are expensive and usually require external investment. That money will probably be found in America as well.

As the company becomes established and gains more customers, it will need to add implementation and support structures. All of these services can be obtained from system integrators. The integrators can also provide a wider geographic coverage than development companies can achieve on their own. It is difficult, though, to convince the integrators to assign staff and resources to new products and brands. Someone has to attract their attention, build the relationships and do all the networking at industry conferences and on technical committees. This is another set of skills that Irish software entrepreneurs can contribute.

Here, in summary, is the formula for a new type of software company. It will probably stay small and highly specialised and is unlikely to seek long-term sustainability. Its geographically dispersed model, though, will make it function in the same way as a large corporation, not like a small enterprise in the conventional sense.

It might be argued that these virtual software companies will make no contribution to the skills pool in Ireland and that any expertise acquired by their employees will be applied in future projects elsewhere.

On the other hand, the co-ordination of a micro-multinational will demand a special knowledge. It actually sounds like the "command and control" model that some international corporations have proposed as an appropriate role for their subsidiaries in Ireland. Whatever happens to the country's software development teams, Ireland's software business managers should find new opportunities to pursue.

Can we get this on the Web for Free?

Developers have always begged and borrowed pieces of software from each other. In generation one they exchanged reels of tape, often without the knowledge of their bosses. Employees in generation five companies routinely download code samples and productivity enhancing tools from websites. Some also obtain database software or e-mail management systems or desktop application suites in this way and pass them on to end users. There is a mass of free code available in the twenty-first century and the web has made it easy to track it down and try it out. Much of this software comes under the jurisdiction of open source groups that draw on the development talents of volunteers around the world.

The Linux operating system is the best-known product of the open source style of software development. Its spread has been mirrored by the Apache web server, the Zope content management framework and the JBoss application server. The users of these products can participate in the development process, proposing enhancements and modifications or submitting new pieces of code. The prominence and popularity of these platforms have attracted large groups of volunteers. Some create ancillary products and distribute them under open source rules. The movement has also discouraged commercial developers from working in the areas that it covers.

Open source licensing has changed the expectations of business software buyers, especially those with enough technical knowledge to access and explore the source code. In many instances they now assume that the products will come free and that their budgets will pay instead for implementation, integration and maintenance. This implies a shift in customer spending from the products trade to the services business.

Iona chief executive Chris Horn points out that organisations are also consolidating their use of software and dispensing with the less essential purchases. Large companies with internal information systems groups, especially in America, are systematically searching for free alternatives to the products they have licensed in the past. "If you are selling something, you will have to have a clear justification for selling it for a fee," Horn says. Iona reached an accommodation with this trend in 2003, when it offered support services for the Java-based JBoss application server under the same terms as it supports its proprietary software. This, the company reckoned, would assist it to sell its development tools into JBoss installations.

The first case of open source altering the role of a development group in Ireland had appeared some years earlier at Sun's European software centre in Dublin. This operation managed the transfer of Sun's StarOffice desktop productivity suite to an independent governance body, the OpenOffice.org foundation, in 2000. It subsequently took on stewardship of portions of Gnome 2.0, an open source desktop environment, and participated in the release of this technology.

Irish-based software organisations were much slower to support open source initiatives and, in contrast with other countries, few service companies promoted free software in the local market. Insofar as there was any interest in the international movement, it took the form of application developers releasing versions of their products for Linux-based computers. They knew how difficult it would be to convince the state agencies or institutional investors to support a business plan based upon the open source model.

Some small operations, usually run by a single developer, offered free products, or shareware, over the web. It was not until 2004, however, that an established company with a substantial product embraced open source licensing.

Wilde Technologies had emerged from the distributed systems group at Trinity College Dublin in 1999 with original ideas on how to tighten the integration between design rules and assembly processes in software development. Within two years it had raised €3 million in private funding. This paid for the recruitment of an experienced management team. In 2002 Wilde launched its Wilde 1.0 application design and development toolset. Microsoft facilitated the promotion of this product across the international developer community that favoured its platforms. In the following year the company previewed Wilde 2.0 and announced that this would be embedded into the Visual Studio system that Microsoft supplied to developers.

When Wilde 2.0 was eventually released in mid-2004 it had a different name, Oscar, and had been re-positioned as an open source technology. Wilde Technologies had shrunk to a fraction of its previous size, but reported that more than 2,500 software architects and developers had registered their interest in Oscar. Company founder Stephen Barrett spoke of harnessing the enthusiasm of a worldwide user group to guide the future of the development toolset. He also emphasised that Wilde would continue to pursue commercial relationships with Oscar's users. Anyone could download the software without paying fees, but the company was confident that it could build up a revenue stream.

Open source licensing continues to spread, but not at the rate that the more enthusiastic advocates had expected, especially when the software is used by people other than software developers. There is little talk of free software to run critical operations in banking or medicine or telecommunications. The buyers prefer vendors with the resources to fix any problems that arise. The e-learning suppliers also seem to have brushed off the concept of free courseware, claiming that these cannot match the quality of their products. Furthermore, as Wilde's strategy suggests, the division between paid-for and free code is not as rigid as it used to be. Established software corporations like BEA Systems, Computer Associates and Novell are offering portions of their product sets under open source licences, while newer companies from the open source movement are charging fees for premium versions of their software. Managed service providers, meanwhile, are supplying the traditional packages and open source products alike under software leasing agreements.

Nonetheless, the open source phenomenon has left a permanent mark on Irish software. The producers of development tools and integration middleware thrived in the 1990s, but have now lost their leadership role in the industry. There is little incentive to be first to market with software based on an industry standard, when that technology is going to be available free of charge. New business models are required. And software entrepreneurs are finding those in product categories other than tools and middleware.

The Next Core Cluster

Generation one companies sold services on the local market in Ireland. Generation two developers, such as Kindle, Insight and RTS, looked further afield, but there was little originality in their products. The companies that prospered in generation three were those, like Iona, that seeded new markets. The successful firms focused on industry standards and middleware rather than business applications. Generation four was spearheaded by the mobile brigade. Generation five has seen a return to the vertical markets.

The best performers since the turn of the century have been companies that combined their knowledge of software architecture and design with an understanding of their customers' lines of business. Firms like Curam Software and Fineos, Performix Technologies and Qumas hark back to the generation two developers that also targeted vertical markets. Unlike their predecessors, though, these companies understand that products are differentiated through a combination of software technology and software functionality.

The reorientation of Norkom Technologies is a sign of the times. When this Dublin company launched its Alchemist customer behaviour analysis software in 1999, it positioned itself as a business intelligence specialist. It always expected that its buyers would come from financial services and telecommunications, but it tried to attract them through its knowledge of customer relationship management, not through its familiarity with their industries. The demand for business intelligence products slowed down in 2001. Alchemist implementations were cancelled and Norkom had to scale down. At this point the company decided to concentrate on risk management in financial institutions and repackaged Alchemist as an analytic application that helps them to combat credit and debit card fraud, money laundering, operational risk and other threats. In May 2004 Norkom announced that its change of strategy had delivered over €15 million in new contracts since the start of the year.

Government policy today aims to support a more research-driven software industry, drawing on the work supported by Science Foundation Ireland. But it is far from clear what sort of products will succeed in the next five to ten years. So many forecasts on the future of software have gone wrong in recent times that analysts everywhere are reluctant to make bold predictions. No one wants to look further ahead than the next year or two.

The last attempt to start a revolution fizzled out. In the late 1990s there was a general consensus that software would soon be managed through the internet instead of installed on customers' computers. Service providers made massive investments in data centres that would house these services. Industry analysts forecast the death of the software package and a dramatic reduction in the number of applications software suppliers. A new breed of applications software providers would shape the market.

What happened instead was that most of the data centres were mothballed and the companies that had built them disappeared. They were unable to recoup their massive investments in new facilities. They also discovered that customers wanted semi-bespoke services that were expensive to deliver. Many software development companies, meanwhile, started to offer their own hosting services. The managed service model did not kill them off. It became another option that they could offer to their customers, who showed a distinct preference for small-scale hosting agreements over the more sophisticated services in large data centres.

Application service providers failed to shake up the software developers' world. No technology that has been commercialised since 2000, indeed, has caused much of a stir. Recent fads and fashions have merely freshened up familiar concepts. Web services and service-oriented architecture, for example, are just the latest variations on application integration. Wi-fi connectivity is merely another style of enterprise networking. Tools for business activity monitoring or the "real time enterprise" add new functions to business intelligence applications without altering the fundamentals of company management. Grid technologies may prove more disruptive by creating an infrastructure where computers share their processing power over the internet as transparently as they now share the contents of web pages. Putting this utility computing concept into practice within organisations, however, has been a long, slow process. Inter-company grids will be much more difficult to establish.

There is thus no obvious rallying point for the next round of software product development. It is possible, indeed, that generation six will be distinguished from its predecessors through its business strategies instead of through its choices of markets or technologies. Nonetheless, the clustering tendency remains strong. It still makes sense for companies with similar interests to be located near each other in the way that the middleware and mobile applications specialists grew up in bunches.

In recent years, moreover, Enterprise Ireland has extended its support services for software developers into related businesses and most notably into digital content creation. This shift became apparent in 1999, when the agency renamed its National Software Directorate as the National Informatics Directorate. One of its new tasks was to select tenant companies for the Digital Hub — a project that designated part of Dublin's southwest inner city as a digital content zone. By mid-2004, this district housed about 30 organisations, including the government-sponsored Media Lab Europe research facility.

The progress of the digital content initiatives has been slow and the average content creation company is still very small. But the strategy has enabled a pool of games developers to get off the ground for the first time in Ireland. It has also assisted suppliers of software tools for digital media production. Havok, another offshoot of software research in Trinity College Dublin, is the most prominent company in this new pack. Its physics engine for games designers determines how on-screen characters and vehicles move and interact.

Havok's area of operation is extremely specialised, but the emergence of the company shows that middleware developers from Ireland can still succeed internationally. Chris Horn at Iona believes that software engineering is due to take another quantum leap, comparable with the introduction of Java in the last decade. This, he suggests, will create opportunities for vendors to launch more intelligent software development tools. In particular, he sees potential for a new cluster around the semantic web initiative, which aims to develop a platform on which data can be shared and processed by software agents — automated tools that perform tasks without human intervention.

Donal Daly at International Ventures, meanwhile, is tracking the evolution of financial applications. The finance industry, he believes, is ready for a new software paradigm, although the form that this will take is not yet clear. Other observers expect a similar wave of change in telecommunications software. Developments in the biotechnology industry may also spark a demand for new categories of software tools.

Niche opportunities will also arise in product categories where Ireland already has proven expertise. These include online security, where Baltimore Technologies built up a knowledge base, and compliance management for regulated industries, where companies like Automsoft International, Qumas and WBT Systems are active. Other companies may identify products that draw on the country's track record in localisation services. Customer interaction technologies, speech recognition and automated translation could be areas to watch.

Wherever the cluster arises, it will need access to new industry standards. One of the challenges for start-ups today is to participate in industry-specific standards groups, as well as tracking the emergence of new software specifications. That involves plugging into the heart of the games community or biotech consortia or financial services regulation — special interest groups that may be harder to join than the middleware and telecommunications committees. The next core cluster, indeed, might arise in the vertical market where Irish companies are best placed to gain access to the standardisation process.

Another Shot at Services

Ireland would never have had an exporting software industry without the packaged product. It is difficult to envisage a future that is not based on product sales, even though some customers will prefer to rent new applications by the month instead of buying them outright. Looking at the global market, however, more money is spent on software-related services than on product licences. Computer installations are steadily increasing the proportion of their expenditure that goes on service contracts and allocating less to enterprise applications. Economists, indeed, still classify software development as a service activity.

The changing mix of IBM's business provides a striking illustration of the trend towards services. The corporation was traditionally a product manufacturer that offered customer services as a sideline. In the 1990s its services division expanded to the point that it became IBM's core business. The company still designs computers and storage systems and writes software. Increasingly, however, these products are introduced into user organisations on the back of the services delivered by IBM Global Services.

Other system integrators and managed service providers have also become hugely influential around the globe. Intermediaries like Accenture and BearingPoint and EDS select combinations of software products, install them on behalf of customers, support end users and manage upgrades. Their product preferences have a significant effect on the fortunes of individual development companies. More and more the software firms must come up with products that will appeal to system integrators.

The system integration companies are normally found in the same locations as their largest customers, even if they transfer part of the workload to low-cost service centres elsewhere. Ireland's position on the edge of Europe and the scarcity of high-spending user organisations inside the country have hindered software service ventures. There is evidence, nonetheless, that the country has been a successful base for specialist services, where customers are willing to pay a premium price and do not seek out suppliers with low labour costs. Vision Consulting, which offers software development behind business strategy and project management services, is the most obvious example. Codec is another. The company started to implement other vendors' financial analytical applications in the mid-1980s and gradually expanded into parts of central and southern Europe where it saw opportunities for skills transfer.

The reputation of software services was tarnished during generation four. In the late 1990s a bunch of newcomers posed as experts in internet-based services, borrowed extravagantly, opened sales offices abroad and declared that they were leaders in e-business transformation. One of the most prominent service companies, Ebeon, also developed software tools to support its internal operations, but decided not to sell this technology because it did not want to be a product vendor. Ebeon emerged at the same time as a bunch of new product companies with internet-related software. Most of these survived when the going got tough in the new century. But the service ventures closed down.

Robert Baker is confident that Irish service companies will find international niches in the coming years. Baker spent the early years of the century in the software product trade, co-founding middleware companies Xiam and PolarLake. His latest venture, Acecedes, has a very different business model. It builds and manages secure private networks for international companies.

According to Baker, software development in Ireland has had its heyday and the experience of the past two decades should now be channelled into managed services. In particular, he foresees an international shortage of security and storage management skills and believes that technically strong service companies can succeed in these areas. "Software development in Ireland is crazy. There are millions in India and even more in China who will do the work for less," he argues. "Where I see growth is in adding value to all the software that will be churned out."

Another prominent industry figure had turned his back on product development some years earlier. Tony McGuire, the creator of Insight, one of the earliest Irish software packages, decided in 1994 that he wanted to run a services business instead. This followed a reunion between McGuire and Insight Software's founder Matt Crotty, who had acquired Blue Rainbow, a developer of electronic document interchange applications. They tried to attract customers, but found little interest and gave up on the Blue Rainbow project in 1993.

This experience convinced McGuire that software development had become too expensive. "What I wanted to do," he says, "was to build a company that looked like a small version of Cap Gemini and was focused on Ireland. I didn't want to develop a product again." First he bought Dascom Open Systems, a Dublin-based services company. In 1996 he acquired System Dynamics from Arrival Holdings and brought the two operations together under the System Dynamics name. McGuire updated the company's offerings to include the implementation of application server technology and business intelligence software. More and more of its work came to centre on IBM software products.

In 2000 System Dynamics announced that it had merged with a California company, Anna Technology, that specialised in embedded computing and remote device management. Anna was much bigger than the Dublin firm, but the partners claimed that their skills were complementary. They spoke of creating a "pervasive computing" practice that could undertake projects on both sides of the Atlantic. But they were unable to raise enough money to proceed with this strategy. In August 2001, after failing to close funding deals in both the US and Germany, the companies separated. Tony McGuire says that their timing was hopelessly wrong. When they went looking for finance, they found that investors just did not want to back software developers.

System Dynamics reverted to its core business as an IBM software partner. The positioning of the company today, indeed, is remarkably similar to that of its earlier incarnation 30 years ago.

In general Ireland's software service companies are a low-profile bunch and do not experience extreme highs and lows in the same way as the product vendors. Most concentrate on contract work inside the country, but there have always been some with international ambitions and activities. The present crop includes Enovation Solutions in Dublin, Galway-based Storm Technology and Original Solutions, which was set up in 2003 and formed a services group in Limerick. Most of this team previously worked at Orygen, before it was shut down by its American parent. Original plans to target mid-tier organisations in the UK, offering expertise in Computer Associates' modelling and development tools.

Brendan Doherty has had a long career on the services side of the industry. Now based at Enovation Solutions, he believes that small entrepreneurial service firms are capable of competing against the global system integrators. According to Doherty, however, the mindset of a product company is very different from that of a software services supplier. People who deal with customer relationships every day do not plan projects in a way that leads to innovative coding. It could, therefore, be difficult for those with a background in product development to cross over to services. Some have made the transition and others may try. But do not expect a rush.

B2B or T2T?

The massive CeBIT fair in Hannover is the best place in the world to track the power plays and strategic shifts in information systems and software. It is the annual gathering where Silicon Valley code goes eyeball-to-eyeball with Taiwanese circuitry in the neutral environs of Lower Saxony. CeBIT is an event with many rituals. The chief executives of major companies present their opinions on the state of the industry in the same timeslots in the same briefing rooms year after year. Regular attendees, some of whom have been going to CeBIT for 20 years or more, are able to catch the subtle nuances. Everyone leaves with their own interpretations of the state of play and adjusts their plans accordingly — until the next year.

The Irish software industry has never taken much interest in this show. Most of the Irish attendees come from sales and implementation companies and go there to find something new to offer to their customers back home. Few software developers bother to make the trip to Hannover. Of the larger firms only Trintech has ever participated effectively in the rituals of CeBIT. The Dublin company, moreover, leaves much of this effort to its German-based employees.

Why do the software exporters stay away? Perhaps it is because most of them have fixed their eyes on the United States and pay little attention to events in Europe. Another part of the explanation is that the CeBIT philosophy of long-term continuity does not chime with a bunch of small firms in a constant state of flux. In addition, the marketing advisers in Enterprise Ireland have often steered companies towards other fairs and conventions instead of towards Hannover.

Most of all, perhaps, the development firms do not see CeBIT as a good forum for the types of software that they produce. They have little interest in the world views of the corporate bosses. They do not need to see the big picture. They are not looking for introductions to chief information officers. What matters instead is what is happening in their niche markets. And in generations three and four those markets usually consisted of other software engineers. Exporters tracked what the members of programming teams were thinking, instead of what the people in suits were saying.

Here, perhaps, is the key to understanding why the software industry has followed a different course to other countries. It is distinctive because the development companies have always performed much better in committee rooms than in exhibition halls.

Another way of examining this distinction is to consider who wants to trade with whom. Back in the years when e-commerce was all the rage, there was much speculation on whether the greatest fortunes over the web would be made from business-to-business transactions or from business-to-consumer services. Expressed in the shorthand of the day, the key question was whether Irish companies should adopt B2B strategies or B2C strategies.

Looking back, however, the answer was neither "B" nor "C" but "T" for techie. Ireland's software exporters have been poor to moderate players of the B2B game and few have ever considered B2C. The successes came where developers sold to other developers. The Irish industry has been led by T2T specialists.

Sometimes their customers worked in other software development or system integration firms. Sometimes they worked in the information systems divisions of large corporations. They were the buyers of development tools and integration middleware. They bought components and building blocks for financial systems or telecommunications networks. Techie-to-techie trading worked.

Generation five has seen a shift away from this approach. More software companies are selling products into business groups other than information systems departments. More companies are becoming experts in the customers' lines of business as well as their computing strategies. There will always be a T2T market for development platforms and testing tools and middleware, but the commercial part of the T2T trade is shrinking. The next generation of vendors must focus instead on selling software to the organisations that will actually use it.

The fate of generation five will depend on how well companies cope with these changing circumstances. They will need to modify the T2T business model. They will need to deepen their knowledge of vertical markets. They will need to apply the networking skills learned on technical standards committees to build contacts in banking or public administration or biotechnology. The T2T formula will not be enough to sustain the industry in the twenty-first century.

The transition is well underway. Companies like Curam Software and Fineos have shown how to marry software engineering savvy with a consultancy capability in their customers' domain. The software development community in Ireland is best known abroad for its middleware. But it has also accumulated solid knowledge about financial services, telecommunications network management and online learning. This is one of the Irish software industry's key assets, particularly when combined with its proven ability to sell non-American software to US customers.

Software technology never stands still. Developers are accustomed to making rapid shifts as new production techniques and delivery mechanisms become available and the twists in direction can be sudden. Generation six may follow a business model quite unlike its predecessors. It is safe to assume however, that the industry will continue to re-invent itself.

A quarter of a century has passed since the first attempts by Irish companies to package and sell software products. The business has retained its distinctiveness and never became boring. What makes the software industry different, perhaps, is its continuing ability to surprise.

Epilogue

WAITING FOR THE BIG ONE

Sooner or later most industries succumb to commoditisation. The diversity of products diminishes, prices fall and the companies that have achieved the greatest economies of scale get hailed as the leaders. It has happened in computer hardware, where the trade is now dominated by a handful of large manufacturers with lookalike products. It has happened in network services.

It has also happened in some of the older subsets of the software industry. Microsoft dominates the personal productivity applications trade. Oracle holds the lion's share of the relational database business, as SAP does in enterprise resource planning and Symantec in internet security. As these product segments matured, the big players were able to erect barriers to discourage new entrants.

The unpredictability of the software industry and the ability of new firms to ride the waves of change have discouraged the tendencies towards homogeneity and consolidation. New product types keep surfacing and more companies keep popping up. These do not need to dislodge incumbent vendors. They define and create new product categories instead. It is still possible for tiny development teams to come up with original product ideas, release new applications and create a buzz on the industry grapevine. Small companies will always find it easier to jump onto new bandwagons than large firms that have customer bases to protect.

The history of the industry offers many examples. When the minicomputer application market slowed down, client-server computing took off and new names arose. This process was repeated on a bigger scale when software developers noticed the potential of the web to support a vast range of computing tasks. More recently there have been innovations in areas like information taxonomies, graphical representations for complex data sets and peer-to-peer computing. Each new strand of the software trade produces its own heroes and role models, its own ground-rules and jargon.

Another reason why the software development business is so fluid is that its key resources are human. New entrants to the industry do not need to raise small fortunes for research equipment or production processes. What they need is a few smart developers, the right computers and a decent internet connection. They also need to be able to adapt to changing circumstances and they need to be well connected with their target markets. Financial planning comes later. The typical software company can get by with little money in the bank until the time arrives to ramp up sales and marketing campaigns. The best software is written by tightly knit, highly motivated teams. Product development is essentially a cottage industry for the global village.

Most software enterprises fail before they get off the ground, often at a personal cost to the founders. Only the most exceptional survive for a decade or more. A support infrastructure has evolved to assist the re-grouping of skills and the formation of new businesses. It is therefore reasonable to assume that the number of small development firms will continue to increase.

Some policy-makers, however, are now advocating a consolidation of the industry. The calls started in the venture capital firms, which have a vested interest in encouraging companies to buy each other, but it has also spread into the state agencies. Their rationale appears to be that if the country could produce a mega-company on the scale of an SAP or a Symantec, the software industry could achieve more stability than it has known in the past. They assume that giant corporations can support large workforces and this make the national employment figures look good. Over and over again Ireland has produced small companies that were bought and dismantled by bigger players from outside the country. If the native outfits were larger, perhaps they would do more acquiring instead of being acquired.

In 2002 Enterprise Ireland selected 38 software ventures as high-potential start-ups. In 2003 it chose another 31. Behind every company that gained approval several others did not make the cut. Many projects fizzled out before their promoters reached the point of registering a company. Some observers suggest that there are as many as 500 attempted software start-ups each year in Ireland.

According to the founder of one of the companies that did not make Enterprise Ireland's high-potential list, the policy of the agency in recent years has amounted to "an extreme form of Darwinism". It only accepts a limited number of new clients each year. Other species of software developers face a culling process. This threat appears to be growing.

Very few software enterprises anywhere in the world achieve annual revenues of $100 million or more from software licence sales. Only a handful of household names have ever reached the $1 billion mark. Almost all of these were American companies that had the benefit of a massive market in their home country. Outside the US, only SAP has penetrated this elite, achieving annual revenues of €7 billion in recent years. Like its American counterparts, SAP grew up in a major market. First, it dominated the German enterprise applications business. Then it expanded its international sales. SAP, moreover, grew up at a time when customers assumed that they must pay hundreds of thousands of dollars or euro for an enterprise software application. Their perception of value has changed since then and the average spend on a software solution has declined dramatically.

In short, it is as difficult as ever to build up a $100 million business, but even harder to aim for the billion dollar bracket than it was ten or twenty years ago.

Iona got closer to the big league than any other Irish-based software company, establishing itself as the pre-eminent supplier of Corba middleware and growing its annual revenues to a peak of $180 million in 2001. It scaled down after failing to win a significant share of the market for application servers and it struggled to adapt to the declining demand for Corba. In addition, Iona's patch in the market was always vulnerable to incursions by mammoths like IBM or Microsoft. If Iona had derived the maximum advantage from each twist of the technology, it would be a bigger organisation today. As a middleware specialist, however, it could never have grown to the size of an SAP.

Twenty years after trying to establish Intelligence Ireland as an international force, Malachy Smith likes the idea of growing a giant enterprise in Ireland. The strategy, he notes, could keep intellectual property ownership inside the country. "I think that we have the capability to have one of the handful of big organisations here. We have the talent," he says.

Malachy Smith returned to Ireland in 2001. On his return he studied the latest crop of software ventures. He found worrying similarities with their underachieving predecessors in generation two. Once again, he says, too many companies are offering near-identical products. He suspects that this decline in originality began with web software. Areas like text messaging and content archiving are also populated by suppliers of lookalike software. Smith has not returned to product development. Instead he took over a Dublin-based software services company that resells and implements other vendors' middleware and development platforms.

Irish software needs start-ups that can break the me-too mould and create intellectual property in new fields. Does the selection process at Enterprise Ireland enable such companies to get off the ground? Has it contributed instead to a proliferation of unexciting products? And what will happen to the cottage industry if the agency promotes consolidation on a larger scale?

Perhaps the state agencies are merely reflecting opinions that have always been held by institutional investors, law firms and financial consultants. These groups see a high level of merger and acquisition activity as desirable. Their stance is perfectly rational, because they can draw high fees and profits from such transactions. History shows, however, that the effects of venture capital investments are not necessarily positive, while mergers and acquisitions have consistently weakened the Irish software industry.

Another fundamental flaw in the bigger-is-better strategy is that a software firm with a large headcount invariably turns into a services company. Mainstream software service contracts go to locations with low labour costs, proven expertise in managed services or close proximity to major customers. Irish service companies can only compete on the margins of this business.

Software product suppliers, of course, sell consulting and customer support services as well. The bigger and older the companies, the more they take on the characteristics of service organisations. Some enterprise application vendors in the US derive three-quarters of their revenues in this way. As technologies change, their customers pull them in the direction of services. When the users need more assistance with modifications and migrations, they become more dependent on the technical support teams. When the vendors become more dependent on services, however, they tend to lose development staff who want to work with the latest tools and concepts.

Like bespoke development contracts, technical support services are drifting towards countries such as India. A large software vendor that depends on service fees would find it difficult to operate from Ireland.

Small is not always beautiful and big is not always bad. But official policy ought to be biased in favour of diversity instead of consolidation. The way forward is for the state agencies to designate more candidates as companies with high potential and not to close the doors on those with unconventional approaches. The software industry should not be subjected to economic models from other industries, where development processes are capital-intensive and manufacturing operations require complex planning and co-ordination.

Policies that aim to create an elite group of a few large companies run counter to the culture of software product development. The cottage industry model works. It has served Ireland very well in the past decade and a half and ought to be preserved. Building a big player should be a secondary objective.

If Ireland ever does produce a billion dollar software company, the process will take years, and more likely decades. It will have to be in an area that can generate high product revenues. The company will also need to be privately owned. Enterprises with stock market listings or board-rooms dominated by venture capitalists will be dragged across the Atlantic as they grow, becoming US corporations with back offices in Ireland. The company must be built up organically by managers with long-term commitment. Software firms that depend on acquisitions to keep growing are easily destabilised and often end up as takeover targets themselves.

SAP is the wrong precedent to follow. Tweaking its name, however, provides a much more appropriate role model for Irish software — SAS. Based in North Carolina, SAS Institute sells analytical software for business planners. Although it is not widely known outside the IT community, the company has a loyal customer base, mostly in medium to large organisations, that keeps buying new editions of its data warehousing and decision support products. It has a reputation among software developers as an exceptionally good employer. The company has grown gradually, but consistently. Its annual revenues broke through the $1 billion mark in 1999 — 23 years after the company's foundation. SAS steered a course through a succession of technology cycles, balancing its generic products with industry-specific applications. Most important of all, its shares are not listed on any stock exchange.

Building a similar company in Ireland would be extremely difficult. But it is not inconceivable.

INDEX